ROUTLEDGE LIBRARY EDITIONS: PHONETICS AND PHONOLOGY

Volume 8

FRONT VOWELS, CORONAL CONSONANTS AND THEIR INTERACTION IN NONLINEAR PHONOLOGY

FRONT VOWELS, CORONAL CONSONANTS AND THEIR INTERACTION IN NONLINEAR PHONOLOGY

ELIZABETH V. HUME

LONDON AND NEW YORK

First published in 1994 by Garland Publishing, Inc.

This edition first published in 2019
by Routledge
2 Park Square, Milton Park, Abingdon, Oxon OX14 4RN

and by Routledge
711 Third Avenue, New York, NY 10017

Routledge is an imprint of the Taylor & Francis Group, an informa business

© 1994 Elizabeth V. Hume

All rights reserved. No part of this book may be reprinted or reproduced or utilised in any form or by any electronic, mechanical, or other means, now known or hereafter invented, including photocopying and recording, or in any information storage or retrieval system, without permission in writing from the publishers.

Trademark notice: Product or corporate names may be trademarks or registered trademarks, and are used only for identification and explanation without intent to infringe.

British Library Cataloguing in Publication Data
A catalogue record for this book is available from the British Library

ISBN: 978-1-138-60364-6 (Set)
ISBN: 978-0-429-43708-3 (Set) (ebk)
ISBN: 978-1-138-31737-6 (Volume 8) (hbk)
ISBN: 978-1-138-31739-0 (Volume 8) (pbk)
ISBN: 978-0-429-45523-0 (Volume 8) (ebk)

Publisher's Note
The publisher has gone to great lengths to ensure the quality of this reprint but points out that some imperfections in the original copies may be apparent.

Disclaimer
The publisher has made every effort to trace copyright holders and would welcome correspondence from those they have been unable to trace.

FRONT VOWELS, CORONAL CONSONANTS AND THEIR INTERACTION IN NONLINEAR PHONOLOGY

ELIZABETH V. HUME

GARLAND PUBLISHING, INC.
NEW YORK & LONDON / 1994

Copyright © 1994 Elizabeth V. Hume
All rights reserved

Library of Congress Cataloging-in-Publication Data

Hume, Elizabeth V., 1956–
  Front vowels, coronal consonants and their interaction in nonlinear phonology / Elizabeth V. Hume.
    p.   cm. — (Outstanding dissertations in linguistics)
  Includes bibliographical references (p.) and index.
  ISBN 0-8153-1697-6 (alk. paper)
    1. Grammar, Comparative and general—Phonology.   2. Distinctive features (Linguistics).   3. Maltese language—Phonology—Case studies. I. Title. II. Series.
P217.3.H86   1994
414—dc20   93-49583
                                                                                CIP

Printed on acid-free, 250-year-life paper
Manufactured in the United States of America

For Zachary and Isobel

Contents

PART I
I. INTRODUCTION
1. Purposes of this Work — 5
   1.1 Front Vocoids and Coronal Consonants — 5
   1.2 Redefining [coronal] — 14
   1.3 The Representation of Consonant/Vowel Interaction — 15
2. Background Assumptions — 20
   2.1 Nonlinear Phonology — 20
   2.2 Underspecification — 21
3. Organization of this Study — 22

II. PHONETIC CORRELATES OF [CORONAL]
0. Introduction — 25
1. Topology of the Tongue — 25
2. Articulatory Description of [Coronal] — 30
   2.1 Hungarian Palatals — 33
3. The Coronality of Front Vowels — 39
4. Acoustic Properties of Coronal Sounds — 52
5. Summary — 54

III. THE FEATURE SPECIFICATION OF CORONALS
0. Introduction — 57
1. Front Vocoids — 57
   1.1 Spanish — 61
2. Coronal Consonants — 71
   2.1 Anterior Coronals — 71
   2.2 Postalveolar Coronal Obstruents — 72
   2.3 Palatalized Consonants — 81
   2.4 Alveopalatals — 83
   2.5 Summary — 86

	3.	Coronal Sonorant Consonants	86
	4.	Summary	87
IV.		THE NONLINEAR ORGANIZATION OF CONSONANT AND VOWEL FEATURES	
	0.	Introduction	91
	1.	Incorporating [coronal] into a Nonlinear Model of Feature Organization	91
		1.1 Sanskrit	94
		1.2 Basque (Baztan dialect)	96
		1.3 Summary	98
	2.	Feature Theory	98
	3.	Feature Organization	99
		3.1 Major and Minor Articulations	100
	4.	Spreading Constraints	104
		4.1 Summary	107
	5.	Cooccurrence Constraints and Dissimilation	107
		5.1 Cantonese	109
		5.2 Akkadian	112
	6.	Root Adjacency as a Necessary Condition on Consonant/Vowel Interaction?	114
	7.	Resolving an Ordering Paradox	115
V.		CONSONANT-TO-FRONT VOWEL ASSIMILATION	
	0.	Introduction	125
	1.	Acadian French	126
	2.	Front Vowels as [-back]	129
	3.	Cross-plane Interaction	134
	4.	Palatalization	137
	5.	Coronalization	140
	6.	Summary	144
	7.	[Continuant] and [Strident]	144
	8.	The Apparent Dorsality of Front Vowels	146
		8.1 Pame	147
		8.2 Romanian	148

PART II
VI.		MALTESE ARABIC: A CASE STUDY	
	0.	Introduction	153
	1.	Preliminaries	155
		1.1 Phonemic Inventory	155
		1.2 Morpheme Structure Constraints	159

Contents ix

	1.3 Tier Conflation	160
2.	Laying out the Problems	161
3.	Typical Formation of the Imperfective, First Measure Triliteral Verb	165
4.	Underlying Vocalism of the Stem	167
	4.1 Summary	181
5.	Plural Imperfectives: Description	182
6.	Metathesis	184
	6.1 Motivating Metathesis	184
	6.2 Syllable Structure Conditions	188
	6.3 Epenthesis	191
	6.4 Syncope and Vocalic Mapping	192
7.	The Realization of the Imperfective Prefix Vowel	195
8.	A Nonlinear Account of Metathesis	197
	8.1 Analysis	197
	8.2 Summary and Implications	202
9.	Further Implications	202
	9.1 Tier Conflation and Total Vowel Assimilation	202
	9.2 Default Rules and Underspecification	205

VII. CORONAL VOWEL AND CONSONANTS PARALLELISMS IN MALTESE ARABIC

0.	Introduction	213
1.	The Realization of the Imperfective Prefix Vowel before Stem-initial Coronal Obstruents	214
	1.1 Description	214
	1.2 Default Assignment	216
	1.3 Vowel Coronal Assimilation	221
	1.4 Summary	226
2.	Consonant Coronal Assimilation	227
3.	Coronal Vowel/Consonant Parallelisms	234
	3.1 Default Segments	234
	3.2 Coronal Assimilation	237
4.	Conclusion	240

VIII. Conclusion 243

References 247

Index 259

Acknowledgments

There are a great many individuals who have contributed their time, concern and interest to the writing of this dissertation. I acknowledge first the members of my committee: Nick Clements, Abby Cohn, John Kingston and Linda Waugh. Although I did not come to Cornell with the intention of specializing in phonology, I was quickly convinced that that was where my interests lie during my first course in phonology given by Professor Clements. To him I owe a debt of gratitude for his interest, encouragement and the many hours he spent going over my work in painstaking detail. But most of all, I am indebted to him for teaching me how to be a phonologist. To Abby, I acknowledge, among many other things, the time she took going over various drafts of this and other work and discussing my newest ideas at a moment's notice. I am grateful to John for his insightful and critical comments of this work, for never ceasing to play the devil's advocate, but most importantly, for sparking my interest in phonetics. Linda contributed to this work in numerous ways among which include the valuable hours she spent discussing with me the works of, among others, Beaudoin de Courtenay, Nicolai Trubetzkoy and Roman Jakobson. In addition to the tremendous influence that all of my committee members have had on this work, I am most appreciative for their friendship and encouragement which did much to make my years in Ithaca an enriching experience.

My gratitude also goes to Ann Bradlow, Kate Davis, Beverley Goodman, Yetunde Laniran, Gita Martohardjono, Sam Rosenthall, David Silva, Veneeta Srivastav, Alice Turk and Renée Zakia not only for discussing various portions of this work with me over the years, but also for encouragement, friendship and fun.

During my third year I was fortunate to be a visiting student in the linguistics departments of MIT and UMASS, Amherst. During that time I benefited a great deal from interactions with Morris Halle, Michael Kenstowicz and John McCarthy. I thank each of them for welcoming me into their courses and Morris Halle, in particular, for going out of his way to encourage me to come and discuss my ideas with him.

There are many people who contributed to this work by providing relevant data and/or discussing certain analyses. For their time and thoughtful comments, I would like to acknowledge Ellen Broselow, Wayles Browne, Walter Cichocki, Gérard Diffloth, Jay Jasanoff, Allard Jongman, David Odden, Stefan Oltean, Keren Rice, Jerzy Rubach, and members of the Permanent Mission of Malta to the United Nations.

The final proofreading of this work was made considerably easier for me due to the invaluable help of Jill Beckman. I am also most grateful to Hyeree Kim for her assistance in preparing this manuscript for publication.

The work in this thesis was funded in part through research fellowships from Cornell University and the Social Sciences and Humanities Research Council of Canada.

My son, Zachary, spent his first six years of life as a graduate student's kid. I thank him for putting up with me during that time and most of all, for helping me to keep things in their proper perspective. Finally, I can say without hesitation that this thesis would not have been accomplished without the undying emotional support of my mother, Isobel. To her I owe a debt of gratitude.

Illustrations

Figure	1	Subdivisions of the tongue (Catford 1988)	26
Figure	2	Subdivisions of the tongue (Ladefoged 1982)	27
Figure	3	Tip and blade of the tongue (Keating 1988)	28
Figure	4	Subdivisions of the tongue (Zemlin 1968)	29
Figure	5	Hungarian palatal [ɟ] (Bolla 1980)	33
Figure	6	Hungarian palatal [c] (Bolla 1980)	34
Figure	7a	Palatal [ç] and velar [x] of German (Wängler 1958)	38
Figure	7b	Palatal nasal [ɲ] of Ngwo (Ladefoged 1968)	38
Figure	8a	Hungarian palatal stop [ɟ] and high front vowel [i] (Bolla 1980)	40
Figure	8b	German palatal fricative [ç] and high front vowel [i] (Wängler 1958)	40
Figure	9a	[i] vs. [u]: Russian (Bolla 1981)	41
Figure	9b	[i] vs. [u]: Canadian French (Gendron 1966)	41
Figure	9c	[i] vs. [u]: Hungarian (Bolla 1980)	42
Figure	10a	[e] vs. [o]: Polish (Wierzchowska 1980)	42
Figure	10b	[e] vs. [o]: Canadian French (Gendron 1966)	43
Figure	10c	[e] vs. [o]: Russian (Fant 1960)	43
Figure	11	[ö] vs. [o]: Hungarian (Bolla 1980)	44
Figure	12	[ɛ] vs. [ɔ]: Canadian French (Gendron 1966)	44
Figure	13a	[æ:] vs. [ɑ]: Swedish (Fant 1959)	45
Figure	13b	[æ] vs. [ɑ]: English (Perkell 1969)	45
Figure	14	Representative 'hard' and 'soft' coronals of Russian (Fant 1960)	47
Figure	15	Vowel Formant Structure (Ladefoged 1982)	53

"Jakobson was...able to overcome one of the most unintuitive aspects of the phonetic frameworks that were then in wide use (and continue in wide use to this day). These frameworks...utilize separate sets of features for vowels and consonants. For some reason, with the exception of some early Hindu grammarians, no one before Jakobson appears to have been struck by the implausibility of such an arrangement, for it implies that different mechanisms are involved in the production of vowels than in the production of consonants, and yet one set of articulators is involved in the production of both types of sound..."

M. Halle 1976:87-88

Front Vowels, Coronal Consonants and Their Interaction in Nonlinear Phonology

PART I

FRONT VOWELS AND CORONAL CONSONANTS

I

Introduction

1. PURPOSES OF THIS WORK

There are three main goals of this study. The first is to provide evidence for the natural class of sounds comprised of front vowels, front glides and coronal consonants. Although the primary evidence for this view is drawn from the patterning of these sounds in phonological rules cross-linguistically, I also draw on phonetic evidence. The second goal of this work is to show that a revised definition of the articulator feature [coronal] properly characterizes this natural class of sounds. As such, I draw on and develop the idea that front vowels are coronals, as first proposed in Clements (1976a). The third goal of this study is to provide a formal representation of front vowels and coronal consonants and their interaction within a nonlinear model of feature organization. Proposals concerning the representation of front vowel/coronal consonant interaction naturally extend to the interaction of vowels and consonants in general.

1.1 Front Vocoids and Coronal Consonants as a Natural Class

The view that front vocoids and coronal consonants are members of a natural class dates back to at least Jakobson, Fant & Halle (1952). However, more recent features theories developed out of the work of

Chomsky & Halle (1968, also referred to as *SPE*) fail to recognize them as such. Rather, front vowels are characterized by the tongue body feature [-back] whereas coronal consonants are characterized by the articulator feature [coronal] (see e.g. Sagey 1986). In this section I provide representative examples illustrating the recurrent patterning of front vocoids and coronal consonants cross-linguistically. That this affinity recurs in a wide range of languages suggests that the traditional classification of these two classes of sounds as [coronal] for consonants and [-back] for vowels is unsatisfactory. Such a classification fails to elucidate why these two classes of sounds should pattern together to the exclusion of all other sounds. Conversely, by recognizing that front vowels and coronals are members of the same natural class, we strongly predict the recurrent patterning of these segments, as evidenced below. Moreover, as I show in subsequent chapters, this affinity is most naturally and simply accounted for by characterizing these sounds by the same place articulator.

1.1.1 The Patterning of Front Vowels and Coronal Consonants

In this section I describe the patterning of front vowels and coronal consonants in a wide range of languages. The purpose of this section is not to provide a complete formal analysis of each case, but rather to illustrate the cross-linguistic affinity of front vowels and coronal consonants.

Perhaps the best-known of all processes involving the interaction of front vowels and coronal consonants takes the form of consonant-to-vowel assimilation, commonly referred to by the cover-term *palatalization* (see chapter V for further discussion). Of particular relevance to the present discussion is the common process in which a velar consonant becomes coronal before a front vowel. I refer to this type of assimilation as Coronalization. Coronalization is not restricted to any one language group but is evidenced cross-linguistically (see e.g. Bhat's 1978 survey). Although frequently triggered by nonlow front vowels, low front vowels may also be triggers. In the historical development of French, for example, velars became nonanterior coronals before all front vowels. Beginning in the 3rd century, velars were coronalized before nonlow front vowels and then towards the 5th century, the low front vowel also triggered the change from velar to coronal, e.g. chaîne (Fr.) < catena (Lat.), chanter (Fr.) < cantare (Lat.), chèvre (Fr.) < capra (Lat.) (Straka 1965).

Similar changes are evidenced in synchronic systems. In Slovak, for example, velars /k g x γ/ are realized as the nonanterior coronals [tʃ dʒ ʃ ʒ], respectively, before a front vocoid /i e æ/ and the palatal glide (Rubach, forthcoming), as illustrated in (1).

(1) k→tʃ vnuk 'grandson'
         vnúk+ik   → [vnútʃik] (dimin.)
         vnúk+æ   → vnútʃæ → [vnútʃa][1](dimin.)
         tʃlovek 'man'
         tʃlovek+e   → [tʃlovetʃe] (voc.)
         tʃlovek+æ   → tʃlovietʃæ → [tʃlovietʃa] 'children'
    g→dʒ cveng 'sound'
         cveng+æ+t'   → cvendʒæt' → [cvendʒat'] 'to sound'
    x→ʃ strach 'fright'
         strach+i+t' → [staʃit'] 'frighten'
    γ→ʒ boh 'god'
         boh+e   → [boʒe] (voc.)
         beh 'run' (N)
         beh+æ+t'   → beʒæt' → [beʒat'] 'to run'

The classification of front vowels as [-back] fails to explain in a straightforward manner why it is that velars become coronal consonants in the context of a front vocoid. That this should be given a natural explanation stems from the observation that Coronalization is commonly attested cross-linguistically. Alternatively, by treating front vocoids and coronal consonants as members of a natural class and specifying them with a common feature, Coronalization can be treated as a natural assimilation rule (see Clements 1976a, and chapter V below). The influence of a front vowel on an adjacent consonant is also evidenced in Eastern Czech, where a labial consonant became coronal before a front vowel, [tivo] < [pivo] 'beer', [tʃetice] < [tʃepice] 'cap, headgear', [niɲ] < [miɲ] 'less' (Jakobson & Waugh 1987:100).

Although consonant-to-vowel assimilations are commonly attested, we also encounter cases in which a coronal consonant exerts an influence on an adjacent vowel. For example, it is not unusual to find vowels being fronted in the context of a palatal consonant. The Ndu language of Iatmul, for example, has an underlying vowel system consisting of a three-way contrast in height among central vowels (Foley 1986, Staalsen 1966): /ɨ ə a/. Front and back vowels are derived from /ɨ/ and /ə/ according to the following rules (examples follow):

(2) /ɨ/ → [i]/__ y, ɲ
[I]/y, ɲ __
[u]/__ w
[ʊ]/w __
[ɨ]/elsewhere

/ə/ → [e]/__ y, ɲ
[ɛ]/y, ɲ __
[o]/__ w
[ɔ]/w __
[ə]/elsewhere

e.g. /ntəw/   → [ndow]   'shrunken'
      /məlɨy/   → [məriy]   'mud flats'
      /ntɨw/   → [nduw]   'man'
      /yɨwɨy/   → [yuwiy]   'grass'
      /malɨy/   → [mariy]   'rat'
      /yətɨwlɨntɨ/ → [yɛtuwrɨndɨ] 'he walks'

The fronting influence of coronal consonants on vowels is not limited to palatal consonants. In Moroccan Arabic, a non word-final /o/ becomes [ö] when immediately preceded by a coronal consonant (D.Odden, p.c.).[2]

(3) qtlo 'he killed him' qtlöh 'they killed him'
    qtlo 'they killed' ma qtlöʃ 'they didn't kill'
    dhɛʃo 'they surprised' dhɛʃök 'they surprised (2s)'
    wuzno 'they weighed' ma wznöʃ 'they didn't weigh'
    ʕaqdo 'tie (s) him!' ʕaqdöh 'tie (pl.) him!'
    ṣəmto 'they were quiet' ma ṣəmtöʃ 'they weren't quiet'
    ktəbt 'I wrote' ktəbto 'I wrote it'
         ma ktəbtöʃ 'I didn't write it'
    xəbzo 'they baked' ma xəbzöʃ 'they didn't bake'
    ḥəbso 'they arrested' ḥəbsöh 'they arrested him'
cf. ləmmo 'they covered' ləmmoh 'they covered him'
    ʒləbo 'they attracted' ʒləboh 'they attracted him'
    dəbʸo 'they tanned' təbʸoh 'they tanned him'
    ḍərbo 'he hit him' ma ḍərboʃ 'he didn't hit him'
    wuqfo 'they stood' ma wqfoʃ 'they didn't stand'
    ḅxxo 'they spit blood' ma ḅxxoʃ 'they didn't spit blood'

In a feature theory in which front vowels are [-back] and coronal consonants are [coronal], accounting for the observed fronting of /o/ in (3) is problematic. Doing so would require specifying all coronals, both anterior and nonanterior, for the vocalic feature value [-back], a specification on consonants which has generally served to characterize secondary palatalization (see e.g. SPE, Sagey 1986, Ní Chiosáin 1991). Specifying all coronals (both anterior and nonanterior) which trigger fronting in (3) as [-back] would then make the incorrect claim that these segments are palatalized, which they are not.

A similar fronting rule is evidenced in Lhasa Tibetan, in which the nonfront vowels /a o u/ were fronted before the coronal consonants /d n l s/ (Michailovsky 1975). This change is observed in the comparison of Written Tibetan with modern Lhasa Tibetan, given in (4). In the forms in (a), the nonfront vowel of Written Tibetan is realized as front before a coronal consonant. The final consonant was subsequently lost in Lhasa Tibetan. Conversely, before labial and velar consonants as in (b), the vowel maintained its original quality. When available, corresponding forms from the modern western dialect of Balti are included as further evidence for the forms of Written Tibetan. In this dialect, no fronting occurred.

(4) Written   Lhasa   Balti
     Tibetan
 a. bod   phö̀ö̀   bodh   'Tibet'
     bdud   tǜǜ   'demon'
     sman   m̃ɛ̃̄ɛ̄   sman   'medicine'
     ston   tȫȫ   ston   'autumn'
     bdun   t̃ü̃ü̃   bdun   'seven'
     bal   phɛɛ   bal   'wool'
     thol   thȫȫ   'extra'
     yul   yüü   yul   'country'
     ras   rɛ̀ɛ̀   ras   'cloth'
     chos   chȫȫ   'religion'
     spos   pȫȫ   'incense'
     lus   lüü   'body'
 b. nub   nùù   nubkha   'west'
     gyag   yàà   hyag   'yak'
     goŋ   qhö̃ö̀   'price'

In Cantonese the occurrence of vowels in syllables containing coronal consonants is highly constrained, as observed by Cheng (1989). As she points out, if the onset and coda of a given syllable are both coronal, a vowel must be front (i.e. [i e ü ö]). The only exception to this generalization is that the central vowels [a] and [a:] may also occur in a syllable with a coronal onset and coda. Thus, although the words [tit] 'iron', [tüt] 'to take off', [tön] 'a shield' are well-formed, back vowels [u o] are excluded from syllables with a coronal onset and coda, e.g. *[tut], *[tsot], *[sut]. Cheng accounts for these facts by vowel-to-consonant assimilation, a rule in which an underlying back vowel is fronted in the context of two adjacent coronal consonants.[3] Such an account is only possible if we assume that front vowels and coronal consonants are specified for a common place feature which, as I argue below, is [coronal]. Thus, an underlying back vowel assimilates to the feature [coronal] of an adjacent coronal consonant and, as a result, surfaces as front.

Vago (1976) describes the fronting of the glide /w/ in Baule, a language of the Ivory Coast. He states: "/w/ is pronounced as the front rounded glide [ẅ] between an alveolar or palatal consonant and a front vowel". After other consonants, the glide surfaces as [w].[4]

(5) tẅi   'gun'
     akpatẅe   'bird'
     adẅi   'amulet'
     sẅi   'elephant'
     sẅɛ   'civit'
     ṇzẅe   'water'
     lẅi   'fat'
     aji̱cẅe   'tortoise'
     mucẅɛ   'eight'
     ɟẅe   'fish'
     a̱ɟẅi   'craft'
     ɟẅeɟẅɛ   'happy'
cf. bwi   'back'
     bwe   'nose'
     bwɛ   'half'
     kwe   'fetus'
     kwɛkwɛ   'comb'

Again we observe the influence of a coronal consonant on the quality of a following vocoid. Similar to Cantonese, fronting is typically contingent upon the relevant vocoid being flanked on either side by a coronal segment.

In Part II of this work I provide an indepth analysis of the realization of the imperfective prefix vowel in Standard Maltese Arabic. It is observed that the prefix vowel surfaces as the high front vowel [i] just in case the following consonant is coronal, anterior or nonanterior. Similar to the cases of vowel fronting shown above, I argue that the frontness quality of the prefix vowel derives from assimilation to the coronality of the following consonant. This rule of vowel-to-consonant assimilation is shown to be a subclass of a more general rule of Coronal Assimilation which affects both the prefix vowel and consonant.

A further example evidencing the patterning of front vowels and coronal consonants is observed in high vowel reduplication in Fe?fe?-Bamileke (in particular, the Petit Diboum dialect) (Clements 1976a; Hyman 1972, 1973). As Clements states: "the normal reduplicative vowel is the high unrounded central vowel *i̵*. The vowel is rounded to *u* when (a) followed by *u* in the next syllable, or (b) followed by a consonant of class A [i.e. p b f v m w] and a rounded vowel of any height. Furthermore, it appears as the front vowel *i* under parallel conditions, that is when (a) followed by ɨ in the next syllable, or (b) preceding a consonant of class B [i.e. t d s z n l c ɟ ʃ ʒ (ɲ) j] and a front vowel of any height" (p.100).

(6)
za	zɨza	'to eat'
to	tɨto	'to punch'
keen	kɨkee	'to refuse'
ben	pɨpɛn	'to accept'
kuum	kukuu	'to carve'
boh	pupɔh	'to be afraid'
siim	sisii	'to spoil'
teen	titee	'to remove'
cen	cicɛn	'to moan'

As evidenced by the above examples, the patterning of front vowels and coronal consonants is common cross-linguistically, particularly in cases in which, by phonological rule, two or more segments become more alike. Perhaps relevant in this respect are the findings of Janson (1986) and Maddieson & Precoda (1990). Janson's cross-linguistic survey of CV patterns suggests, among other things, that there is a tendency for front vowels to occur with coronal (dental or alveolar) consonants. The survey of Maddieson & Precoda confirms that there is an observed preference for front vowels to be preceded by coronal consonants, while not supporting some of Janson's other findings.

Although assimilatory processes involving front vowels and coronals are commonly observed, dissimilatory processes are also attested. In Korean, for example, there is a dissimilatory constraint holding on front vocoids and coronal consonants within the syllable; the palatal glide does not cooccur in any syllable containing a front vowel or a coronal obstruent (Clements 1990c). Thus, the coronal consonants /t t' th c c' ch s s'/ and front vowels /i e ɛ/ are excluded in syllables of the type /CjV/. This cooccurrence restriction receives a straightforward account if we assume that front vocoids and coronal consonants are specified for a common articulator feature (see chapter IV for discussion of similar dissimilatory constraints and their formal representation). As such, the constraint prohibits a palatal glide in a syllable with a homorganic obstruent or vowel.

Sound change in Mon provides a further illustration of dissimilation involving front vowels and coronal consonants (Diffloth 1984, p.c.). In general, word-final palatal consonants [c ɲ] of Old Mon (11th - 13th century) changed to [t n], respectively, in Middle and Modern Mon. However, when preceded by a front vowel, [i e], the palatals instead became the velars [k ŋ].

(7)
	Old Mon	Middle/Modern Mon	
	*phi:c	phek	'to be afraid'
	*kre:ɲ	kreŋ	'parrot'
	*ʔic	ʔik	'excrement'
	*-ndʑic	thnik	'to kick with sole of foot'
cf.	*tdʑa:c	(t)dʑat	'to taste sweet'
	*ta:ɲ	tan	'to weave'
	*kla:ɲ	klan	'to lick'
	*du:ɲ	dun	'bamboo'

In chapter III I argue that palatal consonants are specified for the primary features [coronal, -anterior]. Under the assumption that front vowels are nonanterior coronals, the change from palatal to velar consonant reflects a dissimilatory process: a nonanterior coronal consonant dissimilates just in case the preceding vowel is also (nonanterior) coronal.

The affinity of front vowels and coronal consonants is also observed in cases in which a coronal consonant deletes and is replaced by a vowel. Trigo (1991), for example, discusses a process in Malay (northern dialect of Kedah) in which the final coronals /l/ and /s/ are realized as [i] and [ih] respectively. This is illustrated in (8).

(8)
/VC/	Standard Malay	Kedah	Gloss
al	batal	batai	'to cancel'
al	təbal	təbai	'thick'
ul	pikol	pikoi	'carry'
ul	bətol	bətoi	'right'
as	lipas	lipaih	'cockroach'
as	pluas	pluaih	'to wring'
us	bagos	bagoih	'good'
us	mampos	mãmpoih	'dead'

Trigo (p.15) argues that in Kedah, "final coronals, /l/ and /s/ decompose to an intermediate stage, [il] and [is] and then undergo oral depletion to become [iø] and [ih] respectively (ø is an empty slot)." She attributes the place quality of [i] to that of the coronal consonant. A vowel slot is inserted before the relevant consonants and then in a subsequent stage, the place specification of the consonant maps onto the the empty vowel slot (see Genetti 1990 for discussion of a similar case in Sunwari, a Tibeto-Burman language spoken in Nepal). We find a similar case in Romanian in which final [s] was replaced by [i] in monosyllabic words of Latin origin (Sala 1976).

(9) | Latin | | Romanian |
|---|---|---|
| nos | > | noi |
| uos | > | voi |
| ad pos(t) | > | apoi |
| das | > | dai |
| stas | > | stai |
| habes | > | *has > ai |
| *dos | > | doi |
| tres | > | trei |

In all of the cases that I have observed in which a coronal consonant is replaced by a coronal vowel, the resulting vowel is [i]. The place quality of the vowel, I argue, is acquired from the consonant. The height of the vowel, i.e. [+high], may be attributed to default assignment (see Maltese, Part II).

In the preceding discussion we have seen the recurrent patterning of front vocoids and coronal consonants cross-linguistically. The observation that these sounds function together to the exclusion of all other sounds provides strong evidence that front vocoids and coronal consonants are members of a natural class. In the next section, I briefly discuss the feature which I argue best characterizes this natural class.

1.2 Redefining [coronal]

The second goal of this study, as noted above, is to show that front vowels are naturally included in the class of coronal sounds, as first proposed by Clements (1976a). In recent years, the [coronal] specification of front vowels has been incorporated into a number of papers (e.g. Hume 1988, 1990, 1991a; Broselow & Niyondagara 1989, 1990; Cheng 1989; Clements 1989, 1990c). However, little attention has been paid to what it actually means for a front vowel to be coronal. In fact, given the traditional definition of [coronal] as referring to a sound articulated with the tip or blade of the tongue, this feature is unable to correctly characterize all front vowels. In this study I motivate a revised definition of the articulator feature [coronal], drawing on the original proposal of Halle & Stevens (1979). This redefinition is shown to be independently needed as a means of classifying all coronal consonants. In chapter II I present phonetic evidence illustrating that palatal consonants are produced with the front, as opposed to the tip or blade, of the tongue raised. Consequently, in order to include palatal consonants in the class of coronal sounds we need to redefine [coronal] to refer to an articulation implemented by raising the tip, blade and/or front of the tongue.

With this as a basis, the articulation of front vowels is compared with that of their non-front counterparts. As I will show, the front of the tongue is raised to a greater degree for the front vowel than it is for the non-front counterpart. The revised definition of [coronal] thus naturally extends to front vowels. Consequently, redefining the natural class of coronals so as to include both front vowels and coronal consonants is shown to be well-motivated.

1.3 The Representation of Consonant/Vowel Interaction

The theory of nonlinear phonology serves as the basis in which the analyses in this work are couched. Thus, although my primary focus is on the natural class of front vowels and coronal consonants, a natural extension of this work concerns the formal representation of consonant/vowel interaction in nonlinear theory. The feature organization used in this work is a slightly modified version of the *Unified Features Theory* proposed in Clements (1989, 1990c) and further developed in the work of Herzallah (1990) (see also Goodman 1991; Hume 1990, 1991a,b).

As can be seen in (10), in the model of feature organization developed in this work the degree and location of a segment's constriction comprise a constituent, in a symmetrical manner for both consonants and vowels (based on Clements 1992).

(10)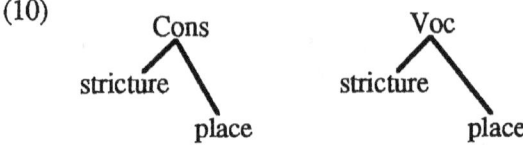

Each constriction is made up of a place node dominating the segment's articulator(s), and a stricture node dominating features referring to the degree of constriction of the segment's articulation. The place node dominates the same set of articulator features in both consonants and vowels, including at least [labial], [coronal] and [dorsal]. Stricture features for consonants include [strident] and [continuant]. For vowels, degree of constriction is characterized by vowel height features [high, low] (and the redundant specification [+continuant] if required).

(11)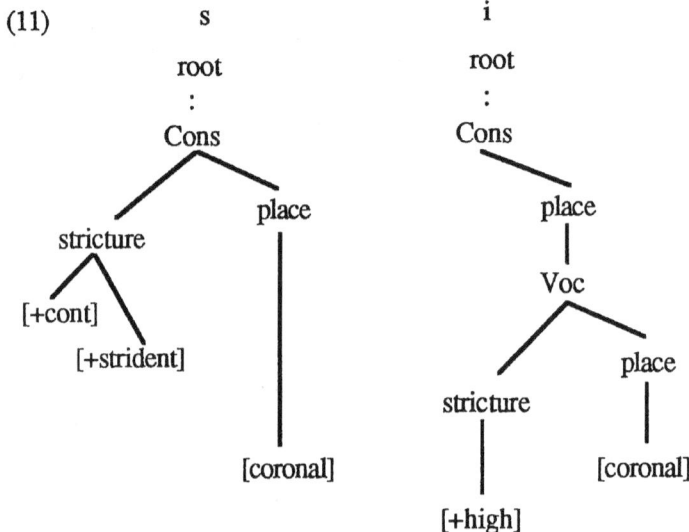

As the partial representations of [s] and [i] in (11) above illustrate, place and stricture features are dominated by a constriction node: CONS for consonantal constrictons and VOC for vocoidal constrictions. Incorporated into these representations is the assumption that features or nodes that occur on the same line are on the same tier. For example,

Introduction

the CONS nodes of both [s] and [i] are on the same tier in (11), whereas CONS and VOC are on independent tiers.

Following Clements (1990c), I assume that the representations of consonants and vowels are partially segregated. The constriction nodes CONS and VOC are arrayed on independent tiers. This provides a straightforward account of the observed transparency of plain consonants in vowel harmony rules (see chapters III, IV). Moreover, with the exception of terminal consonantal features (including articulator nodes), consonant-to-consonant spreading is (correctly) shown to be blocked by an intervening vocoid.

As shown in (11), I introduce the innovation that all instances of a given place feature value are arrayed on the same tier. For example, the [coronal] articulator which characterizes [s] is arrayed on the same tier as [coronal] which characterizes [i]. Thus, although [coronal] is on the same tier in both instances, it is linked to the CONS node for [s] and the VOC node for [i]. This approach makes a number of predictions concerning the interaction of consonantal and vocoidal place features in, for example, cooccurrence constraints and dissimilation rules, phenomena which are generally attributed to the Obligatory Contour Principle (OCP). This principle prohibits adjacent identical autosegments from cooccurring (see e.g. McCarthy 1981, 1986; Yip 1988). Given the commonly accepted view that adjacency is defined on a given tier, in addition to my proposal that all instances of a given place feature are arrayed on the same tier, a number of predictions emerge. First, we would predict cases to exist in which the OCP is defined on the general class of [F], where [F] represents a given place feature. For example, identical adjacent instances of [coronal], [labial] or some other place articulator would be prohibited regardless of whether the feature is arrayed on the consonantal or vocoidal plane. Second, we might expect to find cases in which the OCP is defined on a subset of the general class of [F]. For example, the OCP would hold on instances of [F] arrayed on the consonantal plane, or those instances arrayed on the vocoidal plane. Thus, the OCP scans either the vocoidal plane or the consonantal plane. From this emerges a third prediction. We would expect the OCP to hold on adjacent instances of $[F]_x$ provided that $[F]_y$ does not intervene, where x and y are consonantal or vocoidal, and x is not of the same category as y. If it can be shown that cases such as this do exist, we have strong evidence in support of the view that all instances of a given place feature are arrayed on the same tier. As I show in chapter IV, each of these predictions is borne out, thus supporting my hypothesis.

The single-tier approach which I am proposing differs from that of Selkirk (1988) (see also Clements 1989) who argues that a given consonantal place feature is arrayed on an independent tier from the corresponding vowel feature. In order to maintain this latter approach, the Obligatory Contour Principle (and thus, adjacency) must be allowed to apply across tiers. This has the unfortunate consequence of increasing the power of the OCP and thus creating a less highly constrained theory. Alternatively, I show that by arraying all instances of a given place feature on the same tier we are able to account for rules such as dissimilation without extending the power of the OCP.

In addition to motivating the single-tier hypothesis outlined above, I develop in considerable detail the view that consonantal and vocoidal representations are partially segregated, as proposed in Clements (1989, 1990c). As I stated above, it is argued that each constriction node is arrayed on an independent tier. Given this organization of place features in conjunction with the proposal that a feature from a single tier can link to either the CONS or VOC, it may be the case that a given feature can link to both constriction nodes simultaneously. In this work I claim that a given place feature may, under the marked option, spread from one constriction node to another, thus resulting in a single feature multiply-linked to two different tiers. This is illustrated in (12).

(12)

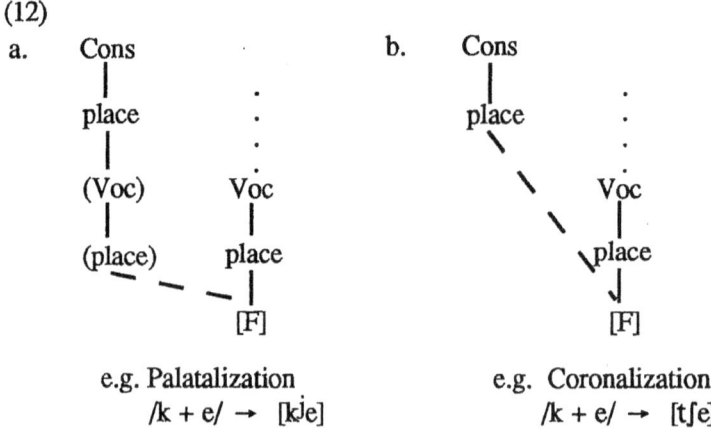

Introduction

In (12a), the feature [F] spreads from the vocoidal plane of a given segment to interpolated vocoidal substructure of the preceding segment. In this instance, the spreading element maintains its original status as a vocoidal feature and is realized as such on both the target and the trigger. In (12b), on the other hand, the feature [F] spreads from the vocoidal plane of the trigger directly to the consonantal plane of the target. The result is a single feature linked to both the consonantal and vocoidal planes. By virtue of being linked to the consonantal plane, [F] will be phonetically interpreted in a manner consistent with the stricture (and other) features that characterize the target. Similarly, by virtue of being linked to the vocoidal plane, the phonetic realization of [F] on the trigger will be consistent with the stricture (and other) features specified for that segment. I propose that the representation in (12a) characterizes Palatalization, a rule in which an i-like articulation is superimposed onto the primary articulation of a consonant, e.g. /k + e/ → [k^{j}e]. (12b), on the other hand, represents Coronalization, a rule in which the primary articulation of a consonant changes to [coronal] in the environment of a front vowel, e.g. /k + e/ → [tʃe] (see chapter V for further discussion).

One of the immediate consequences of allowing articulator features to spread from one plane to another is that Coronalization, as well as Palatalization, may be represented as direct-change rules. In Coronalization, for example, a velar consonant changes into a postalveolar coronal without passing through an intermediate stage of Palatalization, as has been proposed in, for example, Chomsky & Halle (1968), Clements (1989). In the indirect-change approach the realization of a postalveolar coronal before a front vowel can only be indirectly attributed to the quality of the vowel. In other words, the change from velar to postalveolar coronal is not the direct result of assimilation to a following front vowel. Rather, assimilation creates a palatalized consonant. Additional rules not directly related to the front vowel are subsequently required in order to change the palatalized segment into a postalveolar. In the analyses in this work, the change affected in the feature specification of the consonant in both Coronalization and Palatalization is directly attributable to the vowel. Both rules are represented as operations in which a single articulator node spreads from the vowel to the consonantal target. Thus, both rules are represented in simple terms which correctly reflects their common status cross-linguistically.

A number of further implications for phonological theory emerge from this work. For example, in my investigation into coronal vowel/consonant parallelisms in Maltese in Part II (chapter VII), I argue that there is a single default rule assigning place of articulation in the language, i.e. place → [coronal]. This applies regardless of whether the segment in question is a consonant or vowel.

My findings in chapters VI and VII also provide strong counterevidence to the view that the existence of a given default rule necessarily implies that all surface occurrences of this default value are unspecified in underlying representation, as claimed in, for example, Archangeli (1984), Archangeli & Pulleyblank (1986). Instead, we will see that certain segments are crucially specified underlyingly for default feature values. These findings corroborate those of Herzallah (1990) and Hualde (1991) and suggest that default feature values are independent of the underlying feature system of a given language, available perhaps universally or on a language-specific basis as a means of filling in unspecified segments.

2. BACKGROUND ASSUMPTIONS

2.1 Nonlinear Phonology

In this work I assume a general knowledge of phonological theory. As stated above, the analyses in this study are couched in the theory of nonlinear phonology. The development of this theory (and more specifically autosegmental phonology) can be considered among the more influential recent advancements in phonological theory. This emerged when traditional linear representations, as developed out of the work of Chomsky & Halle (1968), failed to account for phonological processes which occur in a wide range of languages. These include, among others, tonal phenomena (e.g. Clements & Ford 1979, Goldsmith 1976, Haraguchi 1977), vowel harmony (Clements 1976b) and nonconcatenative morphology (McCarthy 1979). The problems raised by these phenomena suggest that segments are comprised of feature bundles which are organized on autonomous phonological tiers. Clements' (1985) and Sagey's (1986) investigations of feature organization have shown the need to recognize much more elaborate hierarchical structure for a segment's features than in earlier nonlinear representations. In these models of feature geometry, individual features are organized under class nodes (e.g. place node, supralaryngeal node, laryngeal node) which are ultimately dominated by a root node. The grouping of features under nodes represents their natural classes and by doing so, expresses more accurately natural phonological phenomena such as assimilation (Clements 1985) and the behaviour of complex segments, i.e. those with multiple simultaneous articulations (Sagey 1986), to mention only a few. Since chapter IV of this work presents an indepth discussion of the model of feature organization that I assume, I will leave further discussion to that time.

2.2 Underspecification

The degree to which feature values are underspecified in underlying representation is a controversial issue. There is, however, general consensus among most proponents of underspecification that redundant feature values are absent underlyingly. In one approach researchers argue that only a single value (either + or -) of a given feature is present underlyingly, with the opposite value filled in at a later stage by redundancy rule (see e.g. Archangeli 1984, Archangeli & Pulleyblank 1986, Kiparsky 1982, 1985). One of the principal arguments for this degree of underspecification is based on the notion of simplicity. It is argued that the fewer features present underlyingly, the simpler the grammar. Thus, "the language learner has less to learn and less to memorize" (Archangeli 1984: 41-42). However, Christdas (1988) argues that greater simplicity in underlying representation requires a more complex system of rules in order to eventually fill in the unspecified segments (see also Odden 1991b for additional arguments against the simplicity criterion). Clements (1988) and Christdas (1988) also show that certain potentially unspecified values are needed underlyingly to account for cooccurrence constraints and other phenomena in a range of languages.

In this work, I assume a degree of underspecification based on Steriade (1987) and Clements (1988). In this approach both values of a contrastive feature are generally present underlyingly (see Clements 1988 for further precisions). Articulator features such as [labial, coronal, dorsal] are, however, generally single-valued both underlyingly

3. ORGANIZATION OF THIS STUDY

This work is divided into two parts. Part I (chapters II-V) lays out and develops the specific theoretical claims in this work drawing on evidence from a wide range of languages. Chapter II focusses on the phonetic properties of coronal sounds, both consonants and vowels. Chapter III concentrates on the feature specification of coronal consonants and vowels as motivated by a range of phonological phenomena. In chapter IV, I present the feature theory and nonlinear model of feature organization assumed in this work. This chapter deals in considerable detail with the many predictions made by the model with regards to rules of, for example, assimilation and dissimilation. In chapter V I present my analysis of the well-known consonant-to-vowel assimilations commonly referred to by the cover term *palatalization*.

In Part II (chapters VI-VII), I present a case study of one specific language, Maltese Arabic. I incorporate many of the proposals put forth in Part I as a means of accounting for various interactions among consonants and vowels in this language. Finally, I give a brief conclusion in chapter VIII.

NOTES

1. The low front vowel is backed to [a] by an independent rule after nonlabial consonants. The diminutive suffix that surfaces as [a] in, e.g. vnútʃ+a is the same suffix as in chláp+æ 'man' (dimin.) (see Rubach, forthcoming).

2. Odden's data is taken from his own fieldwork.

3. I assume that the low vowels /a/ and /a:/ are not fronted next to a coronal consonant because they are central, rather than back vowels and thus, are not targets of the coronal assimilation rule. As will be shown in chapter IV, central vowels are not specified for [dorsal] which characterizes back vowels nor for [coronal] which characterizes front vowels. The rule of Coronal Assimilation can thus be defined on the natural class of back (i.e. [dorsal] vowels). To account for the fact that

low vowels are not targets, Cheng proposes that /a/ and /a:/ in Cantonese are [+ATR], a feature specification which is otherwise unmotivated.

    4. He notes that between /ɨ/ and /a/, and word-initially before /i/, /w/ is also fronted.

II
Phonetic Correlates of [Coronal]

0. INTRODUCTION

In its most common usage, the feature [coronal] has served to characterize a consonantal articulation made with the tip or blade of the tongue. Drawing on earlier proposals of, most notably, Halle & Stevens (1979), I plan to show that this definition of [coronal] is unsatisfactory as a means of describing all coronal consonants. Rather, [coronal] can be implemented by the tip, blade and/or front of the tongue. By redefining [coronal] in these terms I will show that this feature naturally extends to the articulation of front vowels.

However, before doing so it is necessary to have a clear understanding of what is meant by the terms *tip*, *blade* and *front* of the tongue. Thus, in the first section of this chapter I review earlier descriptions concerning the topology of the tongue. With this as a basis, I explicate my assumptions concerning the tongue's functional divisions. Next, I present an overview of the term [coronal], as it has been defined in the literature. Then, by drawing on both phonetic and phonological data, I motivate the revised definition and class of coronal sounds. In the final section, I review the acoustic properties of coronals.

1. TOPOLOGY OF THE TONGUE

In this section I focus on descriptions of divisions of the tongue which appear in the literature. Although the root constitutes an important functional part of the tongue, it is not relevant to this discussion and, consequently, I will focus on the divisions of the upper surface of the tongue.

Catford (1977, 1988) divides the upper surface of the tongue (excluding the root) into four regions: the tip (apex), the blade, the antero-dorsum and the postero-dorsum, as illustrated in Figure 1.

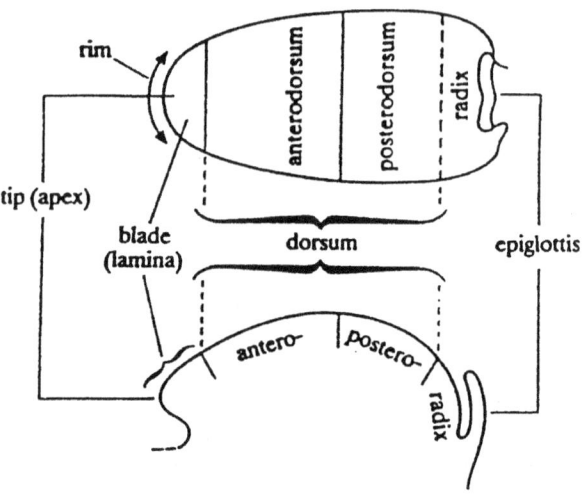

Figure 1. Subdivisions of the tongue (Catford 1988)

Catford classifies the tip as the central point of the tongue's rim, with the rim being the forward edge of the tongue. With respect to the remaining parts of the tongue, he states (1988:82):

> "The blade is that part of the upper surface of the tongue, extending about 1.0 to 1.5 cm back from the apex, that usually lies just under the alveolar ridge when the tongue is at rest, and its rim touching the back of the lower teeth. The remainder of the upper surface of the tongue is the dorsum. The front part of the dorsum (anterio-dorsum) practically always articulates against the roof of the mouth in the palatal zone, while the postero-dorsum articulates in the velar zone."

Ladefoged (1982:4) divides the upper surface of the tongue into the tip, blade, front, center and back as shown in Figure 2.

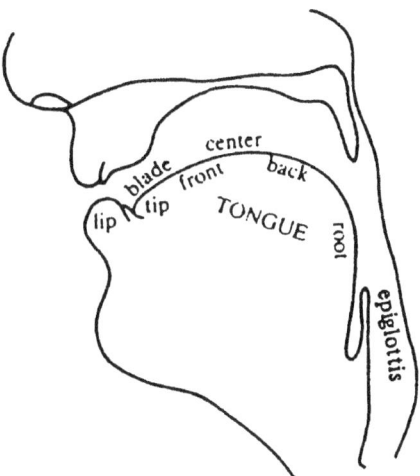

Figure 2. Subdivisions of the tongue (Ladefoged 1982)
Copyright © by Harcourt Brance & Company, reproduced by permission of the publisher.

Ladefoged states (p.4):

> "The tip and blade of the tongue are the most mobile parts. Behind the blade is what is technically called the front of the tongue: it is actually the forward part of the body of the tongue, and lies beneath the hard palate when the tongue is at rest. The remainder of the body of the tongue may be divided into the center, which is partly beneath the hard palate and partly beneath the soft palate, the back, which is beneath the soft palate, and the root, which is opposite the back wall of the pharynx."

Keating's (1990) description of the tongue tip and blade is based largely on those of the above authors. These parts of the tongue are illustrated in Figure 3. She does not include the front or the center of the tongue in her discussion.

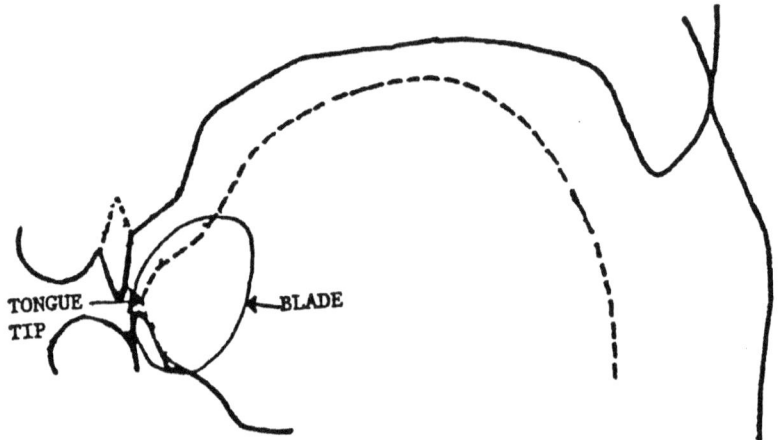

Figure 3. Tip and blade of the tongue (Keating 1990)

Keating notes that: "we will consider the blade of the tongue to be the movable part extending from one to two centimeters behind the tip, and we will consider the tip to include a small rim around the end of the tongue."

Finally, Zemlin (1968:278) states that the upper surface of the tongue is divided into four regions, as shown in Figure 4.

> "This division is based upon the relationship of the tongue to the roof of the mouth...the portion of the tongue nearest the front teeth is called the tip, the portion just below the alveolar ridge is called the blade, the portion just below the hard palate is called the front, and the portion beneath the soft palate is called the back of the tongue."

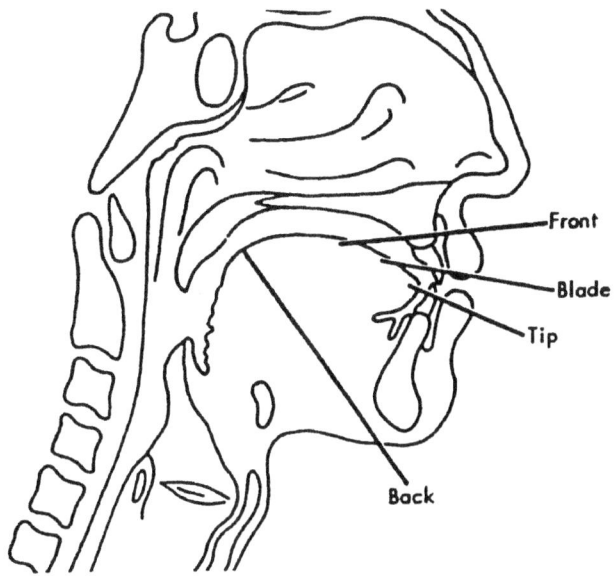

Figure 4. Subdivisions of the tongue (W. R. Zemlin 1968)
Reprinted with the Permission of Prentice-Hall, Inc., Engl. Cliffs, NJ.

From the four diagrams and descriptions given above, it can be seen that there is a great deal of agreement concerning the divisions of the tongue. All authors recognize an area at the most forward part of the tongue referred to as the tip or apex. From a functional point of view, sounds produced with the tip of the tongue are referred to as apical coronals. Retroflex sounds in languages such as Hindi and Urdu are also produced with the tip of the tongue (Ladefoged & Bhaskararao 1983).

There is also general consensus concerning the status of the blade as a functional part of the tongue as well as its general location. Zemlin and Catford refer to the blade as that part of the tongue just below the alveolar ridge. Catford suggests that the blade extends 1.0 to 1.5 cm behind the tip. Keating extends this measurement to up to 2 cm. Ladefoged describes the blade as the mobile part of the tongue between the tip and the front. Based on these descriptions we may take the blade to be the portion of the tongue which extends anywhere from

1 to 2 cm behind the tip and lies just below the alveolar ridge when the tongue is at rest. The blade of the tongue is used in the articulation of laminal sounds such as the palato-alveolar fricative [ʃ] of English.

There is also agreement that the upper surface of the tongue between the blade and the root is divided into at least two general areas. These include what can be called the front and the back of the tongue. Ladefoged includes the center of the tongue as a third region. Functionally, the use of the back of the tongue in the production of speech sounds is uncontroversial, e.g. velar consonants. Moreover, as I show below, palatal consonants are articulated with the front of the tongue. It is not evident, however, whether a third division in addition to the front and back is required. If it can be shown that minimal contrasts exist in a given language among sounds produced with the front, center and back of the tongue, we would have evidence for this third category. At present, I am not aware of any such contrasts. Consequently, I will assume, following Zemlin and Catford, that the region between the blade and the tongue root is divided into two areas: the front which lies below the hard palate, and the back which is located beneath the soft palate.

To summarize, I divide the upper surface of the tongue into four regions: the tip, the blade, the front and the back. The tip is the most advanced portion of the tongue. The blade lies just below the alveolar ridge when the tongue is at rest and extends from 1 to 2 cm behind the tip. The front of the tongue is the portion which lies below the hard palate and the back is located beneath the soft palate.

2. ARTICULATORY DESCRIPTION OF [CORONAL]

The feature [coronal] was introduced into modern phonological theory by Chomsky & Halle (1968). They describe it as follows:

> "Coronal sounds are produced with the blade of the tongue raised from its neutral position; noncoronal sounds are produced with the blade of the tongue in the neutral position. The so-called dental, alveolar, and palato-alveolar consonants are coronal, as are the liquids articulated with the blade of the tongue." (p.304)

We can assume that the blade is intended to refer to the tip as well as the blade since apical sounds are considered to be coronal by these authors. The definition of [coronal] in terms of an articulation produced with the tip and blade of the tongue occurs commonly in the literature. For example, Keating (1990) states that coronals can be defined as segments produced with the blade (including the tip) of the tongue. Moreover, Halle (1983:98) points to the tongue blade as one of three active articulators used in producing speech and states that: "we follow SPE here and postulate that the tongue blade is controlled by the feature [coronal]."

The feature [coronal] as introduced by Chomsky & Halle replaced, to a limited extent, the acoustically-based feature [acute] (or [-grave]) proposed in the work of Jakobson, Fant & Halle (1952). The feature [acute] groups together the consonants that subsequently became classified as [coronal] in SPE as well as front vowels, the palatal glide and palatal consonants. The exclusion of, in particular, palatal sounds from the class of coronals in SPE triggered the emergence of a number of articles providing evidence that palatals pattern with coronal consonants and should thus be included in the same natural class (e.g. Vago 1976, Odden 1978, Hyman 1973, Clements 1976a).

To illustrate, recall from the Introduction that in high vowel reduplication in Fe?fe?-Bamileke the normal reduplicative vowel /ɨ/ is realized as [i] just in case: a) it is followed by /i/ in the next syllable; or b) it is preceded by [t d s z n l c ɟ ʃ ʒ (ɲ) j] and a front vowel of any height (Hyman 1973, Clements 1976a). Furthermore, in Ewe, [l] and [r] are in complementary distribution in CLV syllables: [l] occurs when the initial consonant is labial, velar or labiovelar and [r] occurs when the consonant is coronal, including palatal consonants and the palatal glide (Clements 1976a, Smith 1973, Westerman 1930), as shown in (13).

(13)   blá   'to tie'
       kplɔ   'to accompany'
       kló   'to uncover'
       trɔ́   'to turn'
       ɲrà   'to be enraged'
       dzrá   'to sell'
       jrɔ   'to be dried up'

Moreover, in Porteño Spanish the palatal glide strengthens to a palato-alveolar obstruent in syllable-initial position, e.g. convo[j] 'convoy' vs. convo[ʒ]es 'convoys', le[j] 'law' vs. le[ʒ]es 'laws' (Harris 1983, Morgan 1984; see chapter III below for further discussion). In Sanskrit, a palatal consonant patterns with other coronals in blocking the rule of N-Retroflexion from applying (Odden 1978; see chapter III below for discussion). In Hungarian as well, palatal stops pattern with anterior coronal stops, to the exclusion of labial and velar stops, as trigger and target of rules of affrication, as I show just below.

In light of evidence of this sort, Halle & Stevens (1979) proposed a revision of the feature [coronal] in order to include palatal consonants and the palatal glide. They state (p. 346):

> "In SPE, coronal sounds were said to be 'produced with the blade of the tongue raised from its neutral position,' thus specifically excluding palatal consonants, which are produced by raising not the blade of the tongue, but rather its central portion, i.e. the part connecting the blade with the tongue body. The articulatory correlate of the revised feature of coronality is, therefore, the raising of the frontal (i.e. tip, blade, and/or central) part of the tongue so as to make contact with the palate."

The central part of the tongue referred to by Halle & Stevens corresponds to what I refer to as the tongue *front*.

2.1 Hungarian Palatals

That palatal consonants involve an articulation made by raising the front of the tongue is exemplified by articulatory data from Hungarian (Bolla 1980), which includes the palatal stops /ɟ c/ in its phonemic inventory. As the X-ray tracings in Figures 5 and 6 illustrate, the front of the tongue is raised to form a constriction along the hard palate. Neither the tip nor the blade are involved. This is reinforced by the palatograms (top right of each figure) and linguagrams (bottom right of each figure). In the palatogram, the location of the constriction is indicated by the lightened surface of the palate. The darkened portion of the tongue in each linguagram indicates the area of the tongue involved in the constriction. As seen in the linguagram of, in particular, [ɟ], the constriction is made with the portion of the tongue between the blade and the back of the tongue.

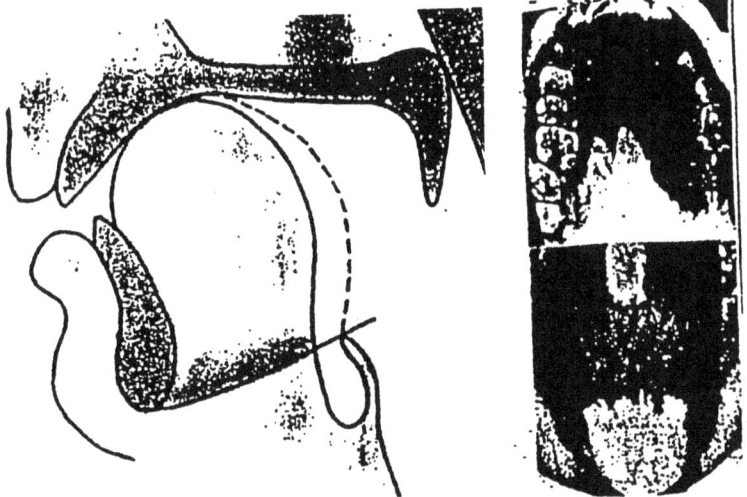

Figure 5. Hungarian palatal [ɟ] (Bolla 1980)
Reprinted with the permission of K. Bolla.

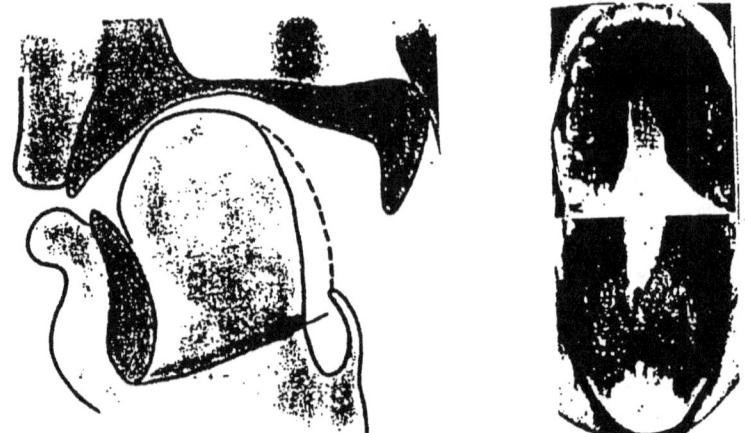

Figure 6. Hungarian palatal [c] (Bolla 1980)
Reprinted with the permission of K. Bolla.

That palatals are in fact coronal sounds is supported by phonological rules of affrication in which the palatal stops function as target and trigger with other coronal stops. In (14a), I provide the phonemic inventory of Hungarian consonants, and in (14b), the fully specified place and stricture specifications of coronal obstruents that I assume (see chapter III for discussion concerning the feature specification and representation of coronals).

(14)   Hungarian Underlying Consonant Inventory
a.

	labial	labio-dental	dental	palato-alveolar	palatal	velar	laryngeal
stops	p b		t d		c ɟ	k g	
fricatives		f v	s z	ʃ ʒ			h
affricates			t͡s d͡z	t͡ʃ d͡ʒ			
nasals	m		n		ɲ		
liquids			l, r				

b. Place and Stricture Specification of Coronal Obstruents

	t	d	s	z	t͡s	d͡z	ʃ	ʒ	t͡ʃ	d͡ʒ	c	ɟ
coronal	+	+	+	+	+	+	+	+	+	+	+	+
anterior	+	+	+	+	+	+	-	-	-	-	-	-
distributed	-	-	-	-	-	-	+	+	+	+	+	+
strident	-	-	+	+	+	+	+	+	+	+	-	-
continuant	-	-	+	+	±	±	+	+	±	±	-	-

There are two interrelated rules which provide evidence for treating palatal stops as coronals. They are Fricative Affrication in which palatal and anterior coronal stops function as triggers, and Stop Affrication in which the same stops function as targets. Both rules are optional. I begin with a discussion of Fricative Affrication.

As Vago (1980) points out, the coronal fricatives /s ʃ/[1] are realized as [t͡s t͡ʃ] respectively, when preceded by /t d c ɟ/, as shown in (15).

(15) hɛɟ   'mountain'   hɛɟ+ʃe:g   [hɛɟt͡ʃe:g]   'mountain range'
     bɑrɑ:t[2] 'friend'   bɑrɑ:t+ʃɑːg   [bɑrɑ:tt͡ʃɑːg] 'friendship'
     öt   'five'   öt+sör   [ött͡sör]   'five times'

Fricative Affrication only applies if the stop and fricative are in the same word, cf. [ke:t se:k] *[ke:t t͡se:k] 'two chairs'; [nɑɟ sobor] *[nɑɟ t͡sobor] 'large statue'; [rövid ʃor] *[rövid t͡ʃor] 'short line'. Furthermore, stops other than /t d c ɟ/ do not trigger affrication, e.g. [tɛpʃi] *[tɛpt͡ʃi] 'baking-tin', [ɛmʃɛ] *[ɛmt͡ʃɛ] 'sow', [vakʃɑ:g] ([vak] 'blind') *[vakt͡ʃɑ:g] 'blindness'. The rule of Fricative Affrication is stated formally in (16a), using the notation introduced by Archangeli & Pulleyblank (1986). The operation of the rule involves spreading [-continuant] from the trigger, a coronal obstruent stop, to the target, a coronal obstruent continuant. Spreading is directional, occurring from left to right, and only applies at the word level. Using the nonlinear model outlined briefly in the Introduction, the rule of Fricative Affication is illustrated in (16b). As can be seen, the fricative acquires the feature [-continuant] from a preceding coronal stop (see chapter III for further discussion of the formalism used). The output is an affricate. Although not crucial to this discussion, I assume that affricates are specified for both values of the feature [continuant] (for alternative representations and discussion see, e.g. Lombardi 1990, Steriade 1989).[3]

36   *The Interaction of Front Vowels and Coronal Consonants*

(16)

a. *Fricative Affrication:*
operation: spread [-cont]
trigger: [coronal, -continuant, -sonorant]
target: [coronal, +continuant, -sonorant]
direction: left to right
domain: word

b.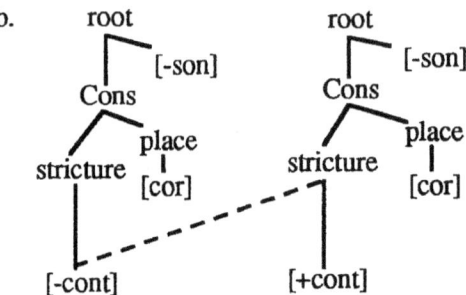

By the second rule, Stop Affrication, coronal obstruent stops /t d c ɟ/ assimilate completely to a following coronal affricate (Abondolo 1988, Vago 1980). The rule may be triggered by an affricate derived as the result of Fricative Affrication as shown in (17a) (and thus within the same word), or by an underlying affricate across a word-boundary as in (17b).

(17)

a.
			Fric. Affric.		Stop Affric.
öt 'five'	öt+sör	→	öt͡sör	→	[ö͡tst͡sör] 'five times'
ötöd 'fifth'	ötöd+sör	→	ötöd͡tsör	→	[ötö͡tst͡sör] 'the fifth time'
bará:t 'friend'	bará:t+ʃá:g	→	bará:t͡ʃág	→	[bará:t͡ʃ t͡ʃá:g] 'friendship'
hɛɟ 'mountain'	hɛɟ+ʃe:g	→	hɛɟt͡ʃe:g	→	[hɛt͡ʃ t͡ʃe:g] 'mountain range'

b.
ke:t t͡sit͡sa	[ke:t͡s t͡sit͡sa]	'two kittens'
ne:ɟ d͡ʒin	[ne:d͡ʒ d͡ʒin]	'four gins'
somse:d t͡ʃala:d	[somse:t͡ʃ t͡ʃala:d]	'neighbouring family'

Phonetic Correlates of [Coronal]

In a), the fricative first becomes optionally affricated by Fricative Affrication. Then as the result of Stop Affrication, the stop optionally assimilates to all features of the following affricate including place of articulation, voicing and continuancy. In b), the final coronal stop of the initial word assimilates directly to the following stem-initial affricate. Total assimilation is characterized as spreading the root node of the affricate to the preceding coronal stop, as stated formally in (18a) and illustrated in (18b). I assume that the output of (18b) is interpreted as a geminate affricate consisting of a long closure plus a release.

(18)
    a. Stop Affrication:
       operation: spread root
       trigger: [coronal],   stricture
                                  /\
                             [-cont] [+cont]
       target: [coronal, -son],   stricture
                                     |
                             [-cont]

       direction: right to left
       domain: phrase

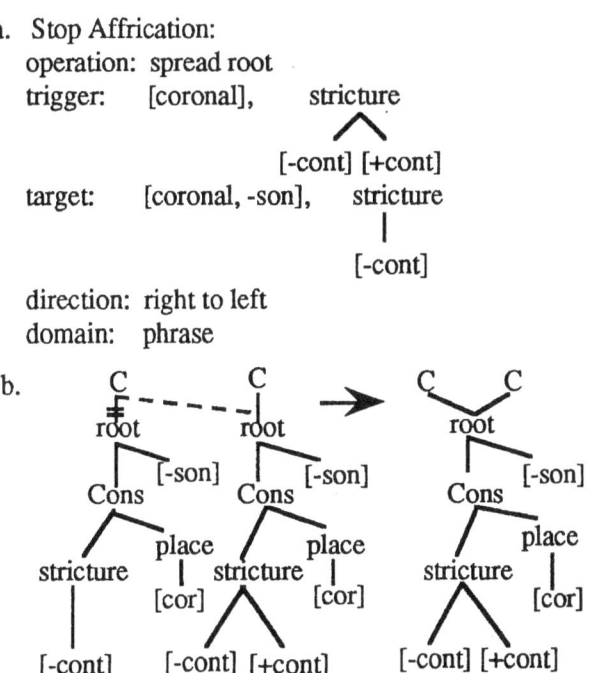

In both Fricative and Stop Affrication the only obstruent stops involved are /t d c ɟ/, in the first rule as trigger and in the second as target. The patterning of Hungarian palatal stops with anterior coronals (to the exclusion of all other stops) is most naturally accounted for by classifying these segments as coronals. Given the articulatory data above showing that the constriction in Hungarian palatal stops is produced by raising the front of the tongue, we have strong evidence in support of the view that the feature [coronal] can be implemented by the tip, blade and/or front of the tongue.

Further support for the view that palatal consonants are articulated with the front of the tongue raised toward the hard palate can be seen in X-ray tracings of the palatal fricative [ç] of German (Figure 7a) and the palatal nasal [ɲ] of Ngwo (Figure 7b). To the right of the German palatal [ç] I give the corresponding velar fricative [x] for comparison. In each instance the constriction of the palatal is made by raising the front, as opposed to the tip or blade, of the tongue.

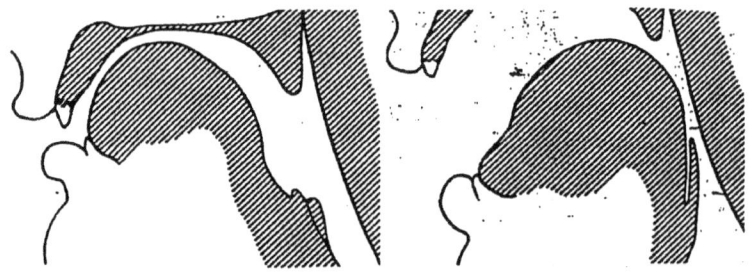

Figure 7a. Palatal [ç] (left) and velar [x] (right) of German
(Wängler 1958)

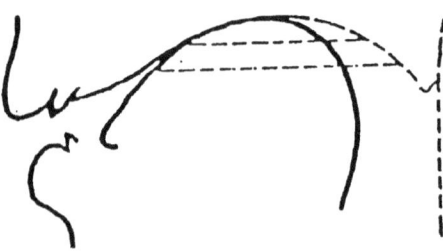

Figure 7b. Palatal nasal [ɲ] of Ngwo (Ladefoged 1968)
Reprinted with the permission of Cambridge University Press.

Keating (1988, 1990) claims that in addition to being specified as [coronal, -anterior], palatals are specified for the tongue body feature [-back]. To anticipate the discussion in chapter III, we will see that specifying palatal consonants for secondary vocalic features is problematic. The evidence is drawn from Hungarian vowel (backness) harmony. As I will show, palatal consonants, like all other consonants in the language, are transparent to vowel harmony. Were palatal consonants specified for secondary vocalic features, this transparency would not be expected. Rather, we would incorrectly predict palatals, to the exclusion of all other consonants, to block the application of vowel harmony. Thus, the specification of palatal consonants for primary consonantal features and no secondary features is supported by both phonetic and phonological evidence.

3. THE CORONALITY OF FRONT VOWELS

In the preceding section I have motivated a redefinition of the feature [coronal] to refer to sounds in which the constriction is made by raising the tip, blade and/or front of the tongue. In this section I show that this revised definition extends naturally to the articulation of front vowels.

By comparing the articulation of the high front vowel with that of the palatal consonant it can be seen that characterizing [i] as [coronal] is well-motivated. As shown in Figure 8a for Hungarian and Figure 8b for German, the parallelism between the two segment types is striking. In both pairs the constriction is produced with the front of the tongue raised toward the hard palate. Given the claim that [coronal] can be implemented with the front of the tongue, and that palatal consonants are [coronal], characterizing the high front vowel as [coronal] is well supported.

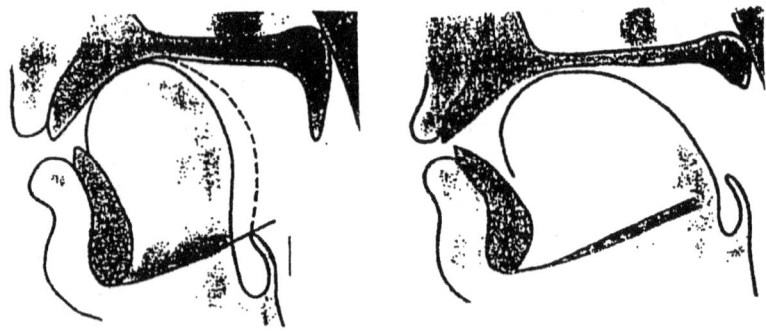

Figure 8a. Hungarian palatal stop [ɟ] and high front vowel [i]
(Bolla 1980) Reprinted with the permission of K. Bolla.

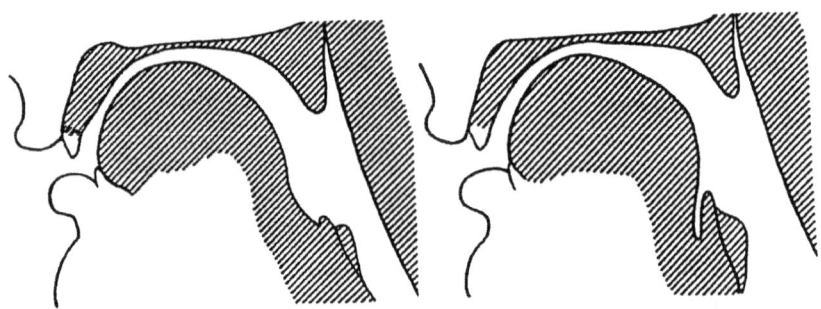

Figure 8b. German palatal fricative [ç] (left) and high front
vowel [i] (right) (Wängler 1958)

The validity of characterizing all front vowels as [coronal] can be verified by comparing a given front vowel with its nonfront counterpart. A given feature is thus interpreted in relative terms. If it can be shown that a given segment displays the defining physical correlate of [+F] to a greater degree than the corresponding [-F] sound, we have evidence for the specification of a given segment as [+F].

To illustrate, consider the X-ray tracings of the vowels [i] and [u] in Russian, Canadian French and Hungarian, in Figures 9a through c, respectively.

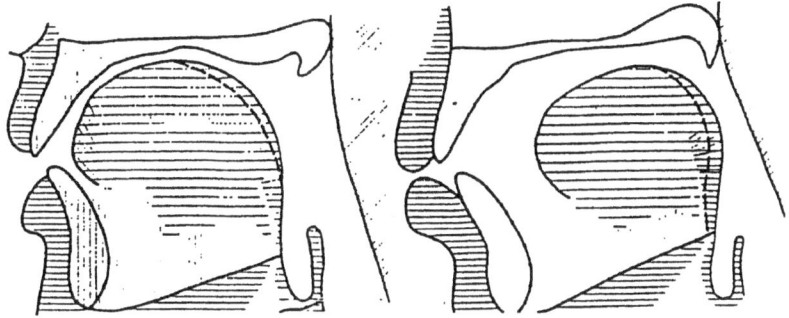

Figure 9a. [i] vs. [u] Russian (Bolla 1981)
Reprinted with the permission of K. Bolla.

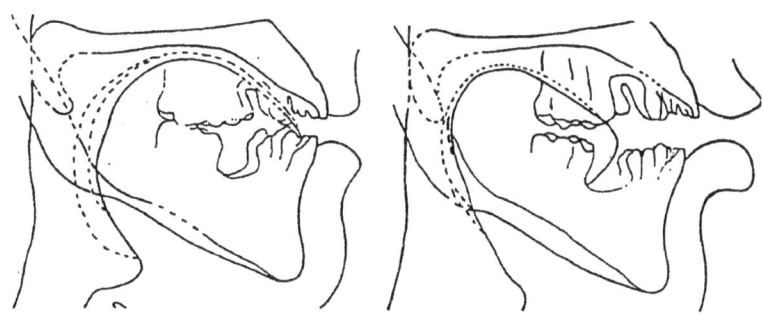

Figure 9b. [i] vs. [u] Canadian French (Gendron 1966)
Reprinted with the permission of Editions Klincksieck.

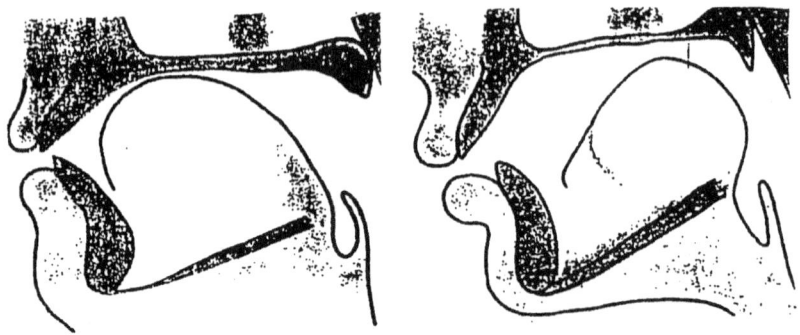

Figure 9c. [i] vs. [u] Hungarian (Bolla 1980)
Reprinted with the permission of K. Bolla.

By comparing each instance of [i] with its back counterpart it can be seen that the articulation of [i] involves raising the front of the tongue to a greater degree than that of [u]. Similar observations hold with respect to the pairs of vowels in the following figures.

In Figure 10 the vowels [e] vs. [o] of a) Polish, b) Russian, and c) Canadian French are compared. Once again we see evidence that tongue front raising is characteristic of front vowels.

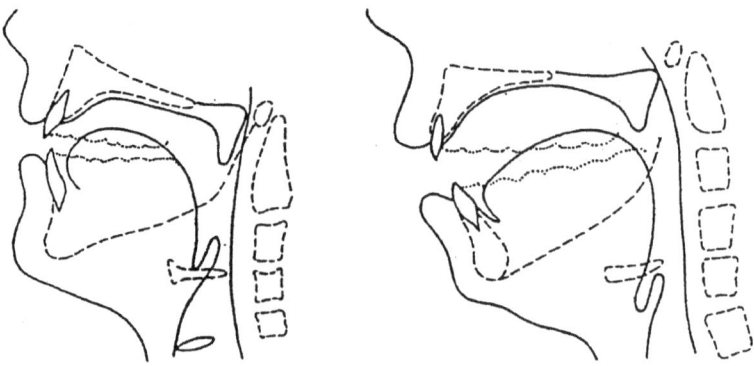

Figure 10a. [e] vs. [o] Polish (Wierzchowska 1980)
Reprinted with the permission of Zakład Narodowy im. Ossolińskich Wydawnictwo.

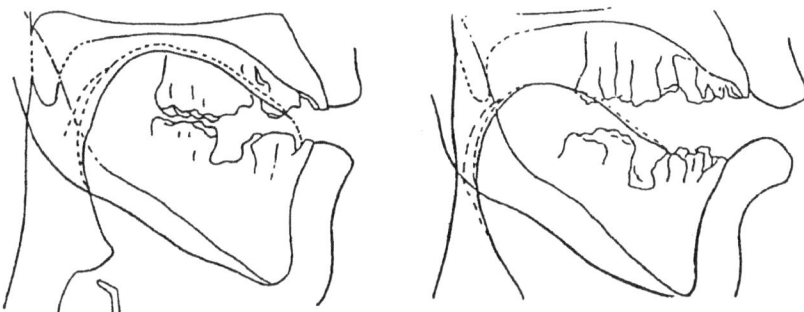

Figure 10b. [e] vs.[o] Canadian French (Gendron 1966)
Reprinted with the permission of Editions Klincksieck.

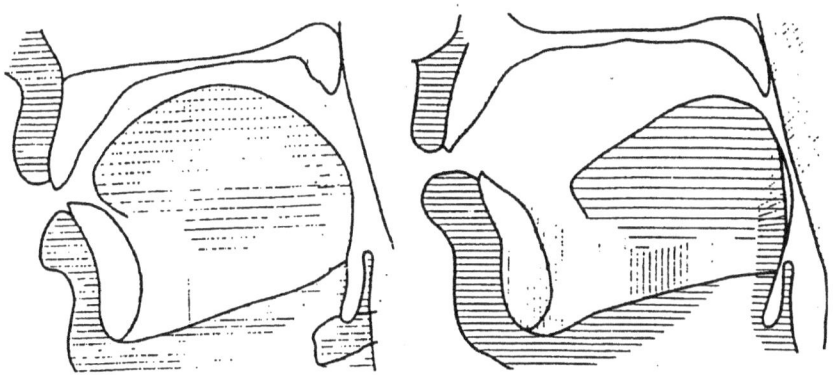

Figure 10c. [e] vs. [o] Russian (Bolla 1981)
Reprinted with the permission of K. Bolla.

In Figure 11, the contrast between the mid vowels [ö] and [o] of Hungarian is shown. Focussing again on the frontal region of the tongue, it will be noticed that in [o] this portion of the tongue is considerably lower than it is for [ö].

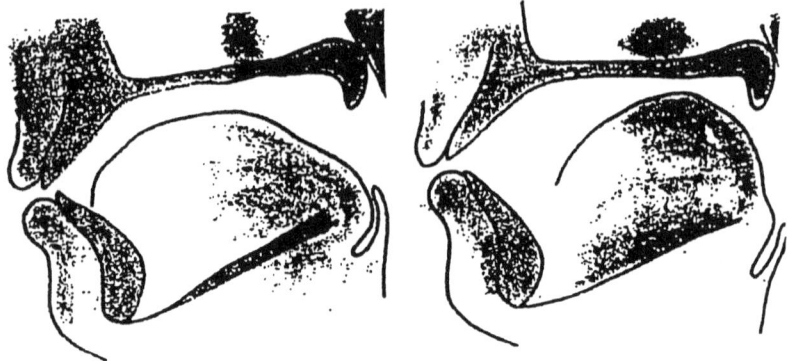

Figure 11. [ö] vs. [o] Hungarian (Bolla 1980)
Reprinted with the permission of K. Bolla.

Figure 12 presents the back vowel [ɔ] compared with the front vowel [ɛ] of Canadian French. Once again the greater degree of front raising in [ɛ] is particularly salient when compared to its back counterpart.

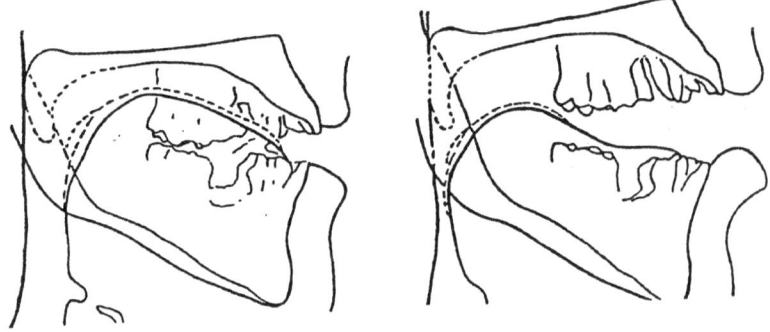

Figure 12. [ɛ] vs. [ɔ] Canadian French (Gendron 1966)
Reprinted with the permission of Editions Klincksieck.

In Figure 13, I illustrate the articulation of the low front vowel [æ] with that of its back counterpart [ɑ] from Swedish and English. Note that by comparing the articulation of [æ] with its noncoronal counterpart [ɑ] it is clear that the front of the tongue is raised to a greater degree in [æ] than it is in [ɑ], even though when examined in isolation this may be less evident.

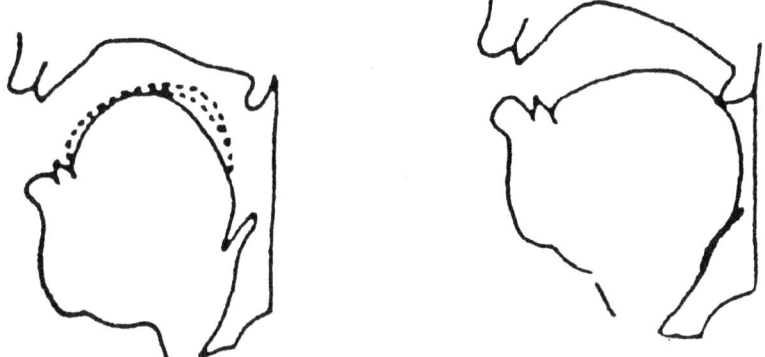

Figure 13a. [æ:] vs. [ɑ] Swedish (Fant 1959)
Reprinted with the permission of Elsevier Science Publishers BV.

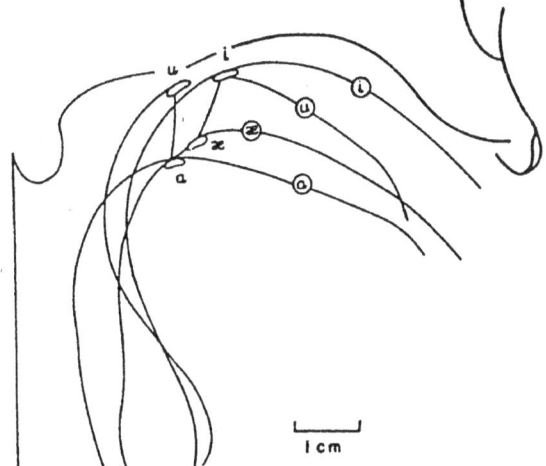

Figure 13b. [æ] vs. [ɑ] English (Perkell 1969)
Reprinted with the permission of MIT Press.

Characterizing front vowels as [coronal] departs sharply from the traditional SPE view in which front vowels are specified as [-back]. In its current usage, [-back] characterizes sounds which "are produced with the tongue body relatively advanced" (Halle & Clements 1983:7). It is this horizontal displacement of the tongue which has been thought to be phonologically salient for characterizing front vowels as a natural class. The view developed in this work is that it is rather the constriction created in the production of front vowels by raising the front of the tongue towards the hard palate which is of phonological importance.

Instead of extending the feature [coronal] to include front vowels one might suggest that we extend the feature [-back] to include coronal consonants. Doing so is problematic, however, since not all coronal consonants are produced with a fronted tongue body. For example, it is well-documented that the phonemic inventory of Russian includes two constrasting series of coronal consonants, with one series ('soft', palatalized) articulated with the tongue fronted, and the other series ('hard', velarized) produced with the tongue in a retracted position. Representative pairs are given in Figure 14 below. Given that the tongue body is not advanced in the articulation of 'hard' coronals, characterizing these sounds as [-back] is unmotivated.

Phonetic Correlates of [Coronal]

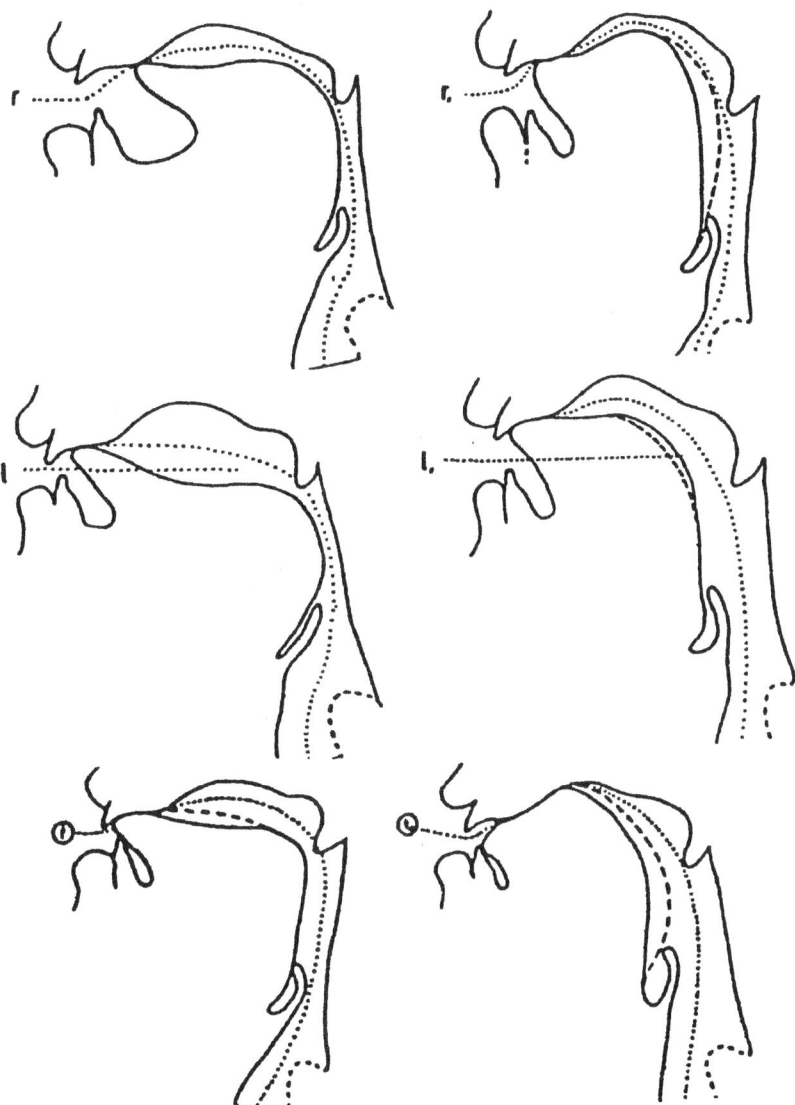

Figure 14. Representative 'hard' and 'soft' coronals of Russian (Fant 1960): [r] vs. [r']; [l] vs. [l']; [t] vs. [t']

Still, one might argue that the 'hard' coronals are not actually coronals but rather segments specified simply for the feature [+back].

In this way, the 'soft' series would be specified as only [-back] and the 'hard' series as only [+back]. However, this specification poses problems for accounting for certain phonological rules in Russian. First, there is a rule which changes 'hard' strident dentals into postalveolars before a postalveolar, i.e. /ʃ ʒ t͡ʃ'/ (C' indicates a 'soft' consonant) (Halle 1959, Wayles Browne p.c.), as illustrated in (19).[4]

(19) s ʃit'   →   [ʃʃit']   'to sew together'
     s t͡ʃ'itat' →   [ʃt͡ʃ'itat']   'to count'
     bez t͡ʃ'est'ijo → [b'iʃt͡ʃ'es't'ijə] 'dishonour'
     bez ʒalost'no → [b'iʒʒalə snə] 'pitiless'
     s ʃum om   →   [ʃʃuməm]   'with noise'

As evidenced by the forms above, the rule is triggered by both (underlying) hard and soft postalveolars. This class of segments can be characterized most simply as [coronal, -anterior]. If we were to propose that 'hard' coronals were specified as only [+back] and 'soft' coronals as [-back], grouping these segments together as a natural class would be problematic.[5]

Specifying 'hard' coronals as just [+back] would have the additional disadvantage of grouping 'hard' consonants with velars, segments which would arguably also be specified as just [+back]. By specifying these two classes of segments as [+back] we would be at a loss to explain the observation that velars /k g x/, but not 'hard' coronals (or labials) are realized as [t͡ʃ ʒ ʃ] before front vowels, e.g. peku 'I bake'/ pet͡ʃet 'bakes', mogu 'I am able'/moʒet 'is able', uspex 'success/uspeʃen 'successful' (Lightner 1965). I conclude then that extending the feature [-back] to include all coronal consonants is not a feasible approach since not all coronal consonants are produced with an advanced tongue body.

As both acoustic and articulatory theories of sound production show, the classificatory dimension used to characterize vowels based on tongue body advancement/retraction, i.e. [-back/+back], is unsatisfactory. For example, Jackson's (1988) cross-linguistic study of vowel articulations reveals that the vowel spaces of individual languages differ systematically from traditional views concerning the organization of the vowel space as based on height and backness. His study shows that a limited number of articulatory primes generate the vocal tract shapes observed in particular vowels. Each of these primes can function as an independent articulatory gesture, with tongue front raising being one of the core articulatory primes (following Harshman et al. 1977). As Jackson points out, tongue front raising is the factor which contributes most significantly to the vowel shapes generated by nonlow front vowels. Although the low front vowel [æ] has a positive value for tongue front raising, it involves a lesser degree of tongue front raising than nonlow front vowels. Tongue front raising in [æ] is particularly salient when compared to the low back vowel [ɑ] which is characterized by negative tongue front raising. Jackson's findings are consistent with the proposal developed in this work with respect to the observation that front vowels are articulated with the front of the tongue raised. However, in Jackson's approach, the property of tongue raising and the degree to which the tongue raises are characterized by a single articulatory gesture. Our approach differs from Jackson's in that the degree to which the front of the tongue raises is characterized by independent height features.

With respect to acoustics, Wood (1982:51) states: "according to a century-old tradition in phonetics, small adjustments of tongue fronting or retraction provide an active and useful means of modifying vowel quality. However, acoustic theory does not support this tradition." By 'century-old tradition', he refers to the classic front/back dimension developed out of the work of Melville Bell (1867), which has been largely preserved in SPE feature theory. Before elaborating further I will briefly present the essentials of the acoustic theory of sound production which serve as a basis for this discussion.

The source-filter theory of speech developed most extensively in the work of Fant (1960) (see also Müller 1848, Chiba & Kajiyama 1941, Stevens & House 1955, Stevens 1972, among others) shows that the formant frequencies which characterize different vowel sounds are determined by the particular shape of the supralaryngeal vocal tract, which acts as an acoustic filter. The development of acoustic theory thus "made possible a quantitative prediction of the filtering effects of particular configurations of the supralaryngeal air passages" (Lieberman & Blumstein 1988:36). This theory is aptly summarized by Stevens (1972:51-52):

> "The acoustic theory may be described, in part, in terms of an area function which specifies the cross-sectional area at each point within the vocal tract between the vocal cords and the lips. The acoustic excitation for this nonuniform tube is either a quasiperiodic source at the glottal end or acoustic noise which may be generated in the vicinity of a constriction in the tube as a consequence of turbulence in the air flow. If this acoustic system is perturbed in some way, such as through modification of a parameter that is used to describe the area function, it is to be expected that the properties of the acoustic output will also be perturbed."

However, not all parameters display the same degree of perturbation of the acoustic signal when modified. As the studies of most notably, Stevens (1972) and Wood (1982) have shown, there are preferred regions for vowel production in the vocal tract in which moderate displacements of the constriction within these regions produce negligible effects in the acoustic signal. Using natural human vocal tract configurations, Wood confirms the findings of Stevens by showing that for the articulation of vowels, the tongue aims to narrow the vocal tract at a particular region. Vowel spectra are relatively insensitive to location perturbations along the hard palate for the nonlow allophones of /i/ and the front allophone of /a/ (Wood 1971). The velar region (with lip-rounding) and the pharyngeal region are also shown to be preferred regions of vowel production (Stevens 1972, Wood 1982[6]). As these studies have shown, "vowels fall naturally into discrete categories instead of being identifiable as points on a continuum" (Stevens 1972:56). It is of significance that the discrete categories signalled by these authors generally align with those which, as discussed in chapter IV, are used in the classification of consonants, e.g. [coronal], [dorsal], [pharyngeal].

A few comments are in order concerning the articulation of the low front vowel [æ] since Wood notes that this vowel falls in naturally with vowels produced in the pharyngeal region thus suggesting a specification of low vowels as [pharyngeal] (for related discussion see Herzallah 1990). As our X-ray data above reveal, the presence vs. the absence of tongue front raising correctly distinguishes the low front vowel [æ] from its back counterpart. In other words, the vowel [æ] is [coronal]. This suggests a specification of the low front vowel as both [coronal] and [pharyngeal] (with perhaps the redundant specification of [+low, -high]). Herzallah (1990) argues that the low back vowel [ɑ] of Palestinian Arabic is properly characterized as both [dorsal] and [pharyngeal], whereas [a] is simply [pharyngeal]. Based on these proposals, the specification of the three low vowels is as in (20), with perhaps the addition of (redundant) height features.

(20)	æ	a	ɑ
coronal	+		
dorsal			+
pharyngeal	+	+	+

Consistent with the findings of Wood, all low vowels form a natural class by virtue of their [pharyngeal] specification. Due to the specification [dorsal], the low vowel [ɑ] forms a natural class with back vowels such as [u, o], and contrasts with central vowels such as [a] which are neither coronal nor dorsal (Clements 1989). Similarly, the [coronal] specification of [æ] signals this vowel's membership in the class of front vowels.

Throughout this discussion I have assumed that front vowels are articulated in a relatively uniform manner across languages. Wood (1979) suggests, however, that the articulation of front vowels can differ in the specific location of the constriction. According to Wood's findings, English and Arabic subjects have significantly different constriction locations for high front vowels. While the English subject's articulation is centered midway along the hard palate, the articulation of the Arabic subject is more anterior (although still in the nonanterior coronal region). He notes that there appear to be language-specific preferences for either a prepalatal or midpalatal tongue position for front vowels. However, Jackson's (1989) study of front vowel articulations reveals no systematic difference regarding the constriction locations in front vowels across languages. Note that even if the differences noted by Wood do exist, such differences do not appear to be constrastive within a given language. Thus, the specification of front vowels as [coronal, -anterior] regardless of the language in question is valid.

In some languages, front vowels are produced with both tongue front and blade raising. Wood (1979) found this to be the case in

Swedish, French, Danish, German and Dutch in which blade raising was shown to contribute to stabilizing the resonance conditions in the production of the high front rounded vowel [y]. A [coronal] articulation in vowels may thus be implemented with both blade and front raising, as it is in consonants. However, unlike consonants it does not appear to be the case that for vowels, blade raising is implemented to the exclusion of front raising.

4. ACOUSTIC PROPERTIES OF CORONAL SOUNDS

The acoustic relatedness of front vowels and coronal consonants has long been recognized within the tradition of acoustic phonetics. Jakobson, Fant & Halle (1952) observe that this natural class of sounds is characterized, in general terms, by a concentration of energy in the upper (vs. lower) frequencies of the spectrum. The underlying assumption in this characterizaion is that the acoustic properties of a given feature are interpreted in relative terms (see e.g. Jakobson & Waugh 1987). As demonstrated for the articulatory correlates of [coronal], the specification of a given segment for this feature is verified if the segment bears the articulatory properties of coronality to a greater degree than its noncoronal counterpart. The same criteria hold with respect to a feature's acoustic properties.

The acoustic properties common to coronal vowels are thus determined by a comparison with their noncoronal counterparts. As shown in Figure 15 above, coronal vowels evidence a second formant located more closely to the third and higher formants (from Ladefoged 1982:177)[7], consistent with Fant's observation (1960) that a tongue constriction in the middle of the oral cavity is optimal for a high second formant. This can be observed by comparing [i] vs. [u], [ɩ] vs. [ω], [ɛ] vs. [ɔ] and [æ] vs. [ɑ]. Thus, consistent with Jakobson, Fant & Halle (1952), energy is more concentrated in the upper frequencies of the spectra.

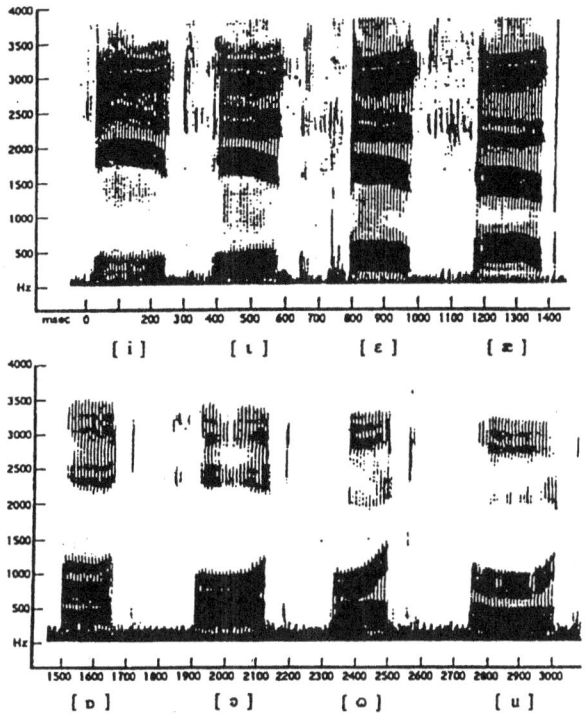

Figure 15. Vowel formant structure (Ladefoged 1982:177)
Copyright © by Harcourt Brance & Company, reproduced by
permission of the publisher.

The number of studies investigating the acoustic correlates of coronal consonants is more limited than that of vowels. Nonetheless, the studies that have been done support the general claim that a coronal consonant is distinguished from its noncoronal counterpart by a greater concentration of energy in the upper frequencies. For example, the spectra of coronal fricatives (anterior and nonanterior) display greater intensity and have higher limits of frequency that those of noncoronal fricatives (Strevens 1967). For stop consonants, Lahiri, Gewirth & Blumstein (1984) show that the shape of the spectrum alone is not sufficient to distinguish between places of articulation. The invariant acoustic properties are drawn from "relative changes in distribution of energy from the burst release to the onset of voicing" (p.398). In particular, coronal consonants are characterized by greater high frequency than low frequency energy at the burst release relative to the onset of voicing. This invariant property is perceptually salient "even in the presence of formant frequency and transitional cues for the alternative place of articulation" (p.403). With respect to coronal nasals, Blumstein & Stevens (1979:1011) note that the spectra of these consonants "should show the same properties as that for a stop consonant with the same place of articulation, although the property may be weaker due to the absence of the burst."

5. SUMMARY

Drawing on the work of Halle & Stevens (1979), in this chapter I have shown the need for a revised definition of the feature [coronal]. As we have seen, the traditional definition of [coronal] as referring to an articulation made with the tip or blade of the tongue is unable to characterize palatal consonants, sounds which are produced by raising the front of the tongue. We thus have evidence that [coronal] may be implemented by the tip, blade and/or front of the tongue. With this as a basis I showed that [coronal] naturally extends to front vowels since they are produced with the front of the tongue raised to a greater degree than their non-front counterparts. Thus, the common articulatory property of coronal sounds, both vowels and consonants, involves an articulation made by raising the frontal region of the tongue, i.e. the tip, blade and/or front of the tongue. Acoustically, the vocal tract configuration created by this articulation results in a sound produced with a greater concentration of energy in the upper frequencies of the spectrum.

NOTES

1. The rule only affects /s ʃ/ since there are no suffixes which begin with /z ʒ/.
2. Throughout the examples, I characterize the low back vowel as [ɑ] regardless of whether it is short or long. On the surface, however, the low back vowel surfaces as rounded [ɔ] when short and as [ɑ] when long. Rounding can be considered the result of a redundancy rule which

assigns the value [+labial] to a [+low, +dorsal] vowel if short (Ringen 1988).

3. The stop may also assimilate in voicing to the following obstruent due to an optional voicing rule which requires an obstruent to agree in voicing with a following obstruent within and across word-boundaries (Vago p.34). This applies independently to give, for example, [hect͡ʃeeg] 'mountain range', in which the palatal stop assimilates in voicing to the following obstruent.

4. For the purposes of this discussion, I ignore additional rules of voicing assimilation, vowel raising and vowel reduction which are also operative in these forms (for discussion see, e.g. Halle 1959, Lightner 1965).

5. One might suppose that all consonants are specified as [+high] and, as a result, the segments /ʃ ʒ t͡ʃ'/ could be characterized as [+strident, +high]. However, this approach would be unable to exclude, for example, the 'hard' anterior coronal /t͡s/ as a trigger.

6. Wood also signals the upper pharynx as a fourth region.

7. It is also feasible to state the properties in terms of the distance between the first and second formants (Ladefoged 1982). In coronal vowels, these two formants are further apart than in the noncoronal counterparts.

III

The Feature Specification of Coronals

0. INTRODUCTION

The focus of this chapter is on the feature specification of coronal consonants and vocoids. Motivation for a particular feature specification is grounded in what we can consider to be two of the fundamental goals of an adequate feature theory. First, a feature theory must be able to distinguish all and ideally only those sounds which are known to be phonemically contrastive in natural language. And second, an adequate feature theory must be able to refer to sounds which regularly pattern together in phonological processes, i.e. natural classes of sounds, by a single nondisjunctive set of feature specifications.

This chapter begins with a discussion of coronal vocoids, i.e. vowels and glides. Following this I examine coronal consonants, beginning with anterior coronals. In the next section I discuss plain postalveolars and then continue with an examination of palatalized consonants. In the final section, the feature specification of coronal sonorants is briefly treated.

1. FRONT VOCOIDS

Following the discussion in chapter II, coronal vowels are specified for the articulator feature [+coronal] which, as illustrated in (21), is linked directly to the VOC place node. Height features link to Stricture with both Stricture and Place immediately dominated by VOC.[1]

(21) e.g. /i/

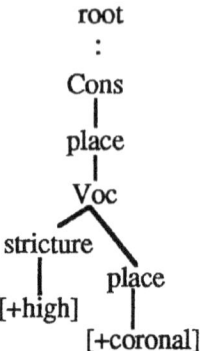

In most current models of feature organization, it is assumed that the articulator feature [coronal] dominates at least the terminal features [distributed] and [anterior] (see e.g. Sagey 1986). The feature [distributed] refers to the length of the constriction involved: "distributed sounds are produced with a constriction that extends for a considerable distance along the midsaggital axis of the oral tract; nondistributed sounds are produced with a constriction that extends for only a short distance in this direction" (Halle & Clements 1983:6). Anterior sounds are produced with a constriction at or in front of the alveolar ridge. The constriction of non-anterior sounds is formed at a point located from behind the alveolar ridge to the front of the soft palate.

As illustrated in the preceding chapter, the articulation of front vowels is produced behind the alveolar ridge, with the constriction extending for a considerable distance along the hard palate. Thus, in articulatory terms front vowels are [-anterior, +distributed] (Clements 1976a). However, unlike consonants in which the features [anterior] and [distributed] can be contrastive, front vowels do not appear to utilize either of these features to distinguish among vowels. The feature values [-anterior] and [+distributed] are then best viewed as redundant values for front vowels (see (22)) and hence, do not form part of a front vowel's underlying specification.

(22) $[+coronal]_{VOC} \rightarrow [-anterior]$
       $[+coronal]_{VOC} \rightarrow [+distributed]$

Phonological evidence supports the view that front vowels are inherently [-anterior], in particular. For example, in many languages the assimilation of a velar consonant to a front vowel results in a non-anterior coronal consonant, e.g. /k+e/ → [tʃe]. Rules of this nature, referred to as Coronalization, are discussed in detail in chapter V. Thus, although the feature value [-anterior] does not play a role in distinguishing among vowels, it is nonetheless relevant when front vowels interact with consonants. This is to be expected given that this feature serves a contrastive function for consonants.

The representation provided in (21) above gives the underlying form of the vowel /i/ in systems in which both [+coronal] and [+high] are nonredundant. This, I claim, is also the representation of the palatal glide. The different phonetic realizations of [i] and [j] can be attributed to syllable position without requiring a change in the feature specification of the segments involved; a vowel is a syllabic nucleus whereas a glide never is (Sievers 1881, Pike 1943, Clements & Keyser 1983, Kaye & Lowenstamm 1984, Levin 1985).[2]

Motivation for this approach comes from the observation that the palatal glide and high front vowel are generally nondistinct underlyingly. In Maltese, for example, the marker of the third person masculine imperfective is realized as a palatal glide in onset position, as shown in (23) below (for more detailed discussion of Maltese see Part II). For comparison, I give the corresponding 2nd person singular form in which the prefix consonant is realized as the anterior coronal consonant [t].

(23) Triliteral Strong Verb

	Imperfective		Gloss
	3rd p.masc.sg.	2nd p.sg.	
1st measure	jaʔtel	taʔtel	'to kill'
5th measure	jitʔattel	titʔattel	'to destroy oneself'

In verbs of the second and third measure, the prefix vowel deletes leaving the palatal glide immediately adjacent to the stem-initial consonant. In preconsonantal position, the same segment is realized as the syllable nucleus [i], as shown in (24).

(24) Triliteral Strong Verb
              Imperfective   Gloss
           3rd p.masc.sg.   2nd p.sg.
2nd measure   iʔattel   tʔattel   'to destroy'
3rd measure   ibierek   tbierek   to bless'

Similarly, in Sanskrit the vowel [i] is realized as the palatal glide when it is in non-nuclear position, e.g. /i + mas/ [imas] 'go, 1st pers. pl.'; /i + tha/ [itha] 'go, 2nd pers. pl.'; /i + anti/ [janti] 'go, 3rd pers. pl.' (J. Jasanoff p.c.). Maltese and Sanskrit are representative of innumerable languages in which the difference between the high front vowel and palatal glide is determined solely on the basis of syllable position. The difference need not be associated with a change in the feature content of the two segments.

The representation of [i] and [j] in (21) incorporates two claims which differ from standard SPE-based feature theory. First, as is apparent, front vowels in addition to the palatal glide are coronals. Second, the palatal glide has a single feature complex. Halle (1989) claims that the palatal glide is typically specified with the major articulator [coronal] thus accounting for the observation that the palatal glide patterns with coronal consonants in phonological processes cross-linguistically. However, he adds (p. 9) that "in many languages, the glides represented as [w, j] have the dorsum as their major articulator; [w] is [+high, -back], [j] is [+high, -back]. Dorsal glides without further specification have been documented in Australian languages...as well as in Mandarin Chinese, where these sounds appear phonetically in onsets of phonologically vowel-initial morphemes." This would suggest that the palatal glide is specified in some languages as [coronal] and in others as [-back] depending on whether the glide is more consonant-like or vowel-like.

As pointed out above, Maltese and Sanskrit are representative of languages in which the difference between the palatal glide and high front vowel depends solely on syllable position. These would presumably be cases in which Halle would characterize the glide as [-back]. There are also languages in which the glide patterns with consonants. At first glance, these might appear to be cases in which we would want the segmental representations of vowels and glides to differ. Along the lines proposed by Halle, the glide [j] would be specified for the articulator [coronal] in order to account for its consonant-like character whereas [i] would be specified as [-back]. Problematic for this view would be a case in which the glide patterns with both consonants and vowels within the same language. In the following section I discuss such a case from the Porteño dialect of Spanish. As I show, specifying the palatal glide, front vowels and coronal consonants as [coronal] provides a straightforward account of the observed alternations. Additional evidence for this approach will be seen in the discussion of Korean syllable structure constraints in chapter IV.

1.1 Spanish

In the Porteño dialect of Spanish, spoken in and around Buenos Aires, the palatal glide is realized as a palato-alveolar obstruent under certain conditions. Of particular interest is the fact that in certain cases, the glide itself is derived from a non-low front vowel by diphthongization. We thus have a three-way alternation among front vowel ~ palatal glide ~ palato-alveolar obstruent. Similar alternations are observed with respect to labio-velar vowels, glides and obstruents. I present the data in this section as evidence for the specification of front vocoids (vowels and glides) and coronal consonants as [coronal]. By contrast, I show that a theory in which front vocoids and coronal consonants are specified for different features can only handle these alternations in an abitrary way or by including additional redundancy into the analysis.

1.1.1 Diphthongization

In Spanish (the Porteño dialect included), the vowels /e, i/ and /o, u/ alternate with the diphthongs [je] and [we], respectively, as shown in the examples in (25) (Harris 1969, 1977, 1983, 1985; Lozano 1979; Morgan 1984).

(25) mer[e]ndáron   'they snacked'   mer[je]nda   'he snacks'
      cal[e]ntámos   'we heat'   cal[je]nta   'he heats'
      s[e]tenta   'seventy'   s[je]te   'seven'
      bib[í]r   'to live'   bib[je]ndo   'living'
      sal[í]r   'to go out'   sal[je]ndo   'going out'
      f[o]rzába   'he forced'   f[wɛ]rza   'he forces'
      n[o]venta   'ninety'   n[wɛ]ve   'nine'
      j[u]gadór   'player'   j[wɛ]go   'game'

Harris (1977) shows that the above alternations are properly accounted for by deriving the diphthongs from simple vowels (I refer the reader to the detailed argumentation and review of alternative approaches in Harris op. cit.; see also Harris 1985). As he points out, diphthongization is directly related to stress: [je], [wɛ] alternate with unstressed /e,i/, /o,u/, respectively. There are no cases in which unstressed diphthongs alternate with stressed vowels. Of particular interest to the present discussion is the important observation that the quality of the glide is directly dependent on that of the underlying vowel: a palatal glide is realized when the underlying vowel is front and a labio-velar glide is derived from an underlying labio-velar vowel. In other words, the place specification of the derived glide is identical to that of the underlying vowel. The rule of diphthongization is described in (26) (irrelevant structure is omitted).[3]

(26)   Diphthongization:

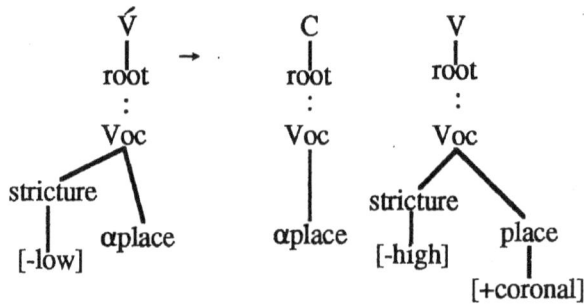

The representation in (26) describes the observation that under certain conditions a stressed non-low vowel is realized as a diphthong. The glide is realized as [coronal] (/j/) when the underlying vowel is [coronal], and [labial]/[dorsal] (/w/) when the vowel is [labial]/[dorsal].

In all instances the nucleus of the diphthong surfaces as the nonlow front vowel [e] which, following Harris (1985), is attributed to default insertion.

Reflected in (26) is the view that vowels and glides are distinguished on the basis of syllable position rather than with respect to their segmental content; as syllable nuclei /i, u/ are realized as [i, u], respectively, whereas when they are nonsyllabic they surface as glides. Examples from Spanish illustrating these alternations occur in phrases such as: mi amor → m[ja].mor 'my love', tu edad → t[we].dad 'your age'. With resyllabification, the vowel of the first word is realized as a glide in the newly-formed initial syllable. However, as Morgan (1984:117) points out, "allowing for the full value of each syllable is a perfectly acceptable solution". Thus, in some speech styles the pronunciations [mi].a.mor and [tu].e.dad are heard. These alternations are the natural consequence of the fact that glides and vowels represent different manifestations of the same underlying segment.

It is important to point out that glides in Spanish, whether or not derived by diphthongization, are phonologically non-consonantal. This is evidenced by, for example, the observation that glides are non-triggers of Sibilant Voicing (see e.g. Harris 1969, Lozano 1979, Morgan 1984). As stated in (27), Sibilant Voicing involves the assimilation of /s/ to the feature [+voice] of a following consonantal segment both within and across word-boundaries.

(27) Sibilant Voicing
      s → z / __ [+cons, +voice]

Representative examples are given in (28) below.

(28) e[z]bozar 'to sketch'
de[z]de 'since'
ra[z]go 'I rip'
la[z] batas 'the robes'
la[z] luchas 'the fights'
lo[z] ricos 'the rich'
a[z]no 'jackass'
tu[z] monedas 'your coins'
cf. e[s]perar 'to wait'
ha[s]ta 'until'
ra[s]co 'I scratch'
la[s] patas 'the ducks (f.)'

Neither vowels nor glides trigger Sibilant Voicing, e.g. lo[s] o[s]os, s[we]vos, de[sj]erto. Note that the glide/vowel sequence in [desjerto] 'desert' is derived by diphthongization, cf. desertar 'to desert'. The fact that glides are non-triggers of Sibilant Voicing falls out from the assumption that they are non-consonantal segments and thus pattern with vowels.

Recall Halle's (1989) proposal that the palatal glide is typically specified as [-back] in languages in which it patterns with vowels. Based on the evidence presented thus far, the palatal glide in Spanish would be most appropriately specified as [-back]. However, as I show immediately below, the palatal glide also patterns with consonants which one might take as evidence for specifying the glide as [coronal]. Given the patterning of the palatal glide with both vowels and consonants, one might argue that the glide is specified for both [-back] and [coronal]. Further below, I discuss problems associated with assuming this dual feature specification for the palatal glide and show that the vowel/glide/consonant alternations observed in Spanish receive a simpler and more natural account within an approach in which all front vocoids are treated as coronals.

1.1.2 Glide Strengthening

In Porteño Spanish, glides are strengthened to obstruents in syllable-initial position. Although this rule affects both labio-velar and palatal glides, I focus on the realization of the palatal glide, in particular. Syllable-initially the palatal glide is realized as a palato-alveolar continuant, e.g. convo[j] 'convoy' vs. convo[ʒ]es 'convoys', le[j] 'law' vs. le[ʒ]es 'laws' (Harris 1983). The rule is stated descriptively in (29) (Harris 1983, Morgan 1984).

(29) Glide Strengthening
      j → ʒ / σ[__
      The palatal glide is realized as a palato-alveolar obstruent in syllable-initial position.

Palatal glides that are derived from underlying front vowels by diphthongization are also subject to strengthening. The forms in (30a) below illustrate the effects of diphthongization in which the final vowel of the infinitive is realized as [jɛ] in the present participle. Glide Strengthening fails to apply given that the derived glide is preceded by a consonantal onset. In (30b), the glide derived by diphthongization is in syllable-initial position and thus surfaces as [ʒ] as the result of Glide Strengthening. Additional examples are given in (30c) showing, on the left, forms with simple vowels, and on the right, the corresponding forms in which the derived glide is strengthened to an obstruent in syllable-initial position.

(30)

	Infinitive		Present Participle			Gloss
a.	bibir		bib[j]endo			'to live'
	salir		sal[j]endo			'to go out'
	komer		kom[j]endo			'to eat'
b.	uir		u[ʒ]endo	(<u.jen.do<u.in.do)		'to flee'
	oir		o[ʒ]endo	(<o.jen.do<o.in.do)		'to listen'
	leer		le[ʒ]endo	(<le.jen.do<le.en.do)		'to read'
	ir		[ʒ]endo	(<jen.do<in.do)		'to go'
c.	errar	[er̄ar]	'to wander'	ierro	[ʒer̄o]	'I wander'
	helar	[elar]	'to freeze'	hielo	[ʒelo]	'ice'

The consonantal status of derived palato-alveolars is evidenced by the fact that these segments trigger Sibilant Voicing, e.g. lo[z] ʒelo 'the ice (pl.)' (/elo/ → jelo → ʒelo). Recall that glides, on the other hand, are non-triggers. Further evidence for the consonantal status of derived palato-alveolars comes from the rule of Nasal Assimilation. As shown in (31), a nasal consonant is homorganic with a following consonant, both within and across words (Lozano 1979, Harris 1969).

(31) tango   [taŋgo]   'tango'
      tambo   [tambo]   'cow-shed'
      tanto   [tanto]   'so much'
      un palo   [um palo]   'a stick'
      un santo   [un santo]   'a saint'
      un gorro   [uŋ goro]   'a cap'
      un mes   [um mes]   'a month'

Before vowels and glides no assimilation occurs and the nasal is realized as [n], e.g. u[n] arbol 'a tree', u[n] oso 'a bear', [nj]eto 'grandson', [nw]evo 'new'. In (32), I give the formal representation of Nasal Assimilation. Informally stated, the place node of a consonant spreads leftward to an interpolated CONS node of a preceding nasal consonant, unspecified for place features (see Sagey 1986 for discussion of node interpolation). I assume that in the event that no assimilation occurs, the nasal consonant receives the feature values [coronal, +anterior] by default.

(32)   Nasal Assimilation

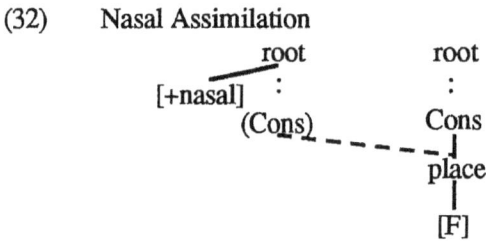

Although vowels and glides are non-triggers of Nasal Assimilation, a palatal glide which has undergone strengthening does trigger the rule, e.g. un hielo [uñ ʒelo]⁴ 'a piece of ice', in which case the nasal is realized as a postalveolar coronal. This is to be expected under the assumption that strengthened glides are obstruents (and hence consonantal).

To summarize, we have seen that the palatal glide may be derived by diphthongization from an underlying front vowel. The phonological patterning of the palatal glide with vowels in the rules of Sibilant Voicing and Nasal Assimilation confirms the glide's status as a vocoid.

The Feature Specification of Coronals

We have also seen that the palatal glide regularly alternates with the palato-alveolar obstruent. The obstruent's patterning with consonants in Sibilant Voicing and Nasal Assimilation indicates that it is consonantal.

1.1.3 Analysis

As illustrated above, under certain conditions the palato-alveolar obstruent is derived from a palatal glide which itself may be derived from a front vowel. As I show just below, the three-way alternation involving front vowel/palatal glide/palato-alveolar obstruent receives a simple and natural account given the view that front vocoids and coronal consonants are specified for the common articulator feature [coronal]. Simplified representations of the three segment types are given in (33). (Parenthesized elements represent redundant feature values.)

(33)

```
        i, e            j              ʒ
        Cons           Cons           Cons
         |              |              |
        place          place          place
         |              |              |
        Voc            Voc
         |              |
        place          place
         |              |              |
      [+coronal]     [+coronal]     [coronal]
         |              |              |
       ([-ant])       ([-ant])        [-ant]
```

All segments in (33) are specified for the articulator [coronal] dominating (redundantly for vocoids) the terminal feature [-anterior]. For vocoids, place features are (indirectly) dominated by a VOC constriction node whereas the place specification of the palato-alveolar is (indirectly) dominated by CONS.

Reference to syllable position alone is sufficient to account for the front vowel/palatal glide alternations discussed above. From vowel to glide, the segment changes from syllable nucleus to non-nuclear position. With respect to the palatal glide/palato-alveolar obstruent alternation (i.e. Glide Strengthening), a change in the status of the glide's articulator feature(s) from vocoidal to consonantal is involved. I express this in (34).

(34)   Glide Strengthening

[F]voc → [F]cons / $_\sigma$[__ V

Informally stated, the vocoidal feature specification of a glide changes to consonantal in syllable-initial position. I assume that the resultant consonant is assigned the feature [-sonorant] by redundancy rule and thus surfaces as an obstruent.

As stated, the rule in (34) correctly predicts that the labial-velar glide will also strengthen to an obstruent in syllable-initial position. As the following examples illustrate, the strengthened glide may be derived from /o/ (or /u/) as the result of diphthongization thus giving, once again, the three-way alternation among vowel/glide/obstruent, e.g. Juan [w̌ɛ]le ~ [o]lía 'John smells ~ smelled' vs. Juan m[wɛ]le ~m[o]lía 'John grinds ~ ground [corn]' ([w̌] represents a labial-velar obstruent) (examples from Harris 1977:263; see also Harris 1969, Lozano 1979, Morgan 1984). Under the assumption that each of these segments is specified for the features [labial] and [dorsal], strengthening can be stated in terms of a change in the features' status from vocoidal to consonantal, as expressed in (34). The rule of Glide Strengthening in (34) thus expresses in simple terms the changes affected in both the labial-velar and palatal glides.

In the remainder of this section I discuss analyses in which front vocoids and the palato-alveolar obstruent are not all specified for a common articulator feature. I consider three potential means of specifying these segments. In all three, front vowels are specified as [-back] and the palato-alveolar obstruent is specified as [coronal, -anterior], as is generally assumed in SPE-based feature theories. The differences reside in the features assigned to the glide. In the first case, the glide is specified as [-back], in the second as [coronal], and in the third as both [-back] and [coronal].

The first approach, i.e. all vocoids are [-back] and consonants are [coronal], is the specification adopted in the model of Sagey (1986) and I use her model to illustrate. In this model, [-back] is dominated by the articulator node [dorsal]. The (simplified) representations of [i], [j] and [ʒ] are given in (35).

(35)

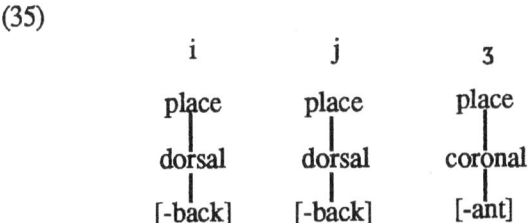

Accounting for the front vowel/glide alternations can be handled in essentially the same way that I proposed above. In other words, the different realizations of a vocoid as glide or vowel are determined solely by syllable position; there is no change in segmental content. But note that the change from glide to obstruent in Glide Strengthening must involve not only a change in the status of the glide from vocoid to consonant but in addition, a change in the place specification of the segment, since the glide is [dorsal, -back] whereas the obstruent is [coronal, -anterior]. Thus, in order to affect the change from /j/ to [ʒ], the consonant must somehow acquire a [coronal] node. Furthermore, by proposing different place specifications for the palatal glide and palato-alveolar obstruent, we fail to express the parallel between palatal glide and labial-velar glide strengthening in a straightforward manner. In the case of labial-velars, strengthening would only involve a change in the status of the segment from vocoid to consonant since both glides and obstruents share common place specifications (in Sagey's terms, [labial,+round] and [dorsal, +back]). However, for the front vocoid/palato-alveolar alternation, the place specification of the consonant must also change. In order to account for both cases of strengthening in terms of a change in the vocoidal status of the segment one might posit an additional rule which would assign the feature [coronal] to the output of palatal glide strengthening. This could arguably take the form of a redundancy rule, e.g. [-back, +cons] → [coronal]. This analysis incorporates a certain degree of arbitrariness since it would be just as simple to posit a redundancy rule of the type [-back, +cons] → [labial]. Moreover, an additional rule would be needed to subsequently eliminate the [dorsal, -back] specification of the strengthened glide in order to obtain the correct feature specification of the palato-alveolar obstruent. The representation of Glide Strengthening in (34), on the other hand, is able to account for the alternations without positing additional rules. It directly predicts the output to be a coronal consonant. Thus, in terms of simplicity and naturalness, (34) is more highly valued.

Consider next the consequences of specifying the palatal glide as [coronal] (instead of [-back]). By treating the palatal glide as [coronal], rules in which the palatal glide patterns with consonants are given a simple account. Glide Strengthening can be handled in essentially the same way as proposed in (34), i.e. change the status of the glide from vocoidal to consonantal without altering the place specification of the input. Yet, with respect to vowel/glide alternations we would be losing the insight that the palatal glide is simply the non-syllabic variant of non-low front vowels. Furthermore, deriving the palatal glide from front vowels in diphthongization would be problematic since front vowels are not considered to be coronal sounds.

As a final alternative, consider the consequences of specifying the palatal glide as both [coronal] and [dorsal, -back]. First, we would once again lose the insight that [i] and [j] are one and the same segment underlyingly since although [j] would be both [coronal] and [dorsal, -back], [i] would be only [dorsal, -back]. Thus, in order to account for the vowel/glide alternations, we would need to posit a rule assigning a [coronal] node to the glide. Furthermore, to account for the glide/obstruent alternation, we would require a further rule eliminating the [dorsal, -back] specification on the derived palato-alveolar obstruent. The parallelism between labial-velar and palatal glide strengthening would also be lost in this analysis. Unlike labial-velar glide strengthening, palatal strengthening could not be handled simply in terms of a change in the status of the segment's features from vocoidal to consonantal. Moreover, as Clements (1989) and E. Pulleyblank (1989) have pointed out, specifying front vocoids for two features referring to 'frontness' is superfluous. Consequently, by specifying palatal glides for both [coronal] and [dorsal, -back] we incorporate additional redundancy which has the unfortunate result of creating a more complex analysis.

1.1.4 Summary

To summarize, I have considered three alternative means of accounting for front vowel/palatal glide/palato-alveolar obstruent alternations. In the first approach, all vocoids are [-back] and consonants are [coronal]. This approach was shown to be less highly valued than my analysis on the basis of naturalness and simplicity. The second approach treats vowels as [-back], and the palatal glide and coronal consonants as [coronal]. This account is unsatisfactory since it is unable to account for vowel/glide alternations in a straightforward manner. Finally, I considered specifying the palatal glide as both [-back] and [coronal]. Similar to approach 2, the insight concerning the underlying identity of vowels and glides is lost. Consequently, accounting for the front vowel/palatal glide alternations would require additional rules. Similarly, additional rules are also necessary to account for the palatal glide/palato-alveolar alternation. Conversely, an analysis which treats front vocoids as [coronal] is not only more highly valued in terms of simplicity but in addition, it provides a natural account of all observed alternations.

2. CORONAL CONSONANTS

In this section, I focus on the feature specification and representation of coronal consonants. Central to this discussion is my claim that place of articulation contrasts in coronal consonants are sufficiently accounted for by the features [coronal], [anterior], [distributed], [strident], and the secondary vocalic feature [coronal].

2.1 Anterior Coronal Consonants

The specification of anterior coronals assumed in this work is consistent with most current approaches (see e.g. Sagey 1986, Keating 1990). Anterior coronal sounds, e.g. dentals, alveolars, interdentals, are produced with the tip or blade of the tongue on the front of the alveolar ridge or on the upper teeth. They are specified with the primary articulator [coronal] dominating the terminal feature [+anterior]. Further distinctions within the class of anterior coronal consonants are made through the use of the feature [distributed] which like [anterior] is dominated by [coronal], and [strident], which is dominated by Stricture.

As indicated above, the feature [distributed] refers to the length of the constriction involved and serves to distinguish, in particular, apical and laminal anterior coronals. Laminal sounds are produced with the blade of the tongue creating a constriction which is longer than that of apical sounds, which are produced with the tip of the tongue. Laminals are thus [+distributed] whereas apicals are [-distributed].

The feature [strident] refers to the level of turbulence produced by the articulation. Acoustically, strident sounds are distinguished from non-strident sounds by the "presence (vs. absence) of a higher intensity noise accompanied by a characteristic amplification of the higher frequencies and weakening of the lower formants" (Jakobson & Halle 1968:740). Strident sounds are "achieved by a supplementary obstacle in the way of the airstream and a consequent intensified turbulence" (Jakobson & Waugh 1987: 142). For anterior coronals, the feature [strident] serves to distinguish the English interdental fricatives [θ ð] from sibilant fricatives [s z] (Jakobson, Fant & Halle 1952; Chomsky & Halle 1968).

2.2 Postalveolar Coronal Obstruents

Postalveolar coronals are produced with a primary constriction made by the tip, blade and/or front of the tongue at a location between the posterior corner of the alveolar ridge and the front of the soft palate. I assume that palato-alveolar, retroflex, palatal and alveopalatal consonants do not constitute discrete places of articulation in the postalveolar region but rather, their differences in realization are encoded in different specifications of the features [distributed] and/or [strident], and/or the presence vs. the absence of the secondary feature [coronal]. In this section, I focus on the features which serve to distinguish among plain (i.e. non-palatalized) palato-alveolar, retroflex and palatal obstruents. Following this, I discuss the representation of palatalized consonants and alveopalatals. Finally, sonorant coronal consonants are treated.

2.2.1 Plain Postalveolar Obstruents

As exemplified by the fricatives in (36), I assume that, all else being equal, the features [anterior], [distributed] and [strident] are sufficient to account for contrasts among plain postalveolar obstruents.

(36)

	retroflex	palato-alveolar	palatal
	ʂ	ʃ	ç
coronal	+	+	+
anterior	-	-	-
distributed	-	+	+
strident	(+)	+	-

As seen in (36), retroflex sounds contrast with palato-alveolars for the feature [distributed]. Retroflex consonants typically involve an articulation made by curling the tongue back such that the tip (or underside of the blade) forms a constriction along the hard palate (Keating 1990). Palato-alveolars, e.g. [ʃ ʒ], are generally produced with a constriction made behind the corner of the alveolar ridge. The articulation is usually laminal, made with the blade of the tongue, though Keating (1990) points out that the tongue tip as well as the blade may be raised in the production of palato-alveolars (see also Ladefoged & Maddieson 1986 for related discussion). The distinction between palato-alveolar and retroflex consonants is characterized as a difference in the length of constriction produced, i.e. palato-alveolars are [+distributed] and retroflex postalveolars are [-distributed]. Underlying contrasts between retroflex and palato-alveolar obstruents are found in a number of languages including Chácobo (Prost 1967), Aranda (O'Grady, Veogelin & Veogelin 1966), Luiseño (W. Bright 1965), Burushaski (Morgenstierne 1945) and Tolowa (J. Bright 1964).

Retroflex consonants contrast with palatals in, for example, Telugu (Lisker 1963, Sastry 1972) and Moru (Tucker & Bryan 1966). As discussed in the previous chapter, true palatal consonants are produced with a contriction made by the front of the tongue extending along the hard palate, a constriction which is significantly longer than that made by retroflex sounds. Thus, similar to the distinction between palato-alveolar and retroflex obstruents, the distinction between retroflex and palatal sounds can be identified as one relating to the length of the constriction. Palatal sounds are thus [+distributed] whereas retroflex sounds are [-distributed].

Hence, both palato-alveolars and palatals are nonanterior distributed sounds. This then raises the question concerning what feature serves to distinguish between these two groups of segments. Jakobson, Fant & Halle (1952) characterize palato-alveolars as [+strident] and palatals as [-strident]. Making use of the feature [strident] to distinguish between these two groups of sounds is well supported by the world's languages. As pointed out by Lahiri & Blumstein (1984) and supported by Maddieson's (1984) language survey, when a given language has both palato-alveolar and palatal obstruents, the most common pattern is for palatals to be stops and palato-alveolars to be affricates or fricatives. I would suggest then, following Jakobson, Fant & Halle and Lahiri & Blumstein, that by definition palatals are [-strident] whereas palato-alveolars are [+strident]. Hence, the difference between these two groups of sounds need not be attributed to differences in place of articulation. With respect to affricates and stops, we may thus conclude that (palato-alveolar) affricates are [+strident] and (palatal) stops are [-strident]. This same distinction is relevant for palato-alveolar and palatal fricatives, as I indicated in (36). When a given language has both palato-alveolar and palatal fricatives, the palato-alveolar is strident and the palatal is non-strident, e.g. German [liʃt] 'extinguishes' vs. [liçt] 'light', [kirʃə] 'cherry' vs. [kirçə] 'church'.

The claim that the feature [strident] serves to distinguish between palato-alveolar and palatal obstruents makes the strong prediction that we would not expect to find languages in which, all else being equal, palatals and palato-alveolars are either both [+strident] or both [-strident]. In Maddieson's (1984) cross-linguistic survey there are three languages which would appear to constitute exceptions to this claim as they are reported to have both palato-alveolar and palatal sibilant fricatives. The languages are Tarascan, Gününa-Kĕna and Paez. However, closer examination of these languages reveals that they are consistent with our claim. According to Foster (1969) and Friedrich (1975), Tarascan has only one postalveolar sibilant fricative phoneme transcribed as /š/ which Foster (p. 22) describes as: "a frontal, alveolo-palatal groove spirant." This contrasts with /s/, "an apical, alveolar voiceless groove spirant". Thus, the contrast between the two sounds is one of anteriority. TarascanWith respect to Gününa-Kĕna, there are two postalveolar fricatives in the underlying inventory. Gerzenstein

(1968) transcribes these sounds as /ʃ/ and /ʂ/, the former being described as a "dorso-prepalatal" fricative and the latter as an "apico-prepalatal" fricative. There is no indication as to whether either one or both of these sounds are strident or nonstrident, although the symbols used typically refer to strident fricatives. Nonetheless, from the description given by Gerzenstein, it is clear that these sounds contrast for properties other than stridency. I assume that the distinction between "dorso-" and "apico-" corresponds to what is typically referred to as laminal/apical. As such, the two sounds can be minimally distinguished by the feature [distributed] with /ʃ/ being [+distributed] (consistent with the specification of palato-alveolars) and /ʂ/ being [-distributed] (in line with the characterization of retroflex sounds). The third language, Paez, is no more exceptional to our claim than the previous two. The primary source Gerdel (1973), points out that the language has only two contrastive postalveolar fricatives transcribed as /š/ and /šʲ/, e.g. [á?ša?] 'it is a scraper' vs. [á?šʲa?] 'mounting (riding animal)'. Both sounds are strident, although the latter is the palatalized version of the former. The distinction between these two sounds can be characterized in terms of the absence vs. the presence of palatalization (see discussion of palatalized consonants below). Thus, these findings are not inconsistent with the view that, all else being equal, palato-alveolar and palatal obstruents contrast for the feature [strident].

Ladefoged & Maddieson (1986) claim that Komi, a Ural-Altaic language, has both palato-alveolar and palatal affricates, all of which are reported to be [+strident]. If correct, this would consitute a counter-example to my claim that the feature [strident] is sufficient to distinguish between palato-alveolars and palatals. The observation that Komi has two series of postalveolar affricates is confirmed by Lytkin (1961) who classifies these segments as 'hard' and 'soft' (p. 35). The 'hard'/'soft' distinction is traditionally used to refer to a non-palatalized/palatalized constrast, respectively, as we find in Russian. It might be the case then, that the 'soft' postalveolar affricate is in fact a palatalized version of the 'hard' affricate. To anticipate the discussion further below, alveopalatals as found in Polish, for example, are articulated with both the front of the tongue raised toward the palate as for palatals and, in addition, with the blade raised as it is for palato-alveolars. Alveopalatals are thus best characterized not as true palatals but rather as palatalized palato-alveolars (Halle & Stevens 1989). Lytkin describes the 'soft' postalveolar affricates of Komi as being articulated with the front part of the tongue raised toward the palate as it is for palatals (p.35). However, there is no indication as to whether or not the blade is also involved and unfortunately no articulatory data are provided. If further evidence shows that the blade is also raised, the 'soft' affricates of Komi would be most appropriately characterized in a way similar to alveopalatals, i.e. as palatalized palato-alveolars (see below for related discussion). Clearly, a more indepth examination of both the phonetic properties and the phonological patterning of these segments is warranted. Komi

No language that I am aware of has a three-way contrast between palato-alveolar, retroflex and palatal obstruents.[5] As a result, all else being equal, the features [anterior], [distributed] and [strident], are sufficient to account for contrasts among plain coronal sounds, as repeated in (37). Note that the feature [strident] is only contrastive for palato-alveolar and palatal obstruents and, as a result, it is parenthesized for the retroflex fricative in (37).

(37)

	retroflex	palato-alveolar	palatal
	ʂ	ʃ	ç
coronal	+	+	+
anterior	-	-	-
distributed	-	+	+
strident	(+)	+	-

2.2.2 Palatal Consonants

In the preceding section I claimed that palatal consonants are nonanterior coronals with no specification for secondary vocalic features. This approach differs from that of Keating (1988) who argues that palatals are specified for the vocalic features [-back, +high] in addition to the consonantal features [coronal, -anterior]. In this section I provide phonological evidence from Hungarian vowel harmony that palatal consonants should not bear secondary articulations under any analysis. As we will see, all consonants in the language, including palatals, are transparent to the spread of vowel features. This contrasts with Turkish vowel harmony in which intervening palatalized consonants block vowel harmony from applying. Under the assumption that palatalized consonants are specified for secondary vocalic features, the opacity of these consonants in vowel harmony is to be expected. However, were palatal consonants also specified for secondary vocalic features, we would incorrectly predict them to be opaque as well. Conversely, their transparency receives a straightforward account under the assumption that palatal consonants bear primary consonantal features with no specification for secondary vocalic features.

2.2.2.1 Hungarian Vowel Harmony

In Hungarian, suffixal vowels typically agree in backness with the preceding root vowel (for detailed discussion of this harmony system I refer the reader to, among others, Booij 1984; Clements 1977; Vago 1980; Hulst 1985 and Ringen 1975, 1977, 1988). This is illustrated in (38) by the vowel alternation in the dative suffix -nɑːk/-nɛk 'from' (from Ringen 1988).

(38)   hɑːz   'house'   hɑːz-nɑk   dat.
       vɑːros   'city'   vɑːros-nɑk dat.
       ür   'gap'   ür-nɛk   dat.
       öröm   'joy'   öröm-nɛk   dat.

Following most analyists of Hungarian vowel harmony, I assume that harmonic suffix vowels enter into the derivation unspecified for frontness (see e.g. Clements 1977, Hulst 1985, Ringen 1988; but cf. Vago 1980). The suffix vowel typically agrees in frontness with the nearest preceding harmonic vowel. Following Clements (1977) and Hulst (1985), I assume that both values of frontness spread from the root to the suffix in a feature-filling manner. This is characterized as spreading [αcoronal] (where α may be either - or +), as shown in (39).

(39)

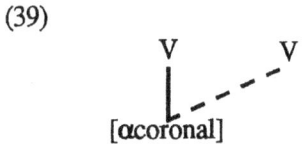

With this as a basis consider the examples in (40).

(40) a) -unk/-ünk (1st person plural present indefinite)
olvas-unk 'to read'
vaɟ-unk 'to be'
mɛɟ-ünk 'to go'
jöv-ünk 'to come'

b) -nok/-nök (derivational suffix)
gond 'care' gond-nok 'caretaker'
fö: 'head' fö:-nök 'boss'
üɟ 'matter' üɟ-nök 'agent'

As the examples in both (38) and (40) illustrate, vowel harmony freely applies across any intervening consonant. Of particular relevance to the present discussion is the fact, observed in (40), that the palatal stop [ɟ] is transparent to vowel harmony. If palatal consonants were to bear secondary articulations, as proposed by Keating (1988), we would not expect this observed transparency. Rather, we would predict palatals to block vowel harmony in a manner similar to the palatalized consonants of Turkish, as shown just below.

In Turkish, a suffixal vowel generally agrees in backness with a root-final vowel[6] (Clements & Sezer 1982; see also Lewis 1967, Swift 1963), as illustrated in (41).

(41)
Nominative singular	Accusative singular	Gloss
deniz	deniz - i	'sea'
diʃ	diʃ - i	'tooth'
akʃam	akʃam - ɨ	'evening'
kadɨn	kadɨn - ɨ	'woman'
kitap	kitab - ɨ	'book'
satʃ	satʃ - ɨ	'hair'

However, when the root-final vowel is followed by a palatalized velar or lateral consonant [kʲ, lʲ], the suffixal vowel surfaces as a front vowel instead of the expected back vowel, as illustrated in (42) below.

(42)   Nom. sg.   Acc. sg.   Gloss
       sualʲ   sualʲ-i   'question'
       hilʲalʲ   hilʲalʲ-i   'crescent'
       istikʲlʲalʲ   istikʲlʲalʲ-i   'independence'
       indrak⁷   indrākʲ-i   'perception'
       iʃtirak   iʃtirākʲ-i   'participation'
       imsak   imsakʲ-i   'fasting'
       inhimak   inhimakʲ-i   'addiction'
  cf. tʃatal   tʃatal-i   'fork'

Thus, in Turkish, vowel harmony fails to apply just in case a palatalized consonant intervenes. The suffixal vowel surfaces instead as front which, following Clements & Sezer, is attributed to assimilation to the root-final /kʲ lʲ/.

We have seen that palatalized consonants in Turkish block vowel harmony from applying. In Hungarian, on the other hand, all consonants, including palatals, are transparent. Accounting for the different phonological behaviour of palatalized and palatal consonants is straightforward under the assumption that palatalized consonants are specified for secondary vocalic features whereas palatals are not.

As illustrated in (44), the secondary articulation of a palatalized consonant (C') is linked to VOC place. Spreading the vocalic feature (also linked to VOC place) of a vowel across an intervening palatalized consonant will violate the No Line-Crossing principle (Goldsmith 1976), as stated in (43) (see chapter IV for detailed discussion). As a result, spreading is correctly predicted to be blocked.

(43)   No Line-Crossing (Clements 1990c):
       Association lines may not cross on a plane.

(44)

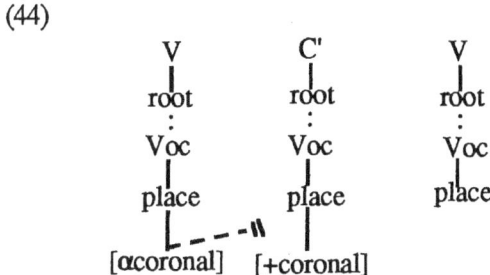

Yet, if Hungarian palatals also bore secondary features, we would incorrectly predict them to be opaque as well, as shown in (45). Turkish

(45)

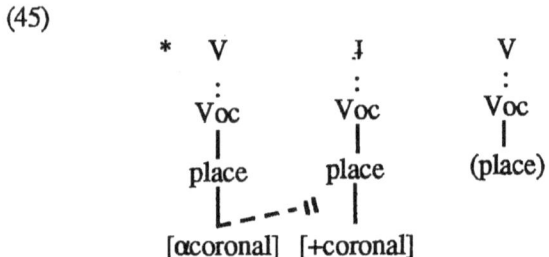

The transparency of palatal consonants receives a straightforward account given my claim that palatal consonants are specified only for primary consonantal features, i.e. [coronal, -anterior].[8] Given that the consonantal feature [coronal] is on a independent plane from vocoidal [coronal] (see chapter IV), vowel harmony is correctly predicted to apply across an intervening palatal, as shown in (46).

(46)

```
        V           ɟ           V
        ⋮           ⋮           ⋮
       Cons        Cons        Cons
        |           |           |
        Voc       place        Voc
        |                       |
       place                  (place)
        └──[αcoronal]──[coronal]──┘
```

Note that these same predictions hold if we were to assume that palatals are specified for the vocalic feature [-back] (see Ringen 1988 for an analysis in which the harmonic feature in Hungarian is [-back]). In this approach, specifying palatals for the feature value [-back] would also (incorrectly) predict palatals to be opaque since they would be specified for the same feature that spreads from the vowel trigger, i.e. [αback].

The phonological behaviour of Hungarian palatals in vowel harmony provides strong evidence that palatal consonants cannot be specified for secondary vocalic features. If they were, we would expect them to behave like the Turkish palatalized consonants and block vowel harmony. This evidence supports the redefinition of [coronal] in chapter II. It will be recalled that the X-ray tracings of Hungarian palatal stops showed that the constriction is made with the front of the tongue raised toward the hard palate. Given the phonological evidence presented in this section, tongue front raising in palatals cannot be characterized by vocoidal features. Rather, it must be viewed as a consonantal articulation, thus providing crucial evidence that primary [coronal] can be implemented by tongue front raising.

2.3 Palatalized Consonants

In this section I elaborate on the feature specification and representation of palatalized consonants, segments with an i-like vocalic articulation superimposed on a consonantal articulation. Such consonants frequently result from assimilation to an adjacent front vowel (see chapter V), although underlying contrasts between palatalized and non-palatalized consonants are also attested in a number of languages, e.g. Russian, Lithuanian, Paez. The palatalized velar, as shown in (47), exemplifies the representation of palatalized consonants assumed in this work.

(47)

```
                    k'
                   root
                    |
                   Cons
              ┌─────┴─────┐
          stricture     place
              |         ╱  ╲
           [-cont]     ╱    Voc
                  [dorsal]   |
                            place
                             |
                          [coronal]
```

In the unmarked case palatalization is characterized by the vocalic feature [coronal] (redundantly [+high]) (see chapter V for a more detailed discussion of rules of palatalization). I state that [coronal] consitutes the *unmarked* specification since given the assumption that vocoidal articulators are potentially binary-valued, it might be the case that the specified value of frontness under VOC in a given language is [-dorsal], with [coronal] being assigned by redundancy rule. Note, however, that regardless of whether the value is [coronal] or potentially [-dorsal], the specification of secondary palatality on consonants must be consistent with the specified value of frontness on vowels.[9] Conversely, if we were to allow secondary palatalization to be specified as, for example, [coronal] and front vowels as [-dorsal] the predictive power of the theory would be substantially weakened. For example, given a vowel harmony rule defined on the feature value [+coronal], a palatalized consonant specified for secondary [+coronal] would be predicted to block the rule (as the result of line-crossing) whereas a palatalized consonant specified for secondary [-dorsal] would be transparent. Consequently, in order for the theory to be able to predict in a principled and consistent manner the interaction of palatalized consonants and front vowels, it must be the case that within a given system the value of secondary palatalization is consistent with the specified value of vocoidal frontness.

If we are correct in characterizing palatalization by secondary vocalic features, we should expect to find palatalized counterparts of palato-alveolar, retroflex and palatal consonants as shown in (48).

(48)

	palato-alveolar		palatal		retroflex	
CONS						
coronal	+	+	+	+	+	+
anterior	-	-	-	-	-	-
distributed	+	+	+	+	-	+* (see below)
strident	+	+	-	-		
VOC						
coronal		+		+		+

As noted above, contrastive palatalized vs. nonpalatalized palato-alveolars are attested in Paez (Gerdel 1973) and are commonly found in Slavic languages. Palatalized palatals would presumably be more difficult to find given the similarity in articulation between palatal consonants and front vowels. However, Hammarberg (1971) claims that [c] is palatalized to [cʲ] in Moksha Mordvinan. True palatalized palatals are also attested in Nupe (Hyman 1970:65). In the discussion

The Feature Specification of Coronals

of Polish immediately below, we see evidence for palatalized retroflex consonants.

2.4 Alveopalatals

Alveopalatal consonants, e.g. [ɕ ʑ], are found in languages such as Polish and Standard Chinese (Pekingese). In Halle & Stevens' (1989) study of Polish fricatives, they show that alveopalatals are articulated like palato-alveolars in that the blade of the tongue is raised toward the alveolar ridge. In addition, the front of the tongue is raised as it is for palatal consonants. Thus, alveopalatals are properly characterized as palatalized palato-alveolars (see also Ladefoged & Maddieson 1986). The specification of secondary palatalization on these segments receives support from the observation that in Polish alveopalatals are the only consonants which fail to undergo Surface Palatalization, a low-level rule which adds secondary palatalization onto a consonant (Rubach 1984). Under the assumption that alveopalatals are underlyingly palatalized, it is clear that the reason they fail to palatalize is because they are already specified for secondary vocalic features. I assume then that alveopalatals are specified for the primary consonantal features [coronal, -anterior, +distributed, +strident] and the secondary vocoidal feature [coronal] (see also Clements 1990b). Based on this feature specification, alveopalatals are not 'true' palatals but rather palatalized palato-alveolars. This predicts that we should not find a language in which alveopalatals and palatalized palato-alveolars contrast. As far as I can tell, this prediction is true.

In addition to alveopalatals, Polish has two other series of postalveolars, one plain and one palatalized, which following Halle & Stevens (1989), I refer to as retroflex. As will become apparent, distinguishing between the language's alveopalatals and palatalized retroflex sounds presents a potential counterexample to my claim that, all else being equal, distinctions among coronal sounds may be made on the basis of the consonantal features [coronal, anterior, distributed, strident] and secondary [coronal]. Both the alveopalatals and palatalized retroflex consonants are [coronal, -anterior, +distributed, +strident] with secondary [coronal]. As I show, however, the distinction between these two series of sounds is attributed to the presence (palatalized retroflex sibilants) vs. the absence (alveopalatals) of lip rounding. I begin with a brief discussion of plain retroflex postalveolars.

In Polish, alveopalatals contrast with plain retroflex postalveolars, e.g. /ṣ ẓ/, koś [ɕ] 'reap!' vs. kocz [ṣ] 'basket'. Halle & Stevens (1989:11) state: "the two fricative sounds /ṣ/ and /ɕ/ differ not in the location of the constriction, but rather in the shape of the constriction and the tongue-body position. In /ɕ ʑ/ the constriction is [+distributed] whereas it is [-distributed] (retroflex) in /ṣ ẓ/. This contrast is clearly seen in the palatograms....As first brought out by Ladefoged & Maddieson (1986),...the most striking difference between the two classes of sounds is in the configuration of the tongue body: in /ɕ ʑ/ the tongue body has the configuration found in front high vowels like /i/, whereas in /ṣ ẓ/ the tongue body is in a configuration that approximates its neutral rest position." Hence, the retroflex postalveolars can be characterized by the consonantal features [coronal, -anterior, -distributed] with no secondary articulation.

Polish has a low-level rule which adds secondary palatalization onto consonants (see Surface Palatalization in Rubach 1984). Although alveopalatals are not affected by this rule, as mentioned above, retroflex postalveolars are. On the surface then, the inventory of Polish includes, for example, the postalveolar fricatives [ṣ ṣʲ ɕ], all of which are phonetically distinct, one from another (Dogil 1990). Based on the linguagrams and palatograms of Wierzchowska (1980), Dogil points out (p.10) that "there is practically no difference between [ɕ ʑ] and [ṣʲ ẓʲ] as far as the position of the lingual articulators is concerned...Both are distributed and palatalized." In addition, there is no significant difference in the level of amplitude between retroflex postalveolars and alveopalatal fricatives, as supported by the acoustic analyses of Halle & Stevens (1989); all are [+strident]. We may thus assume that [+strident] is a redundant specification of postalveolar obstruents in Polish.

We can consider the distributed property of palatalized postalveolars to be a consequence of superimposing one non-anterior coronal (vocalic) articulation onto another non-anterior coronal (consonantal) articulation, thus creating a long constriction extending along the hard palate. As such, the feature [+distributed] is a redundant specification of palatalized postalveolars and need not be specified underlyingly. Given this claim, we would not expect to find palatalized and non-palatalized postalveolars contrasting for the feature [distributed]. I am not aware of any examples showing such a contrast. Hence, both the alveopalatals and palatalized retroflex sibilants of Polish are specified for the consonantal features [coronal, -anterior] (redundantly [+distributed, +strident]) and the secondary vocalic feature [coronal].

The identical specification of Polish alveopalatals and palatalized retroflex sibilants presents a potential counterexample to my claim that, all else being equal, the features [coronal, anterior, distributed, strident] and secondary [coronal] are sufficient to distinguish among coronal sounds. However, as Dogil (1990) suggests, all else is not equal. According to Dogil, the distinct realizations of alveopalatals and palatalized retroflex postalveolars are directly related to the shape of the lips in the articulation; [ʂʲ ʐʲ] "have distinctly protruded lips, whereas in the case of [ɕ ʑ] the lips are nonprotruded, slightly spread, and offer a relatively narrow escape for the outcoming air" (p.10). Acoustic analyses support this observation. He points out that what distinguishes the retroflex postalveolars from the alveopalatals is "the presence vs. absence of the major amplitude peak in the F2 frequency region" (p.19). The strong spectral prominence in the F2 region can be attributed to lip rounding in the retroflex consonants. Lip rounding lengthens the sublingual cavity created by raising the tongue tip/blade which lowers the frequency of its principal resonance into the region of F2. Consequently, both the lingual and labial articulations of the retroflex postalveolars contribute to producing the strong spectral prominence in the F2 frequency region. By contrast, spreading the lips in the alveopalatals shortens the resonating cavity and hence, raises the frequency of its principal resonance away from the F2 region (J. Kingston, p.c.). These findings indicate that it is the shape of the lips that contributes to the distinction between the palatalized retroflex postalveolars and the alveopalatals. Thus, as illustrated in (49), the Polish retroflex postalveolars are specified with a secondary [labial] articulator whereas the alveopalatals lack specification for this feature. In view of this, Polish postalveolars do not present counterevidence to the specification of coronal sounds assumed in this work.

(49)   Polish Postalveolars

		Retroflex				Alveopalatals	
		ş	ẓ	ṣʲ	ẓʲ	ç	ʑ
CONS	coronal	+	+	+	+	+	+
	anterior	−	−	−	−	−	−
VOC	coronal			+	+	+	+
	labial	+	+	+	+		

2.5 Summary

In the preceding sections I have shown that attested contrasts among coronal obstruents are sufficiently accounted for by the use of the primary features [coronal], [anterior], [distributed], the stricture feature [strident], and the secondary place feature [coronal]. This is illustrated in the fully specified chart in (50) showing contrasts among representative coronal fricatives.

(50)   Coronal fricatives

	s	ʃ	ş	ç	ç
CONS					
coronal	+	+	+	+	+
anterior	+	−	−	−	−
distributed	−	+	−	+	+
strident	+	+	+	+	−
VOC					
coronal				+	

3. CORONAL SONORANT CONSONANTS

In the preceding section I have claimed that, all else being equal, palato-alveolar and palatal obstruents are distinguished by the presence vs. the absence of stridency. For sonorant consonants, however, stridency is generally not available as a means of distinguishing between palato-alveolars and palatals: [+sonorant] typically implies [−strident] (see e.g. Stevens & Keyser 1989). This then predicts that we should not expect to find minimal contrasts between plain palato-alveolar and palatal sonorants within a given language. In other words, a language would not be expected to have, for example, a plain palato-alveolar nasal stop contrasting with a palatal nasal stop. In Maddieson's survey, contrasts between retroflex and palatal sonorants (e.g. nasals, lateral approximants) are attested in a number of languages. Retroflex sonorants are also reported to contrast with palato-alveolar sonorants. No language is reported to have a contrast between palato-alveolar and palatal sonorants.

However, Ladefoged & Maddieson (1986) claim that the Australian language, Yanuwa, has a three-way contrast among postalveolar sonorants which they categorize as retroflex, palato-alveolar and palatal nasal plosives. If correct, Yanuwa would constitute a counterexample to the above claim. Kirton & Charlie (1978), the original source, describe these sounds as lamino-alveolopalatal, apico-domal and palato-velar, corresponding to Ladefoged & Maddieson's palato-alveolar, retroflex and palatal, respectively. Kirton & Charlie's discussion of, in particular, the 'palato-velars' suggests, however, that these segments are best characterized as underlying front (palatalized) velars, as opposed to palatals. First, they point out that in their earlier descriptions of Yanuwa, the 'palato-velars' were not included as phonemes but rather were analyzed as a sequence of a palatal glide and velar consonant. Second, they state (p.188) that "when the velar consonants /g/ and /ŋ/ precede the high front vowel /i/, fronted variants occur which the writer finds indistinguishable from the palato-velar stop and nasal phonemes." The descriptions suggest then that there are only two series of postalveolar coronals (as opposed to three) with the 'palato-velar' characterizing an underlying fronted velar. Thus, the evidence from Yanuwa in support of a three-way contrast among plain postalveolar sonorants is inconclusive.

4. Summary

In the preceding sections I have outlined the feature specification of coronal sounds. Front vowels and glides, referred to by the cover-term *front vocoids*, are specified for the articulator feature [coronal] which is immediately dominated by the VOC place node. Plain coronal consonants, i.e. those without a secondary articulation, are specified with a [coronal] articulator dominated by CONS place. Distinctions within the class of coronal consonants are made by use of the feature [anterior], which divides [coronal] into two regions. Within these two regions, coronal consonants are distinguished by the features [distributed] and [strident]. 'True' palatal consonants are specified for the primary articulator [coronal] dominating (when nonredundant) the features [-anterior, +distributed] with no specification for secondary articulations. Palatal obstruents are distinguished from palato-alveolar obstruents on the basis of stridency: palatals are [-strident] and palato-alveolars are [+strident]. Finally, alveopalatals are analysed as palatalized palato-alveolars.

NOTES

1. My focus is on the organization of features below the Root node. What the Root node itself links to is not crucial to this discussion and for my purposes I assume that syllabic segments are linked to V and non-syllabic segments are linked to C on the skeletal tier (Clements & Keyser 1983; see e.g. Levin 1985, Hayes 1989a, McCarthy & Prince 1989 for alternative representations and related discussion).

2. Although I focus on the palatal glide and high front vowel, the proposals in this section extend naturally to the front rounded glide [ɥ] and vowel [ü], as well as to the glide [w] and the back rounded vowel [u].

3. The descriptive formulation of diphthongization in (26) is sufficient for the purposes of this discussion. For two current formal accounts of diphthongization and related discussion I refer the reader to Hayes (1989b) and Clements (1990a).

4. Following a nasal or lateral consonant, /ʒ/ undergoes further strengthening and is realized as an affricate (see Morgan 1984:108).

5. Ladefoged & Maddieson (1986) mention an additional strident fricative transcribed as [ŝ] (based on Bgazba 1964). This occurs in the North West Caucasian language of Abkhaz and contrasts with /s, ṣ/ and the alveopalatal /ɕ/. In the X-ray tracings provided, the articulation of /ŝ/ is similar to /ʃ/ in that the constriction is in the postalveolar region at the back of the alveolar ridge. Like /ʃ/, I assume that /ŝ/ is specified as [+coronal, -anterior, +distributed, +strident] (see also Clements 1990b). No language that I am aware of is reported to contrast the two

sounds. The sounds /š/ and /ç/ are distinguished by the absence vs. the presence of a secondary [coronal] specification (see further below for discussion of alveopalatals).

6. High suffixal vowels also agree in roundness with the preceding root-final vowel. This aspect of harmony does not bear crucially on the present discussion.

7. Stem-final [k] is underlyingly /kʲ/ which is realized as [k] in syllable-final position (see Clements & Sezer (op. cit.) for discussion).

8. In Hume (1990), it is argued that in Korean palatal consonants block the spreading of vocalic [coronal] in the rule of umlaut. A re-evaluation of these data, however, suggests that the consonants in question are alveopalatals as opposed to palatals. As I show in the discussion in section 2.4, alveopalatals are best analyzed as palatalized palato-alveolars. For obstruents, this means that alveopalatals are [+strident] (whereas palatal obstruents are [-strident]). My re-evaluation of Korean postalveolars as alveopalatals as opposed to palatals comes from the observations that: 1. the Korean postalveolar obstruents in question are [+strident]; 2. these segments block vowel harmony; and 3. perceptually, the Korean postalveolar fricative is indistinguishable from the corresponding Polish alveopalatal. In the future, I plan to test the hypothesis that the Korean postalveolars are in fact alveopalatals (similar to those of Polish) with the aid of articulatory and acoustic data.

9. Assigning the feature value [+coronal] to a [-dorsal] vowel would, of course, not be an option in a system with central vowels. This is because central vowels are neither coronal nor dorsal and as a result, positing the redundancy rule [-dorsal] → [+coronal] is not feasible.

IV

The Nonlinear Organization of Consonant and Vowel Features

0. INTRODUCTION

In this chapter I focus more exclusively on the nonlinear representation of coronal consonants and vocoids, and on consonant/vowel interaction in general. I motivate the specific model of feature organization assumed in this work and discuss in considerable detail various predictions and theoretical implications of the model.

In chapter II, I showed the need to redefine the class of coronal sounds so as to include front vocoids and coronal consonants. With front vowels specified for the articulator feature [coronal], the next step is to incorporate [coronal] into a nonlinear model of feature organization. As stated in the Introduction, the model that I assume in this work is a slightly modified version of the *Unified Features Model* proposed in Clements (1990c). I discuss this model in detail in section 3. By means of introduction, however, I examine two alternative models and show why neither is adequate. Both alternatives employ the organization proposed in Sagey (1986) as a basis.

1. INCORPORATING [CORONAL] INTO A NONLINEAR MODEL OF FEATURE ORGANIZATION

Halle (1983) and Sagey (1986) claim that the sounds of natural language are produced by a limited set of articulators. In this approach, consonants and vowels are characterized by a largely disjunctive set of features. In the feature organization of Sagey (1986), vowels are characterized by a [dorsal] articulator referring to sounds produced with the tongue body, dominating vowel place and height features. For front vowels, the articulator node [dorsal] dominates the tongue body feature [-back]. Conversely, coronal consonants bear a [coronal] articulator node dominating, when relevant, the terminal features [anterior] and [distributed]. Both [coronal] and [dorsal] are dominated by the class node *Place*. In (51), I give the (partial) feature representations of [s] and [i] to illustrate.

(51)   Feature representation (based on Sagey 1986):

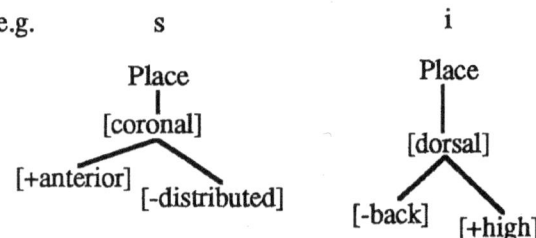

Given the view that front vowels are coronal sounds, our move is to incorporate the coronal specification of front vowels into feature organization. One means of doing so is to simply adjoin a [coronal] articulator to the representation of front vowels in (51), as I proposed in Hume (1988) (see also Cheng 1989), thus giving (52).

(52)

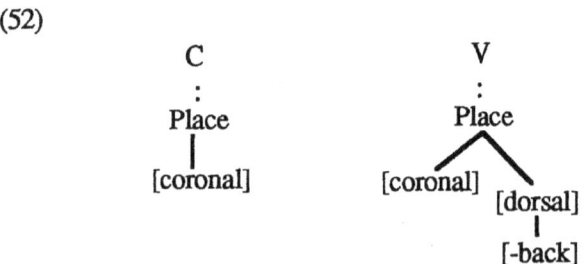

The representation of front vowels in (52) correctly incorporates the insight that front vowels are coronal sounds. Yet, as correctly pointed out by Clements (1989) and E. Pulleyblank (1989), specifying front vowels for [-back] in addition to a common feature shared with coronal consonants is superfluous; two features denoting "frontness" are unnecessary as a means of distinguishing front vowels from central and back vowels. The proposed solution is to redefine the content of the

The Organizaton of Consonant and Vowel Features 93

natural class [coronal] in order to include both front vowels and coronal consonants. By doing so, the feature [-back] becomes superfluous and is eliminated from feature theory.

With the feature [-back] removed, the representation in (52) can be revised such that both coronal consonants and front vowels are specified for a [coronal] articulator. As I show in (53), this results in a representation in which the [coronal] articulator of both consonants and vowels is arrayed on the same plane, as proposed in Lahiri & Evers (1991).

(53)

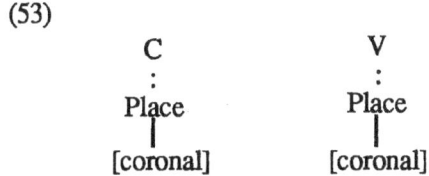

Arraying [coronal] on the same plane for both consonants and vowels, as in (53), makes strong predictions concerning the opacity effects of front vowels and coronal consonants in, for example, assimilation rules. Given the commonly accepted view of assimilation as spreading, we would predict that spreading the feature [coronal] in vowel harmony would be blocked by an intervening coronal consonant since it would result in crossed association lines (see (54)). However, as we saw in the discussion of Hungarian and Turkish vowel harmony in chapter III, this prediction does not obtain; plain consonants are not opaque to spreading vocalic features.

(54)

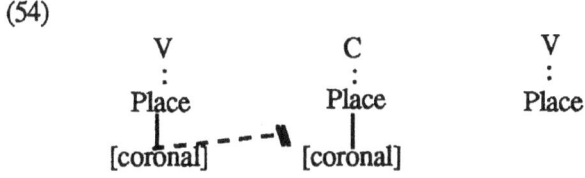

Along these same lines, an intervening front vowel is predicted to block the spread of [coronal] from consonant-to-consonant. Once again this hypothesis is falsified. To illustrate, I provide evidence from Sanskrit and Basque which show that [coronal] freely spreads from consonant-to-consonant across an intervening front vocoid. Consequently, arraying the articulator [coronal] on the same plane for consonants and vowels is problematic.

1.1 Sanskrit

N-retroflexion characterizes the process by which the anterior coronal nasal /n/ is realized as retroflex [ṇ] when preceded by a retroflex continuant, i.e. ṣ r ṛ.[1] Otherwise, the nasal surfaces as [n] (Whitney 1889, Odden 1978, Steriade 1985, Schein & Steriade 1986). The data in (55) illustrate.

(55) Context for rule met: Context for rule not met:
   -na- (passive suffix)
   vṛk - ṇa   'cut up'   bhug - na   'bend'
   kṣi: - ṇa   'destroy'   di - na   'divide'

   -na:m (genitive plural suffix)
   sarga: - ṇa:m   'ocean'   deva: -na:m 'god'
   bha:ṣa: - ṇa:m 'language'
   re:pha: - ṇa:m 'letter r'
   priya: - ṇa:m   'lovely'

   -nas (nominal suffix)
   dravi - ṇas   'wealth'   ap - nas   'acquisition'
   pari: - ṇas   'fulness'
   rek - ṇas   'riches'

Retroflexion fails to occur when a coronal consonant intervenes between the target and trigger, as shown in (56).

(56) krśa: - na:m   *krśa: - ṇa:m   'weak'
    rodha: - na:m *rodha: - ṇa:m 'obstacle'
    dṛpti: - na:m   *dṛpti: - ṇa:m   'crazy'

Before proceeding with the analysis, I give the underlying specification of coronal consonants which I assume.

(57)

	anterior	distributed
t, s, n	+	
ṭ, ṣ, ṇ	−	−
c, ś, ɲ	−	+

The feature [distributed] serves to contrast retroflex and postalveolar coronals. Conversely, for anterior coronals the feature [distributed] is noncontrastive and thus, remains unspecified.

The Organizaton of Consonant and Vowel Features

From the table in (57), it can be seen that the change from anterior to retroflex coronal crucially involves a change in the feature [anterior]. At first sight, it would appear that the rule of N-retroflexion could be defined as spreading the single feature [-anterior] from a retroflex consonant to a following anterior nasal. Although this would correctly change the value of anteriority on the nasal, the output would remain unspecified for the feature [distributed]. In order to obtain the correct output, the nasal must also acquire the feature value [-distributed]. The most straightforward means of doing this is to spread the entire [coronal] node dominating [-anterior] and [-distributed] from a retroflex consonant to an anterior nasal, as shown in (58).

(58)   N-Retroflexion

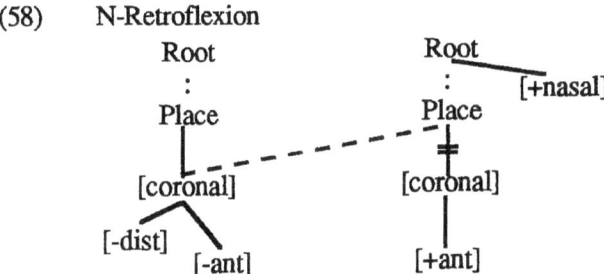

Note that attributing the feature value [-distributed] to redundancy rule assignment is not possible since [distributed] is contrastive for nonanterior coronals and thus, not predictable. Consequently, assimilation in the rule of N-retroflexion must be defined on the [coronal] node.[2]

Recall that N-retroflexion fails to apply just in case a coronal consonant intervenes. As pointed out by Steriade (1985) and Schein & Steriade (1986), the opacity of coronal consonants derives in simple terms from the assumption that these consonants are also specified for [coronal]. Thus, as shown in (59), spreading [coronal] across an intervening segment also specified with [coronal] would violate No Line-Crossing (for simplicity only relevant structure is given).

(59)
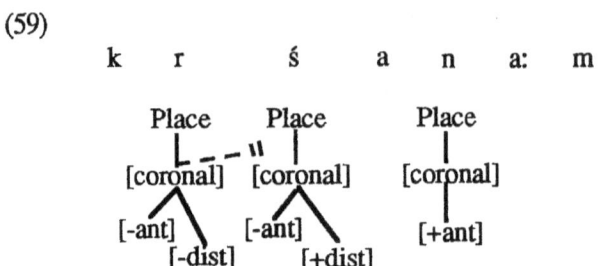

Of relevance to the present discussion is the observation that N-retroflexion applies across front vocoids (vowels and glides), as the examples in (60) show.

(60) kṣi: - ṇa   'destroy'
      re:pha: - ṇa:m 'the letter r'
      priya: - ṇa:m   'lovely'
      dravi - ṇas   'wealth'
      pari: - ṇas   'fullness'
      rek - ṇas   'riches'

If we were to assume that [coronal] is arrayed on the same plane for both consonants and vowels, as proposed by Lahiri & Evers (1991), we would incorrectly predict front vocoids to be opaque to the spreading of consonantal [coronal], as illustrated below.

(61)
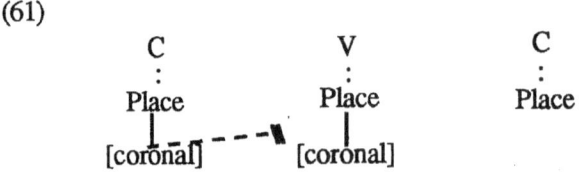

1.2 Basque (Baztan dialect)

As a further example, consider the rule of Sibilant Harmony in the Baztan dialect of Basque, as discussed in Hualde (1988). In Basque, there is a morpheme structure constraint which requires that all sibilants within a morpheme agree in place of articulation. This holds exceptionlessly. Affected by this constraint are the language's three series of sibilants: apico-alveolar (orthographically *s ts*), lamino-

The Organizaton of Consonant and Vowel Features 97

alveolar (orthographically *z tz*) and postalveolar (orthographically *x tx*), as shown in (62) (from Hualde 1988:223).

(62) asots, eltsuntse, urtxintx, samats, zuzen, zezen, azazkal, zimitz, sasoin, eskasi, osasun, zintzur, itseso, sasi, zozo, sos, zorrotz, izotz, zortzi, zize, zizeri, zizel, zurruzte, zapelatz

The features [anterior] and [distributed] are sufficient to account for contrasts among Basque sibilants, as shown in (63).

(63)

	s ts	z tz^3	x tx
coronal	+	+	+
anterior	+	+	−
dist.	−	+	+

Following Hualde, I assume that the constraint on sibilants is accounted for by Sibilant Harmony, a rule attested in a number of languages, e.g. Chumash, Navajo. However, Basque differs from the languages just mentioned in that there are three (as opposed to two) series of sibilants. Consequently, a rule spreading just [anterior] or [distributed] is not sufficient. Rather, both [anterior] and [distributed] must spread. Since both features are dominated by [coronal], we may formulate the rule as spreading the [coronal] node (Odden 1991a). Following Hualde, I assume that Sibilant Harmony applies from left-to-right, as shown in (64). For expository clarity, I incorporate the feature organization outlined in the Introduction.

(64)   Sibilant Harmony

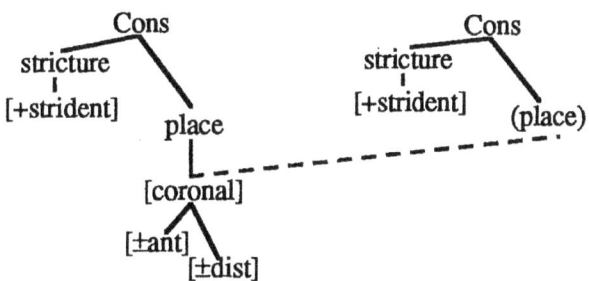

Similar to Sanskrit, an intervening front vowel does not block Sibilant Harmony from applying,[4] e.g. urtxintx, zezen, zimitz, itseso. The transparency of these vowels would not be expected if the [coronal]

specification of both consonants and vowels were arrayed on the same plane.

1.3 Summary

In this discussion I have shown that while maintaining the view that coronal consonants and front vocoids are specified for a common articulator feature, it cannot be the case that both instances of [coronal] are arrayed on the same plane. Consequently, our representation of coronal vowels must incorporate two crucial points. First, in order to capture the insight that front vowels are coronal sounds, they must be specified for a [coronal] articulator. Second, in order to account for the observed transparency of coronal consonants and vowels in spreading rules, the [coronal] specification of vowels and consonants must be sufficiently segregated. In the following section, I outline the feature theory and model of feature organization which serves as the basis for the analyses in this work. These, I will show, allow for the representation of front vowels and coronal consonants as a natural class without the added problems associated with the alternative approaches above.

2. FEATURE THEORY

The *Unified Features Theory* proposed in Clements (1989, 1990c [1993]) incorporates the view that place of articulation in both consonants and vowels is characterized by the same set of features. These include [labial, coronal, dorsal] and a feature of pharyngeal constriction which, following Herzallah (1990) and McCarthy (1989), I refer to as [pharyngeal]. It should be noted that while in Sagey's framework [dorsal] refers to an articulation made with the tongue body, Clements restricts this feature to refer to an articulation made with the back of the tongue. [Dorsal] thus serves to classify velar consonants and back vowels, in particular. A vowel inventory consisting of the three vowels, /i a u/, is characterized as in the redundancy-free specification in (65a). For vowels at least, I assume, following Clements, that both values of a given articulator are potentially available resulting in the fully specified feature chart in (65b).

(65) a.   i   a   u⁵   b.   i   a   u
      Labial   +   Labial   -   -   +
      Coronal   +   Coronal   +   -   -
      Dorsal   Dorsal   -   -   +
      Pharyngeal   +   Pharyngeal -   +   -

3. FEATURE ORGANIZATION

The model of feature organization assumed in this work is based on the *Unified Features* model proposed in Clements (1990c [1993]) (for related discussion see Herzallah 1990; Hume 1990, 1991a,b; Goodman 1991). I incorporate certain terminological changes which serve to emphasize the view that features characterizing the degree and location of a segment's constriction comprise a constituent, in a symmetrical manner for both consonants and vocoids, as illustrated in (66) (based on Clements 1992).

(66)

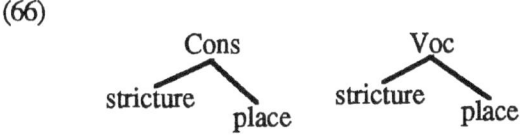

Each constriction is comprised of a place node dominating the segment's articulator(s), and a stricture node dominating features referring to the degree of constriction of the segment's articulation. I assume that stricture features for consonants include [strident] and [continuant]. For vowels, degree of constriction is characterized by the vowel height features [high, low] (and perhaps the redundant specification [+continuant] if required). Place and stricture features are dominated by a constriction node: CONS for consonantal constrictions and VOC for vocoidal constrictions. The division of place and stricture into two separate constituents correctly expresses the observation that place and stricture features can function independently of one another in phonological rules (see e.g. Odden 1992 regarding vowel features, and Clements 1992, regarding consonantal features). This organization also reflects the observation that a segment's place and stricture features can function as a constituent in phonological processes (see e.g. Clements 1987; for related discussion see Browman & Goldstein 1989). Structure superordinate to the constriction units is given in (67), using [s] and [i] as examples. As can be seen, CONS links directly to the root node. VOC links indirectly to the root through intermediate place and CONS nodes. As will be shown further below, the presence of intermediate nodes in the latter case is required to account for the opacity of vocoids in consonantal spreading rules.

(67)

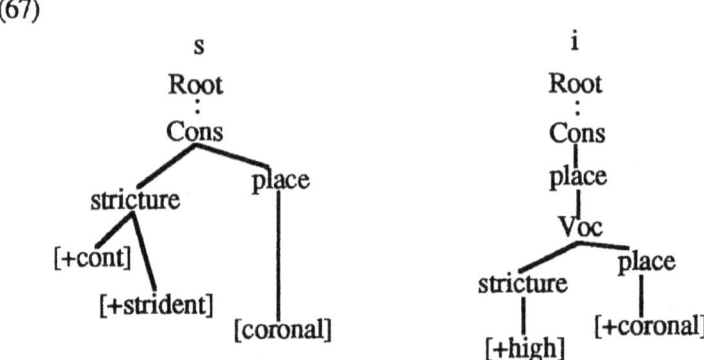

3.1 Major and Minor Articulations

I follow Sagey (1986) in defining the primaryness of an articulation as a phonological relationship between the segment's degree of closure (stricture) features, and the major articulator. She defines *major articulator* as follows:

(68)   Major Articulator:
       The major articulator of a segment is the articulator
       to which the distinctive degree of closure features apply.

Stricture features of the minor articulator are not specified underlyingly as they are predictable either within a given language or by universal default rules.

In Sagey's model, identifying the major articulator is achieved by means of a pointer, as illustrated in (69). Here I give the representation of the palatalized consonant [pʲ] in which, following her organization, the stricture feature [-cont] links directly to the root node. A pointer is used to indicate which of the two articulators is major (in this case the [labial] articulator), the articulator to which [-cont] applies.

(69)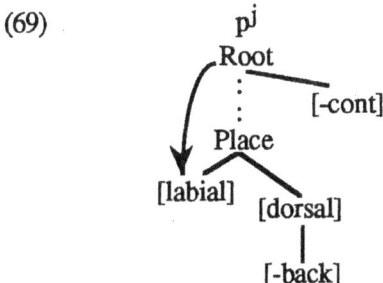

In the present model, the relationship between major and minor articulators is integrated directly into the representation. As a result, the otherwise unmotivated pointer device is unnecessary. As shown in (70), a consonant with a minor articulation is characterized as a vocoidal constriction superimposed on a major consonantal constriction (as based on Clements 1990c).

(70)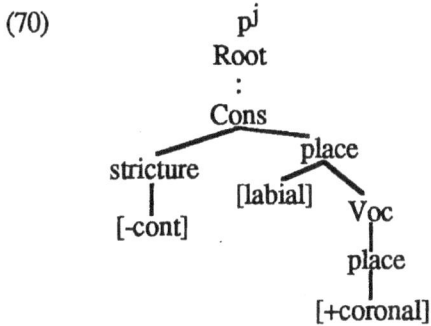

The stricture feature [-cont] applies to the articulator feature immediately dominated by CONS place. Note that were [-cont] to refer to the vocoidal as well as the consonantal articulation in this case, we would incorrectly predict [coronal] to be realized with complete closure. Consistent with Sagey, I assume that the stricture features of the minor articulator need not be specified underlyingly as they are generally predictable. We may formalize the relationship between stricture and place features as in (71).

(71) Constriction Relationship Principle (CRP):[6]
Feature [F] immediately dominated by a stricture node S applies to articulator [G] immediately dominated by a place node P if S and P are sisters.

This is schematized in (72).

(72)
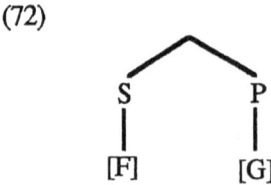

With respect to the representation in (70) further above we see that by the CRP, the stricture feature(s) dominated by CONS will always apply to the articulator feature also dominated by CONS (and not to those dominated by VOC). This then prohibits [-cont] from applying to [coronal]$_{VOC}$ as opposed to [labial]$_{CONS}$. Following Sagey's definition of *major articulato* in (68), [labial] then constitutes the major articulator since the distinctive degree of closure feature, i.e. [-cont], applies to this articulator. Of course, in the event that a segment has only a single articulator, all stricture features will apply to that articulator.

It will be noticed that the theory does not rule out the representation of vocoids with major and minor articulators, as shown in (73).

(73)
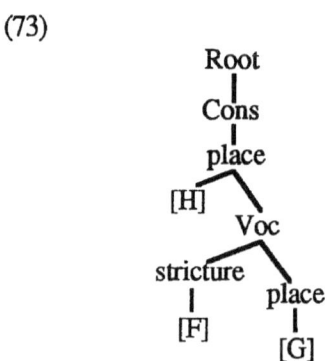

Feature [F], being specified as the segment's distinctive degree of constriction, applies to articulator [G] by the CRP, thus signalling [G] as the segment's major articulator. The degree of constriction of the segment's minor articulator, i.e. [H], remains unspecified underlyingly. Potential examples of vocoids with what might be construed of as major and minor articulations are vowels with both vocalic and consonantal constriction. Neo-Aramaic (Garbell 1965), for example, is reported to have pharyngealized vowels. This includes a pharyngealized low vowel, a case in which [pharyngeal] would arguably constitute both a major and minor articulator. In the Chinese dialect of Nantong, high central vowels are produced with a coronal fricative articulation (Ao 1990, personal communication), a potential candidate for [coronal]$_{CONS}$. It has also been proposed that the in- and out-rounded vowels of Swedish are characterized with a place feature of consonantal constriction in addition to one of vocalic constriction (Clements 1990c). Admittedly, with the exception of Swedish, many of these examples remain impressionistic at the present time. Further investigation is clearly warranted into the phonological as well as the phonetic status of the vowels in question.

It will be noticed from the representations above that a segment's status as consonantal or vocoidal is generally predictable from the representation itself. For example, in the unmarked case a consonant has the structure in (74a) with only a specification for consonantal constriction. Similarly, vocoids are represented as in (74b) with only specification for vocoidal features. In such cases, the major class feature [±consonantal] is essentially superfluous.

(74)

    a.   Root   b.   Root

           Cons = consonant   Cons = vocoid

  stricture   place   place

    [F]   [G]   Voc

                                 stricture   place

                                    [F]   [G]

For segments with both a major and minor articulator, the status of a given segment as consonantal or vocoidal is also generally predictable. In the unmarked case, any segment with a consonantal articulation will be consonantal, as shown in (75a). If further evidence shows the need to recognize vocoids, in addition to consonants, with major and minor articulations, the status of the segment may be predicted from reference to the segment's major articulator. (Recall that distinctive stricture features will apply to the major articulator.) Thus, in (75a) the result will be a segment with a major consonantal constriction (=consonant) whereas in (75b), the major constriction is vocoidal (=vocoid).

(75)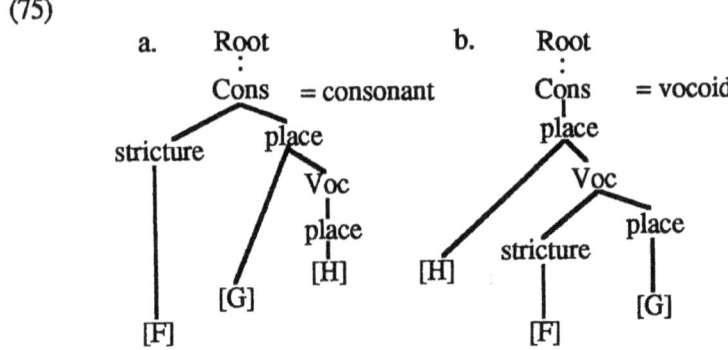

Additional information contributing to our knowledge of a given's segment status as consonantal or vocoidal is generally accessible from reference to the higher structure such as the skeletal tier (e.g. C vs. V) and/or to other feature specifications (e.g. [±sonorant]). It may be the case that with the segmental representations of consonants and vocoids given above, in conjunction with additional information, the major class features [±consonantal] (or [±vocoidal]) can be completely predictable from the feature organization itself. I leave this issue open for future consideration.

4. SPREADING CONSTRAINTS

In the discussion of Hungarian and Turkish vowel harmony in chapter III, I made brief mention of some of the predictions made by this model with respect to operations involving spreading association lines. In this section, I focus more exclusively on these predictions. As noted in chapter 3, spreading is constrained by the prohibition against crossed association lines (Goldsmith 1976), as expressed in the well-formedness condition in (76) (from Clements 1990c).

(76) No Line-Crossing:
Association lines may not cross on a plane.

This condition set limits on what constitutes a possible phonological representation, be it underlying or derived. To illustrate, I present representations characterizing possible spreading rules involving consonants and vowels (for simplicity I leave out stricture features).

The Organizaton of Consonant and Vowel Features 105

The first, as shown in (77), involves vocoid-to-vocoid spreading across an intervening consonant specified only for a major consonantal articulation.

(77)
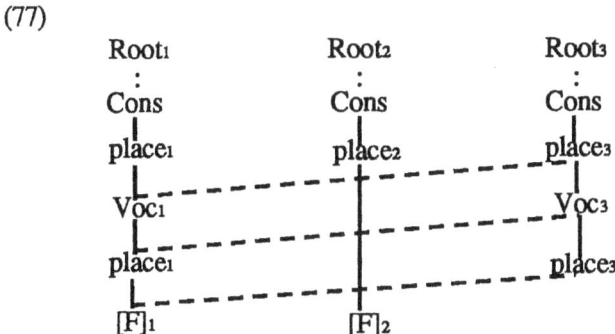

Given the structure of segments in (77), there are three well-formed spreading operations which may occur from $root_1$ to $root_3$. These involve spreading the terminal feature $[F]_1$ to VOC $place_3$, spreading $place_1$ to VOC_3, and spreading VOC_1 to CONS $place_3$. No line-crossing is incurred on a single plane in any of these operations. Such spreading rules commonly occur cross-linguistically. For example, in Turkish and Hungarian, as was seen in chapter III, a vocoidal articulator feature spreads across intervening plain consonants. Examples of vowel harmony involving VOC place are also attested. In Eastern Cheremis, for example, vowels assimilate to the backness and roundness (but not height) of a preceding vowel, across intervening consonants (Odden 1992; for related discussion see Clements 1989). Total vowel spreading, i.e. spreading VOC, across an intervening consonant is also attested, as exemplified by Maltese (Part II).

Spreading is blocked, however, when a feature or node of the same category as the spreading element intervenes on the same plane. This is illustrated in (78) using features dominated by VOC as an example. Between $root_1$ and $root_3$, no spreading rules are possible since all elements are defined on the same plane.

(78)

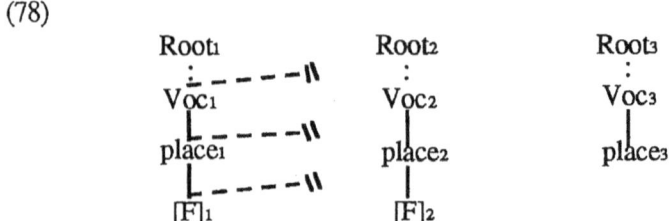

Within this model, consonants with minor articulations are represented with place features dominated by VOC place. This makes the strong prediction that in rules of vowel harmony, an intervening consonant specified for minor place feature [±F] will be opaque to the spreading of [±F]$_{VOC}$ from the vowel. As was seen in Turkish vowel harmony in chapter III, palatalized consonants block vowel harmony, thus supporting this hypothesis.

The model further predicts that no blocking will be incurred when an intervening segment specified for the same category as the harmonic feature or node occupies a different plane. This was also seen for Turkish. With the exception of palatalized consonants, all other consonants including coronals consonants are transparent to vowel-to-vowel assimilaton. This same prediction holds with respect to consonant-to-consonant assimilation. As we saw in both Sanskrit and Basque in sections 1.1, 1.2, respectively, [coronal] spreading from one consonant to another freely applies across intervening coronal vowels.

As is well-known, vowel-to-vowel assimilation across an intervening consonant is commonly attested cross-linguistically. Conversely, consonant-to-consonant assimilaton across an intervening vowel is less frequent. Rules of this type are generally restricted to spreading place articulators (and/or the features that they dominate), as in the case of Sanskrit and Basque. Such rules are correctly predicted to occur by the present model. On the other hand, total consonantal place assimilation across an intervening vowel is predicted not to occur. As illustrated in (79), the only spreading rule possible between root$_1$ and root$_3$ involves [F]$_1$. Place assimilation would result in crossed association lines, as would spreading CONS.

(79)

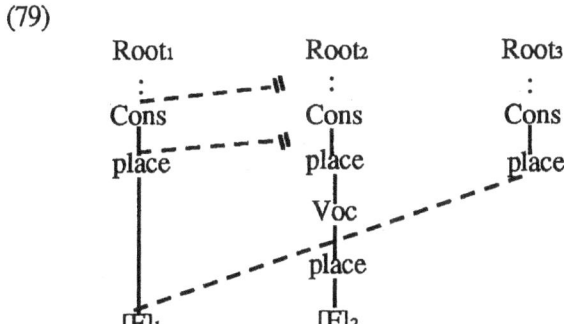

The failure of consonantal place assimilation to apply across an intervening vowel is evidenced in English, for example. It is well-known that under certain conditions a nasal consonant assimilates to the place specification of an adjacent consonant, e.g. i[m]polite, i[n]tolerable, i[ŋ]consistent. Place assimilation does not apply, however, when a vowel intervenes between target and trigger, e.g. i[n]accessible (*i[ŋ]accessible), i[n]ability (*i[m]ability). This receives a straightforward account under the assumption that both consonants and vocoids are specified for CONS place.

4.1 Summary

In this section I have outlined how the organization of the Unified Features model correctly accounts for observed opacity and transparency effects in assimilation rules. Central to this account is the claim that the place features of consonants and vocoids are arrayed on independent planes.

5. COOCCURRENCE CONSTRAINTS AND DISSIMILATION

In this work I claim that all instances of a given place feature are arrayed on the same tier regardless of whether the feature is defined on the vocoidal or consonantal plane. Such an approach makes strong predictions concerning the interaction of consonantal and vocalic place features in, most notably, cooccurrence constraints and dissimilation rules, phenomena commonly attributed to the Obligatory Contour Principle (OCP) (see e.g. McCarthy 1981, 1986; Yip 1988), stated in (80).

(80)   Obligatory Contour Principle:
        Adjacent identical autosegments are prohibited.

Central to the OCP is 'adjacency', a notion assumed in most current works in nonlinear phonology. This is expressed in (81).

(81)   Adjacency:
        The elements x and y are adjacent on tier n iff no element z on tier n intervenes.

Given the commonly accepted view that adjacency is defined on a given tier, added to the assumption that any given place feature [F] of consonants and vocoids is arrayed on a single tier, a number of predictions emerge. First, we would expect to find languages in which the OCP holds on [F] regardless of whether [F] is consonantal or vocoidal, as in (82). The OCP is thus defined on the general class of [F]. In other words, the rule scans the [F] tier.

(82)   *   [F] [F]

Second, we might expect cases to exist in which the OCP is defined on a subset of the general class of [F]. For example, we might expect the OCP to hold only for instances of [F] defined on the consonantal plane, or for those defined on the vocoidal plane, as shown in (83a,b), respectively. Thus, in (83a) the OCP scans the CONS plane whereas in (83b), the OCP scans the VOC plane.

(83) a.   * $[F]_{cons}$ $[F]_{cons}$ b.   * $[F]_{voc}$ $[F]_{voc}$

Under the assumption that all instances of [F] are arrayed on the same tier, a further prediction emerges with respect to the constraints in (83). In particular, we would expect the OCP to hold on two adjacent instances of $[F]_x$, provided that $[F]_y$ does not intervene, where x and y are either consonantal or vocoidal place features, and where x is not of the same category as y. (84a), for example, illustrates a hypothetical cooccurrence constraint prohibiting adjacent instances of $[F]_{cons}$ on tier F. Under the assumption that $[F]_{cons}$ and $[F]_{voc}$ are arrayed on the same tier, an intervening $[F]_{voc}$ will block adjacency of the two consonantal features and as such b) is well-formed.

(84) a.   b.
F-tier * [F]cons [F]cons   [F]cons [F]voc [F]cons

In this section I show that these predictions are borne out.

The view that all instances of a given place feature are arrayed on the same tier differs from the approach taken by Selkirk (1988) who argues that the place features of consonants and vowels are arrayed on different tiers (see also Clements 1990c). In order to maintain this latter multiple-tier approach, the OCP (and thus, adjacency) must be allowed to apply across tiers. This has the unfortunate consequence of increasing the power of the OCP and thus, creating a less highly constrained theory. Moreover, this approach would not predict blocking of the OCP in situations such as (84b). Since, as I show below, such cases are attested, the multiple-tier approach is problematic. Alternatively, by maintaining the view that all instances of a given place feature are arrayed on the same tier we are able to account for dissimilation and cooccurrence facts in a principled manner without extending the power of the OCP.

5.1 Cantonese

First, consider Cantonese as discussed in e.g. Cheng (1989), Hashimoto (1972), Yip (1982, 1988). In general, two labials do not cooccur within a single morpheme, with a morpheme typically corresponding to a single syllable. This holds of the labial consonants /p, m, f/, the labialized velar /k^W/, the labial glide /w/, back rounded vowels /o, u/ and front rounded vowels /ü ö/. As a result, we do not find morphemes in which both the onset and coda are labial[7] (from Cheng 1989, Hashimoto 1972), e.g. *pim, *fap, *k^{W}am, *mip, *wam. Furthermore, there are no morphemes in which a labial coda follows a rounded vowel, e.g. *up, *om, *uw, *öp, *üm, *öw. In onset-nucleus position, only front rounded vowels do not cooccur with a labial onset, back rounded vowels are permitted, e.g. *pü, *fö, *k^{W}ü, *wö. Setting aside this further restriction on onset-nucleus pairs (for discussion and proposed accounts see e.g. Cheng 1989, Yip 1988), the generalization can be stated as a cooccurrence constraint on adjacent labial specifications, as formulated in (85). In other words, the Obligatory Contour Principle is defined on the [labial] tier in Cantonese. Of particular interest is the fact that this constraint holds of any [labial] specification, regardless of whether it is consonantal or vocoidal.

(85)   *[labial]   [labial]

Yip (1982, 1988) describes a secret language in Cantonese referred to as La-mi in which the constraint in (85) serves as a rule blocker. As shown in (86), La-mi turns a given base into a derived morpheme comprised of two syllables.

(86)   ma   →   la mi
        kei   →   lei ki
        t'aw →   law t'i
        ha:ñ →   la:ñ hiñ
        jat   →   lat jit

Yip claims that La-mi involves reduplication of the base onto a template to which /l/ and /i/ are pre-associated, as shown in (87a). (87b) gives the formation of *lat jit* (< *jat*) (from Yip 1988:83).

(87)
a.   l   i   b.   l   i
      | | | |
      C V C   C V C   C V C   C V C   → lat jit
                                | | | |
                                j a t   j a t

When the coda consonant of the base is labial, the final consonant is realized as a coronal consonant instead of the expected labial.

(88)   sap → lap sit (< lap sip)
        t'im → lim t'in (< lim t'im)

As pointed out by Yip, labial dissimilation serves to eliminate the violation of (85). Following Odden (1988), Yip (1988), among others, I analyze dissimilation as deletion. In the present case, as shown in (89), dissimilation involves delinking the [labial] node of the second segment. Subsequent to dissimilation, the features values [coronal, +anterior] are assigned by default.

The Organizaton of Consonant and Vowel Features 111

(89)   Labial Dissimilation:

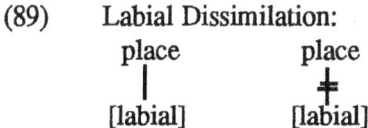

This is illustrated in (90) for the derived morpheme *lap sit*.

(90)

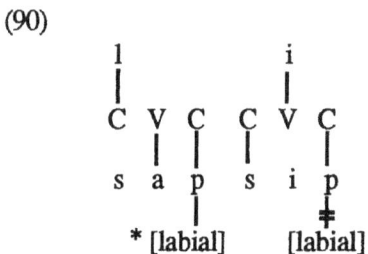

Yip notes that there is an additional rule which affects a change in the /i/ of the second syllable when the preceding vowel is also /i/. In this case, the second /i/ changes to [u], e.g. kin → lin kin → [lin kun]. Of particular interest is the fact that this rule fails to apply when the base has a labial coda (note that Labial Dissimilation applies regardless).

(91)   t'im   →   lim t'im   →   lim t'in (*lim t'un)

Yip argues that the i→u rule is blocked from applying as it would result in two adjacent [labial] nodes, thus violating the OCP (i.e. (85)), as shown in (92).

```
                 labial dissim.            i→u
(92)   l i m  t' i m  →  l i m  t' i n  ≢>  l i m  t' u n
       |         |              |                |     |
     *[labial] [labial]      [labial]        *[labial] [labial]
```

An alternative is to assume that the i→u rule does apply and then Labial Dissimilation takes place to eliminate the OCP violation. Choosing between the two analyses is not crucial to this discussion. In either case, it is crucial that the OCP holds on [labial] regardless of whether it is defined as consonantal or vocoidal. Recall that the OCP makes crucial reference to the notion of adjacency, which is defined on a given tier. By maintaining the view that instances of a given feature are arrayed on a single tier we are able to account for the interaction of consonantal and vocoidal place features in OCP driven rules such as dissimilation in a straightforward manner.

A similar interaction between consonantal and vocoidal place features is discussed in Clements (1990c) where he motivates a dissimilatory constraint in Korean involving the articulator feature [coronal]. As Clements points out, the palatal glide /j/ is excluded from cooccurring in a syllable with a coronal obstruent /t t' t^h c c' c^h s s'/ or a front vowel /i, e, ɛ/. Similarly, the labial glide /w/ is excluded from syllables containing a labial obstruent or labial vowel /u o ɔ/ (see Selkirk 1988 for discussion of a similar phenomenon involving [labial] in Berber). Clements states: "If we take the distinctive place of articulation features of Korean glides to be [coronal] and [labial], we may conflate these two constraints into a more general one disallowing glides in syllables containing homorganic obstruents or vowels."

In this section I have shown that the OCP holds on a given feature category regardless of whether or not the specification in question is consonantal or vocoidal. In what follows, we will see the OCP defined on a subset of a given feature category, in this case consonantal. Of particular interest is the fact that the rule is blocked from applying just in case a feature from the corresponding vocoidal class intervenes, as predicted by the model.

5.2   Akkadian

In Akkadian, the nominal prefix consonant typically surfaces as [m-], as shown in (93a) (data from von Soden 1969; for related discussion see McCarthy 1979, Odden 1991a). When the prefix consonant is followed by a labial consonant anywhere in the root, the prefix dissimilates to [n], as in (93b). Note that labial vocoids do not trigger the rule, nor does the mimation suffix [-m].[8]

The Organizaton of Consonant and Vowel Features 113

(93) a.   ma-luuṭu   'tire'
       ma-zuukt   'mortar'
       ma-ʃkanu-m   'place'
       me-ereʃu-m   'plantation'
       mi-i-ʃaru-m   'justice'
       ma-ṣallu-m   'camp'
   b.   ne-ereb   'entrance'
       na-rkabt   'chariot'
       na-pteetu-m   'key'
       na-ʃpartu-m   'letter'
       ne-lmenu   'loss, damage'
       na-raamu-m   'favourite'

Similar to Cantonese, dissimilation is formulated as delinking the labial node of the first segment with the features values [coronal, +anterior] assigned by default, as in (94). Note that in this case dissimilation is crucially defined on consonantal [labial] in order to exclude labial vocoids as triggers.

(94)   Labial Dissimilation:

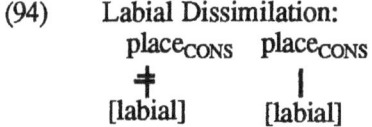

     [labial]   [labial]

Of particular interest is the observation that dissimilation fails to occur if a labial vowel or glide intervenes, as shown in (95).

(95)   mu-uʃabu-m   'seat'
       ma-amiitu-m   'oath'   (< /ma-wmii-t-u-m/)
       mu-ʃpalu-m   'deep'
       mu-nnab(it)tu-m   'fugitive'
       mu-ʃeepiʃu-m   'work leader'
       mu-ʃteepiʃtu   'to leave one baffled'

According to the rule formulation in (94), the two labial$_{CONS}$ nodes must be adjacent for dissimilation to occur. Since, as shown in (96), the vocoidal [labial] specification intervenes on the same tier, the adjacency requirement is not met. Consequently, the rule fails to apply.

(96) muʃpalum

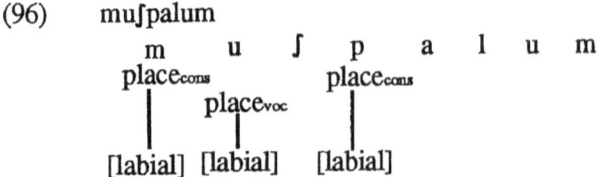

The condition that Labial Dissimilation applies provided that a labial vocoid does not intervene receives a straightforward account under the assumption that the [labial] specification of consonants and vocoids is on the same tier.

6. ROOT-ADJACENCY AS A NECESSARY CONDITION ON CONSONANT/VOWEL INTERACTION?

It has been suggested that the interaction of consonantal and vocoidal place features in OCP-related phenomena is limited to cases in which the two segments are root-adjacent (e.g. Selkirk 1988). In assimilation phenomena, however, root-adjacency does not appear to be a necessary condition. In Tulu, for example, a back unrounded vowel becomes rounded in the context of a labial consonant which may be non-root-adjacent.

As described by Bright (1972) (for related discussion see Odden 1991a, Sagey 1986), in Tulu [u] occurs when a rounded vowel occurs in an adjacent syllable (97a) or when preceded by a labial consonant, either root-adjacent to the vowel or separated from it by an intervening consonant (97b). Otherwise, the high unrounded back vowel [ɯ][9] generally occurs (97c).

(97)
    a.   uccu   'kind of snake'
          moroḍu   'empty'
          kukku   'mango'
          kaṇṇulu   'eyes' cf. kaṇṇuɯ 'eye'
          eeḍulu   'goats' cf. eeḍuɯ 'goat'
    b.   bolpu   'whiteness'
          kappu   'blackness'
          avu   'that'
          iimḷu   'kind of leech'
          avtu   'out'
    c.   kaṭṭuɯ   'bond'
          kaṇṇuɯ   'eye'
          pudaruɯ   'name'
          ugaruɯ   'brackish'

As the forms iimḷu 'kind of leech' and avtu 'out' illustrate, root-adjacency is not a necessary condition for labial assimilation to occur. In each case, the triggering consonant is separated from the target vowel by an intervening consonant.

Recall also that in the analysis of La-mi in Cantonese further above, the OCP holds on non root-adjacent instances of [labial]$_{CONS}$ and [labial]$_{VOC}$. The examples from Cantonese and Tulu then suggest that root-adjacency is not a necessary condition for the interaction of consonantal and vocoidal place features.

7.   RESOLVING AN ORDERING PARADOX

As just shown, by arraying all instances of a given place feature on the same tier we are able to provide a principled account of deletion rules and cooccurrence constraints involving consonantal and vocoidal place features without abandoning the view that adjacency (and the OCP) is defined on a single tier. In addition, I follow Clements (1990c) in claiming that the place features of consonants and vocoids are defined on independent planes. Consonantal place features link (indirectly) to the constriction node CONS, while vocoidal place features link (indirectly) to VOC; CONS and VOC are themselves arrayed on independent tiers. As shown further above, the partial segregation of consonantal and vocoidal place features correctly accounts for observed asymmetries in consonantal and vocoidal spreading rules across intervening segments.

Allowing features on the same tier to link to different planes could potentially result in a configuration like (98) in which feature [-F] of segment 2 follows feature [+F] of segment 3 (for simplicity, I omit the intervening place node). Such a configuration could be the result of an assimilation process.

(98)
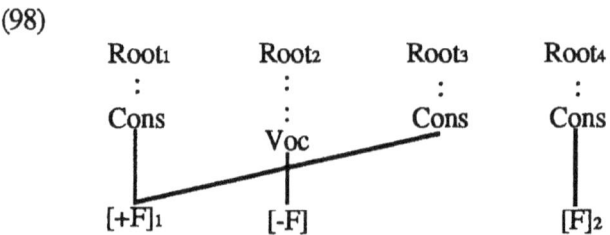

It is commonly assumed that the sequencing of elements on a given tier encodes linear precedence (<). Thus, $root_1 < root_2 < root_3 < root_4$. Similarly, $[+F]_1 < [-F] < [+F]_2$. It will be observed, however, that although $root_2$ precedes $root_3$, the feature $[+F]_1$ which links to $root_3$ precedes [-F], which links to $root_2$. The organization of elements in (98) thus presents a ordering paradox. As a result, it is predicted that on tier F the feature $[+F]_1$ is non-adjacent to $[+F]_2$ even though the root nodes dominating these features are adjacent at the level of the root (i.e. $root_3 < root_4$). Note that the ordering paradox in (98) is not ruled out by No Line-crossing since the association lines cross on different planes. This then differs from the configuration in (99) which *is* ruled out by No Line-Crossing.

(99)
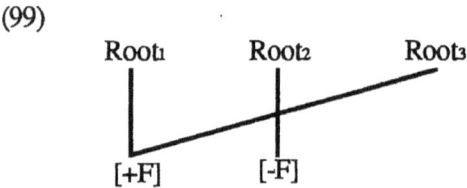

In this section, I argue that the ordering paradoxes in both (98) and (99) result from violations of a universal ordering principle, along the lines proposed in Hammond (1988). Although a rule which would create a configuration such as (99) is blocked by No Line-Crossing, a rule creating a representation like (98) is not and, as a result, may occur. The ordering violation, I argue, is eliminated at a later stage in the derivation.

The Organizaton of Consonant and Vowel Features 117

In nonlinear representations, features and nodes are hierarchically organized by means of association lines. Given a representation such as (100) where A and B are features or nodes and where A dominates B, the relationship between these two elements is interpreted as B *characterizes* A (Laughren 1984, Clements 1985; but cf. Sagey 1986, Hammond 1988).[10]

(100)   A
         |
         B

As stated in (101), 'characterization' (=>) has the properties of transitivity, asymmetry and irreflexivity.

(101)   Characterization ("=>")
   a.   transitivity: if F=>G and G=>x, then F=>x
   b.   asymmetry: if F=>G, then NOT G=>F
   c.   irreflexivity: NOT F=>F

To illustrate these properties consider the simplified representation in (102). Since by transitivity [coronal] characterizes Place, and Place characterizes Root, then [coronal] will characterize Root. Asymmetry incorporates the notion that association is one-way, i.e. [coronal] characterizes Place but the reverse does not obtain. Finally, irreflexivity states that [coronal], for example, does not characterize itself.

(102)   Root
            |
           Place
            |
         [coronal]

Along the lines proposed by Hammond, ordering relations between segments are constrained by a general ordering principle. I formulate this as the Ordering Constraint in (103).

(103)   Ordering Constraint (OC)
        Given the elements X<Y on tier M and A, B on tier N, where A characterizes X and B characterizes Y, B cannot precede A.

The configuration in (104) is ruled out since A characterizes X and B characterizes Y, yet B precedes A. As pointed out by Hammond, No Line-Crossing is thus a natural consequence of general ordering principles.

(104)

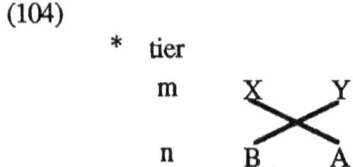

Recall, however, that No Line-Crossing will not rule out a configuration such as (105) since the association lines cross on different planes.

(105)

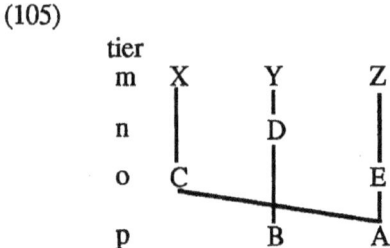

The configuration in (105) does nonetheless violate the OC. This is due to the fact that, by transitivity, A characterizes X and B characterizes Y yet, B precedes A.

The OC is a condition on the well-formedness of representations. No Line-Crossing serves to blocks rules from applying whose output would otherwise violate the OC. However, since No Line-Crossing is not available as a means of blocking rules which would create configurations like (105), we might suppose that such rules apply but that the OC violation is subsequently eliminated at some point in the derivation. In order for violations such as that in (105) to be eliminated, A must precede B when it characterizes X, yet follow B when it characterizes Z. Such a representation is impossible given the multiple-linking of A to both X and Z. What we need then is a means of eliminating the multiple-linking of A to both X and Z, but at the same time preserving the association of A to X and that of A to Z. I would suggest that this is achieved by the universal repair convention, Cloning, as stated in (106).

(106) Cloning
  i. Associate, in accordance with well-formedness conditions, a copy of $[F]_1$ to X, where X represents a given node;
  ii. Delink the original association line from X to $[F]_1$.

Applied to (105), and illustrated in (107a), Cloning applies as follows: i. associate a copy of A_1 to C; ii. delink the association line from C to A_1. The output of these operations gives the well-formed configuration in (107b).

(107)

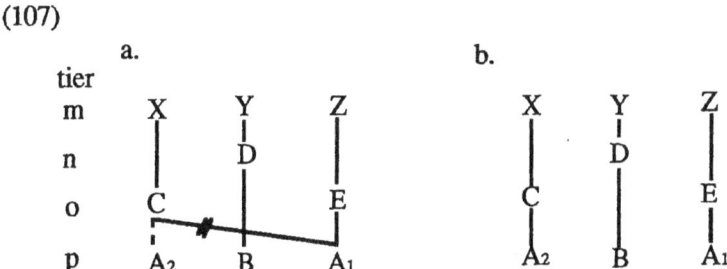

Thus, although No Line-Crossing prevents violations of the Ordering Constraint from occurring, Cloning eliminates violations that do occur. As I show just below, Cloning is independently required in phonological theory (see Cohn 1990:56-57 for related discussion). Although a full treatment of this issue must be left for future consideration, two cases in which the application of Cloning may be warranted will be discussed.

The first involves configurations resulting from the application of Tier Conflation. McCarthy (1979, 1981) motivates the complete segregation of consonant and vowel melodies in Classical Arabic, to mention one example. The eleventh binyan perfective of the root 'write' has the following representation, with the /a/ vocalism multiply-linked to three V-slots of the template, and the consonant /b/ linked to two C-slots.

(108)

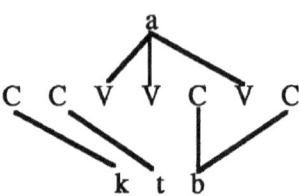

McCarthy (following Younes 1983) claims that at a particular point in the derivation, consonant and vowel melodies become linearly ordered with respect to one another. The operation which affects this change is referred to as Tier Conflation. By the application of Tier Conflation, the representation in (108) changes to (109).

(109)

```
C C V V C V C
| |  \|/  | |
k t   a   b a b
```

It will be noticed that Tier Conflation has split apart certain melodies: /a/ is no longer multiply-linked to all three vowel slots, nor is /b/ linked to two C-slots. Rather, a new instance of both /a/ and /b/ have been created. If each of these elements were not split, Tier Conflation would create the representation in (110) which is ill-formed, precisely because it violates the Ordering Constraint.

(110)

In a previous discussion of this phenomenon, Archangeli & Pulleyblank (1986) suggest that the splitting apart of these elements in Tier Conflation is the result of universal rule. We might suppose that the universal rule responsible for accomplishing this splitting is Cloning. I should point out that Cloning simply makes explicit the type of mechanisms that have been implicitly assumed in order to create a well-formed representation with the application of Tier Conflation.

A second case in which Cloning might also be operative involves the splitting apart of elements which result from assimilation. In Part II, I show that in Maltese the imperfective prefix vowel is realized as

The Organizaton of Consonant and Vowel Features

[i] before coronal consonants as the result of assimilation. Of particular interest is the fact that assimilation is triggered by all coronal obstruents, both anterior and non-anterior. Assimilation involves spreading the articulator [coronal] to a preceding V-slot, which necessarily requires that any features dominated by [coronal] also spread. Thus, when the trigger is a non-anterior coronal consonant, the feature [-anterior] spreads onto the vowel whereas when the trigger is an anterior coronal, [+anterior] spreads.

I claim throughout this work that front vowels are inherently [-anterior]. However, as just pointed out, assimilation to an anterior coronal consonant results in the vowel being multiply-linked to the consonant, as shown in (111) where both the vowel and the consonant are specified as [coronal, +anterior].

(111)

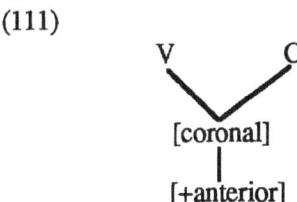

The configuration in (111) predicts that the output of assimilation to an anterior coronal consonant will be a vowel with a constriction in the anterior coronal region. Conversely, when assimilation involves a non-anterior coronal consonant, the prediction is that the vowel's constriction location is in the non-anterior coronal region. Unfortunately, at present I do not have access to phonetic data which would assist in determining whether or not these predictions hold up. If it is the case that the front vowel is articulated in the non-anterior coronal region regardless of the consonant to which it assimilates, the representation in (111) would need to be repaired. Note that simply changing the value of [+anterior] on the vowel to [-anterior] would be unsatisfactory given the multiple-linked structure. If we were to do this, both consonant and vowel would become specified as [-anterior] which would incorrectly predict that the consonant surfaces as a postalveolar coronal. An alternative solution would be to invoke Cloning whereby each segment would be independently linked to [coronal, +anterior]. By phonological rule, the [+anterior] specification of the vowel could then be changed to [-anterior] without affecting the feature specification of the consonant. I leave these issues open for further consideration.

NOTES

1. A further conditioning factor is that the nasal target must be followed by a nonliquid sonorant (for related discussion see Schein & Steriade 1986: 720ff.).

2. This is the same conclusion drawn by Steriade (1985) and Steriade & Schein (1986). They, however, assume that anterior coronals are specified for the feature value [+distributed] and thus, differ from retroflex consonants with respect to both the values of [distributed] and [anterior]. Specifying anterior coronals for [+distributed] is unmotivated though since it is noncontrastive for these consonants. Furthermore, according to Whitney's (1889) description of anterior coronals (on which they base their specification), it is not completely clear that these segments are in fact [+distributed]. Whitney describes the anterior coronals as being "formed at the teeth (or at the roots of the teeth), by the *tip of the tongue*" (p.47) [my emphasis]. He adds a further description of these sounds as they are spoken by 'modern Hindus'. It is this comment that Steriade and Schein & Steriade crucially employ to motivate the specification of anterior coronals as [+distributed]. Whitney notes that "the modern Hindus are said to pronounce their dentals with the tip of the tongue thrust well forward against the upper teeth, so that these sounds get a slight tinge of the quality belonging to the English and Modern Greek th-sounds." (p.48). In Whitney's initial description, he states that anterior coronals are produced with the tip of the tongue. This would lead us to suspect that these sounds are apical and hence, [-distributed]. However, according to his second description, the specification [+distributed] is perhaps more appropriate. Given the fact that the feature [distributed] is noncontrastive for anterior coronals, deciding between these two specifications is not crucial to the present analysis.

3. Hualde (p.226) specifies the lamino-alveolars as [-anterior] although given his description of these sounds as alveolars, I assume that they are [+anterior] sounds.

4. Sibilant Harmony also applies across intervening anterior coronal consonants. I assume that non-strident anterior coronals are unspecified for [coronal] and for the features that [coronal] dominates in underlying representation. This is supported by the fact that non-strident coronal consonants do not contrast for place in Basque; underlyingly there is only a single series of anterior non-strident coronals. Consequently, the feature values [coronal, +anterior] are predictable for non-strident coronals and can be filled in by redundancy rule.

5. An alternative is to specify /u/ as [+dorsal] with [+labial] being the redundant feature value.

6. An interesting parallel can be drawn between the CRP and the notion of government in syntax (see e.g. Chomsky 1981, 1986).

7. This constraint may be violated in onomatopoeic and loan words (see Cheng 1989).

8. It is not possible to determine from the data whether this suffix fails to trigger Labial Dissimilation because it is not a root consonant (as proposed by McCarthy 1979) or because the case vowel [u] which precedes it blocks the rule from applying. The blocking effect of labial vocoids is discussed further below.

9. Sagey treats this vowel as the high front vowel [i] whereas Bright, the original source, and Odden refer to this vowel as a high back unrounded vowel. I follow Bright and Odden in assuming that the vowel in question is a high back unrounded vowel.

10. Sagey (1986) interprets association in terms of simultaneity. Hammond (1988) convincingly shows that this approach is untenable as a means of accounting for, in particular, the notion of overlap in multi-tiered representations. Hammond, on the other hand, argues that association lines be viewed as elements which issue instructions to a given node. However, as pointed out to me by Nick Clements, the notion 'issuing instructions to' gives association, which is a phonological relation, a phonetic definition (such as that employed in phonetic implementation).

V
Consonant-to-Front Vowel Assimilation

0. INTRODUCTION

Any work dealing with the interaction of front vowels and consonants would clearly be incomplete without discussing palatalization, undoubtedly the most commonly attested rule involving these segments. Palatalization is generally used as a cover-term to refer to the various assimilations that consonants undergo in the context of front vowels (see e.g. Bhat 1978). These may result in, for example, the addition of an i-like articulation to a consonant, e.g. /k + e/ → [kʲe], or a complete change in the major place of articulation of the consonantal target, e.g. /k + e/ → [tʃe].

To quote McCarthy (1988), "the goal of phonology is the construction of a theory in which cross-linguistically common and well-established processes emerge from very simple combinations of the descriptive parameters of the model....if the representations are right, then the rules will follow." Given the fact that palatalization is quite common cross-linguistically, we would then expect an adequate representation of these processes to be relatively straightforward. This, however, has not been the case, particularly with respect to the representation of rules in which the major place of articulation of the consonant changes e.g. /k + e/ → [tʃe]. In this chapter, I illustrate how a feature theory in which front vowels are [coronal] elucidates such processes, thus building on the proposal originally developed in Clements (1976a). Consonant-to-front vowel assimilation in Acadian

French, a Canadian French dialect, provides a typical example illustating these rules.

1. ACADIAN FRENCH

Acadian French is spoken in the Canadian maritime provinces of New Brunswick, Nova Scotia and Prince Edward Island. The variety discussed here is characteristic of that spoken in the Moncton region of New Brunswick. My data are drawn primarily from Lucci (1972) and Flikeid (1988), supplemented with examples provided by W. Cichocki (p.c.). The phonemic inventory is given in (112) for reference.

(112) Phonemic inventory:

a. Oral vowels:

	Front		Central	Back
	unrounded	rounded		
	i	y		U
	e	ø		o
	ɛ ɛː	œ		ɔ
			a	ɑ

Nasal vowels:

Front	Back
ɛ̃	ɔ̃
	ɑ̃

b.

	bilabial	labiodental	dental	palato-alveolar	palatal	velar	laryngeal
	p b	f v	t d			k g	
			s z	ʃ ʒ			h
			l r				
	m		n		ɲ		

Palatalization is an optional rule characteristic of all varieties of Acadian French. Before a front vowel, a velar consonant may be realized as a velar, a palatalized velar or a palato-alveolar affricate. Thus, we find the realizations [k g]~[kʲ gʲ]~[t͡ʃ d͡ʒ], as shown in (113a).

Before a back vowel, only the velar pronunciation is attested,[1] as seen in (113b). Lucci notes that the affricate pronunciation is most characteristic of older speakers in rural areas although even among speakers in these communities all three variants are heard.

(113)
a. [kø]~[kʲø]~[t͡ʃø]   'tail'
    [kyir]~[kʲyir]~[t͡ʃyir]   'leather/to cook'
    [okɛ̃]~[okʲɛ̃]~[ot͡ʃɛ̃]   'no, not any'
    [ki]~[kʲi]~[t͡ʃi]   'who'
    [kɛ]~[kʲɛ]~[t͡ʃɛ]   'quay'
    [kœr]~[kʲœr]~[t͡ʃœr]   'heart'
    [sarkœj]~[sarkʲœj]~[sart͡ʃœj]   'coffin'
    [gɛte]~[gʲɛte]~[dʒɛte]   'to watch for'
    [gœl]~[gʲœl]~[dʒœl]   'mouth'
b. [ka]   'case'
    [kUt]   'cost'
    [kote]   'side'
    [gar]   'station'
    [gUt]   'drop (N.)'

The palatalized velars and palato-alveolar affricates in (113) are best considered to be derived from underlying velar consonants as the result of assimilation to a following front vocoid. Positing /k g/ as underlying as opposed to /kʲ gʲ/ or /t͡ʃ dʒ/ is motivated first, by the observation that palatalized velars and palato-alveolar affricates only occur before (underlying) front vocoids whereas velars have a wider distribution, e.g. word-finally, [sark] 'circle'; preceding a consonant, [griʃe] 'ruffled'; prevocalically, [kUt] 'cost'. In addition, the change from velar to palatalized velar or palato-alveolar in the context of a front vowel is a common rule attested cross-linguistically. I will refer to the rule which adds secondary i-like articulation onto a consonant's major articulation as *Palatalization* and to the rule which derives a postalveolar as *Coronalization* (Hume 1988, Itô & Mester 1989).

Palatalization and Coronalization are best viewed as phonological as opposed to phonetic rules in Acadian French. As Lucci points out, they occur only word-internally, yet not in an exceptionless manner. Words such as [pike] 'to sting, prick', [debarke] 'to get out of a car', [mokø] 'teasing' are always pronounced with a plain velar consonant.

Neither the palatalized velar nor palato-alveolar pronunciations are attested. In addition, the trigger of, in particular, Coronalization may undergo further phonological rules. Some varieties of Acadian French have an optional rule which lowers and backs /ɛ/ to [a] before /r/. Thus, we find alternations such as [sɛrtɛ̃]~[sartɛ̃] 'certain', [pɛrʃ]~[parʃ] 'perch' (Flikeid 1988: 75-78). We also find the palato-alveolar surfacing before the low central vowel in, e.g. [d͡ʒaːr] 'war'. Including the vowel [a] as a trigger of Coronalization would incorrectly predict the rule to affect the initial velar of, e.g. [gaːr] *[d͡ʒaːr] 'station'. Conversely, by positing that the underlying vowel of 'war' is /ɛ/ the rule of Coronalization will first change the velar to palato-alveolar, then ɛ-lowering will apply to change the vowel to [a], i.e. /gɛr/ → d͡ʒɛr → d͡ʒar → [d͡ʒaːr].[2]

Dental consonants in Acadian French undergo similar conditioning before a front vocoid, as shown in (114). However, only a non-syllabic front vocoid triggers the change and is subsequently deleted. Note that glide deletion also occurs in cases in which the consonantal target is a velar, e.g. /ɛkietyd/ → [ɛ̃tʃetyd] 'anxiety'. Lucci states that a dental stop is realized as either a dental, palatalized dental or a palato-alveolar affricate before an underlying non-syllabic palatal vocoid.

(114)
UR	SR	Gloss
/ɛ̃diɛn/	[ɛ̃djɛn]~[ɛ̃dʲɛn]~[ɛ̃d͡ʒɛn]	'indian (fem.)'
/kanadiɛ̃/	[kanadjɛ̃]~[kanadʲɛ̃]~[kanad͡ʒɛ̃]	'Canadian'
/diamã/	[djamã]~[dʲamã]~[d͡ʒamã]	'diamond'
/diø/	[djø]~[dʲø]~[d͡ʒø]	'god'
/pitie/	[pitje]~[pitʲe]~[pit͡ʃe]	'pity'
/tiɛ̃/	[tjɛ̃]~[tʲɛ̃]~[t͡ʃɛ̃]	'your'
/amitie/	[amitje]~[amitʲe]~[amit͡ʃe]	'friendship'
/kartie/	[kartje]~[kartʲe]~[kart͡ʃe]	'quartier'
/tiɛd/	[tjed]~[tʲed]~[t͡ʃed]	'lukewarm'
cf. /dyp/	[dyp]	'dupe'
/tip/	[tip]	'type'

Palatalization and Coronalization are common phenomena not limited to any particular language group but rather attested in a wide range of languages cross-linguistically. As stated in the introduction, our formal representation should thus be able to account for these rules in a principled and straightforward manner. An adequate analysis must also account for the fact that although the conditioning environment in each rule is identical, the outputs are different. In Palatalization, the consonant acquires a vowel-like articulation while maintaining its original major place of articulation. In Coronalization, a front vocoid affects a change in the consonant's major place of articulation, either from velar to nonanterior coronal, or from anterior coronal to nonanterior coronal.

In the following section, I review the assumptions necessary to account for Palatalization and Coronalization within a framework in which front vowels are specified with the tongue body feature [-back]. Drawing on the model of feature organization proposed in Sagey (1986), it will be shown that the representation of Coronalization, in particular, fails to reflect the observation that the rule in question is a natural assimilation process. Conversely, by incorporating the view that front vowels are coronal sounds, both Palatalization and Coronalization are represented in a principled manner as natural assimilation processes.

2. FRONT VOWELS AS [-BACK]

In SPE, vowels are characterized by the tongue body features [back, high, low]. Front vowels form a natural class by virtue of their common [-back] specification. Sagey (1986) maintains this vowel specification in her model yet, as mentioned previously, introduces the innovation that these features are dominated by the node [dorsal], referring to an articulation produced with the tongue body. Front vowels are thus [-back] dominated by [dorsal]. Velar consonants, like vowels, are specified for a [dorsal] node yet generally unspecified for terminal tongue body features. Consonants produced with the tip or blade of the tongue have a [coronal] articulator dominating the terminal features [anterior, distributed]. To illustrate, the representations of the anterior coronal [t], the postalveolar [t͡ʃ], the velar [k] and the front vowel [e] are given in (115) (irrelevant structure is omitted).

130   The Interaction of Front Vowels and Coronal Consonants

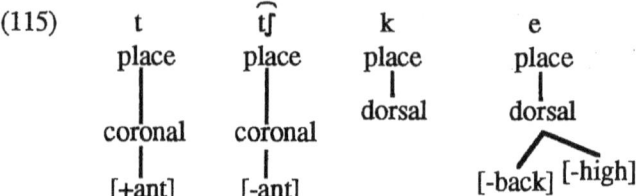

(115)

Following Sagey, the representation of Palatalization, e.g. /k/ → [kʲ], is shown in (116) where the feature [-back] spreads to the [dorsal] node of the velar consonant.

(116)
```
      C              V
      ⋮              ⋮
    place          place
      |              |
    dorsal         dorsal
            ------   |
                  [-back]
```

The result is a palatalized (or fronted) velar. The naturalness of this rule derives from the fact that in the output, both the target and trigger are specified for a common feature, i.e. [-back]. The change affected in the target is thus directly attributable to the vocalic trigger. In other words, the consonant acquires the quality of frontness as the result of assimilation to an adjacent front vocoid.

Representing Coronalization, e.g. /k/ → [t͡ʃ], is less straightforward in Sagey's framework. In order to affect the change from velar to nonanterior coronal, the velar consonant must somehow acquire a [coronal] node. Since front vowels are specified for [dorsal, -back], it is not obvious where the [coronal] node comes from. Sagey does not address this issue. She does, however, provide an analysis of the change from an anterior coronal to postalveolar, e.g. /t/ → [t͡ʃ], from which we might attempt to generalize in order to account for velar Coronalization.

As shown in (117), Sagey claims that the change from /t/ → [t͡ʃ] involves spreading the feature [-back] from the vowel trigger to a [dorsal] node (interpolated in this case).

Consonant-to-Front Vowel Assimilation

(117)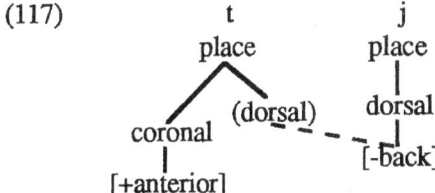

As Sagey points out, the output of (117) is not a postalveolar consonant but rather [tʲ]. In order to affect the change from [tʲ] to the desired output [t͡ʃ] she states: "what is at work is a process reanalyzing ([tʲ]) as a [-anterior] coronal, rather than as a [+anterior] coronal doubly-articulated with a [-back] dorsal glide. This, then is the common process whereby adding the feature [-back] to a coronal results in the coronal becoming [-anterior]" (p.109). She continues: "what seems to occur is that the coronal and dorsal articulations, because they are so close to each other, are not pronounced as two independent constrictions, but rather fuse to a single, [-anterior] coronal articulation -- halfway between the original coronal articulation and the dorsal articulation" (p.110). We might formulate Fusion as in (118).

(118)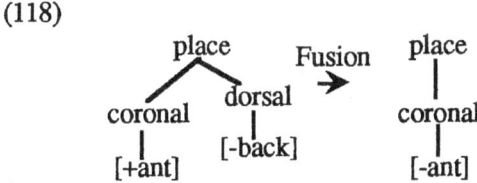

The change from /t/ to [t͡ʃ] before a front vowel within Sagey's analysis is not, properly speaking, assimilation. Assimilation to a front vowel creates a palatalized anterior coronal, whereas the postalveolar is derived from the palatalized anterior coronal as the result of Fusion, a process independent of the front vowel trigger. The fact that a [-anterior] coronal results is therefore only indirectly attributable to the quality of the front vowels which condition this change.

We might attempt to account for the change from /k/ to [t͡ʃ] as evidenced in, e.g. /kɛ/ → [t͡ʃɛ] 'quay', in a similar manner. First, the velar consonant assimilates to the frontness of an adjacent front vocoid as shown in (119).

(119)

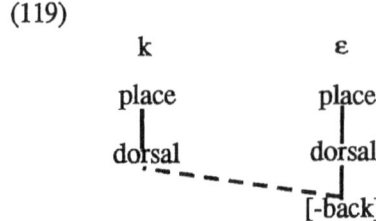

As in (117), the immediate output of assimilation is a palatalized consonant, in this case, [kʲ]. Yet, Fusion is unfeasible as a means of accounting for the fact that the ultimate result is a [-anterior] coronal since there is no pre-existing coronal node on the consonantal target. Thus, in order for Fusion to be employed the velar would need to acquire a [coronal] node specified for [+anterior]. (Recall that Fusion results from the merger of a [coronal, +anterior] articulation and a [dorsal, -back] articulation.) However, positing that an [+anterior, coronal] specification is generated on the velar consonant just in order to allow Fusion to apply is ad hoc. This then raises the question of where the [coronal,-anterior] specification on the output of Coronalization comes from. Since, in this approach, it cannot be attributed to the vowel, a restructuring rule of the type [dorsal, -back] → [coronal, -anterior] would be required to assign a [coronal] node to the fronted velar, with perhaps an additional rule that subsequently deletes the original [dorsal] articulator.

There are a number of weaknesses with an aproach along these lines. First, similar to the change from /t/ → [tʃ], the fact that a non-anterior coronal results would once again only be indirectly attributable to the front vowels which clearly condition this change. Thus, although Palatalization is characterized in simple terms as an assimilation rule, Coronalization is not. Rather, it must be the result of additional independent operations applied to the output of Palatalization. Second, the relationship expressed in this model between [-back] and [coronal, -anterior] is a formally arbitrary one. There is nothing inherent in the theory that would predict that a velar consonant in the context of a [-back] vowel would result in a nonanterior coronal. Third, and perhaps the most important, is the fact that restructuring rules would be permitted to account for common phonological processes. Rules of this nature are excessively powerful and arbitrary. By incorporating restructuring rules into our theory, we seriously weaken one of the fundamental goals which is to seek a formal representation capable of expressing common processes as simple rules.

It is important to point out that this account is not unlike the analysis proposed in SPE. Chomsky & Halle employ linking rules to affect the change from, for example, velar to non-anterior coronal. Similar to Sagey's account, a fronted velar is first formed. Then, through a succession of rules, the fronted velar is ultimately realized as a nonanterior coronal.

To summarize, in Sagey's account, Palatalization is characterized as a common phonological process. The consonant assimilates to the quality of a front vowel by spreading a single feature. However, in Coronalization, the change from dental or velar to palato-alveolar can only be indirectly attributed to the quality of front vowels which condition this change. Coronalization is not assimilation, per se. This account fails to reflect the observation that Coronalization, like Palatalization, is a common phonological process attested in a wide range of languages and, as a result, should be represented in simple terms.

As I show further below, the claim that front vowels are coronals provides a straightforward account in which both Palatalization and Coronalization are treated as natural assimilation rules. In both instances, the consonantal target acquires the feature value [coronal] (redundantly [-anterior]) from a front vowel. The account of Coronalization given below draws on my earlier analysis of Polish in Hume (1988) (see also Broselow & Niyondagara 1990, Hume 1990). The present account differs from my earlier analysis concerning one significant aspect, in particular. In Hume (1988), the place features of consonants and vowels are arrayed on the same plane which, as shown in chapter IV, incorrectly predicts consonants to be opaque in vowel harmony rules, and vowels to block consonant-to-consonant assimilation. In the analyses of Palatalization and Coronalization below I show that the bi-planar representation of consonantal and vocoidal place features allows for a natural account of both rules. As will be seen, the realization of the consonantal target as either a palatalized consonant or a post-alveolar consonant is determined by the plane to which the vocalic features link. Before dealing with the rules of Palatalization and Coronalization further, I will outline my assumptions concerning cross-planar spreading.

3. CROSS-PLANE INTERACTION

In chapter IV it was shown that OCP-driven rules involving the interaction of consonantal and vocoidal place features provides strong evidence for the view that a given articulator feature is arrayed on the same tier for both consonants and vocoids. However, as was also seen, in order to account for consonant/vocoid asymmetry in spreading rules, consonantal and vocoidal representations are partially segregated such that each constriction tier defines its own plane. Given the bi-planar organization of place features in conjunction with the view that a given feature can link to either the consonantal or vocoidal plane, one might suppose that a given feature may link to both planes simultaneously, perhaps as the result of spreading. In this section I focus on the interaction of consonantal and vocoidal place features and claim that a given place feature may, under the marked option, spread from one constriction plane to another.

Consider the representations in (120), which illustrate possible spreading rules applying (a) within and (b) across constriction planes.

(120)

a. Cons   b. Cons
    | |
    place   :   place   :
    | :   \   :
    (Voc)   Voc   \ Voc
    | | \ |
    (place) _ _ place   \ place
             _ _ | \ |
                [F]   [F]

In (120a), the feature [F] spreads from the VOC plane of a given segment to interpolated vocoidal substructure of a preceding segment. In this instance spreading takes place within the same constriction plane. The spreading element maintains its original status as a vocoidal feature and is realized as such on both the target and trigger. Conversely, in (120b) [F] spreads from the vocoidal plane of the trigger directly to the consonantal plane of the target. In this case, spreading occurs across constriction planes.

Consistent with the view of assimilation as spreading, the output of both (120a,b) results in a single multiply-linked feature. In particular, in (120b) [F] is linked (indirectly) to both CONS and VOC.

In other words, [F] is present on both the consonantal and the vocoidal plane. I assume that the phonetic implementation of vocoidal [F] will be consistent with the stricture (and other) features which characterize the segment to which it is linked. Similarly, by virtue of being linked to CONS, consonantal [F] will be realized phonetically in a manner consistent with the consonantal stricture (and other) features which apply to that particular articulator.

In the spirit of Paradis (1988), Piggott (1988), among others, I assume that the two options characterized in (120) take the form of a parameter included in the statement of a given rule. This is stated in (121).

(121)   Constriction Status Change (CSC)? no/yes

In consonant-to-consonant or vocoid-to-vocoid assimilation rules there seems little doubt that the 'no' option would be chosen, as shown in (122 a,b), respectively. In each instance, [F] spreads within a given constriction plane.

(122)
a. option: no

```
    C           C
    :           :
    Cons        Cons
    |           |
    place       place
    L _ _ _ _ _ _|
    [F]
```

b. option: no

```
    V           V
    :           :
    Voc         Voc
    |           |
    place       place
    L _ _ _ _ _ _|
    [F]
```

c. option: no

```
    V                   C
    :                   :
    :                   Cons
    :                   |
    Voc                 place
    |                   |
    place               (Voc)
    L _ _ _ _ _ _ _ _ _ |
    [F]                 (place)
```

d. option: no

```
    C                   V
    :                   :
    Cons                Cons
    |                   |
    place               place
    L _ _ _ _ _ _ _ _ _|\
    [F]                  Voc
                         |
                         place
                         :
```

(122) cont.

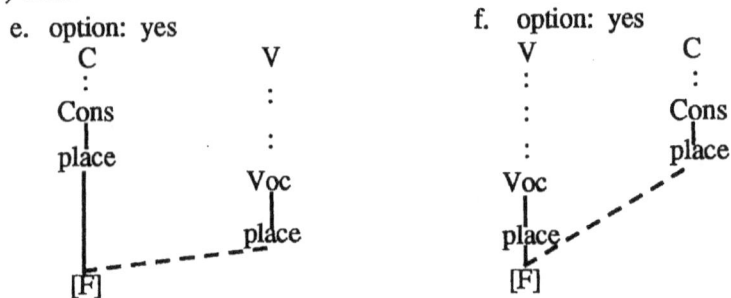

In vocoid-to-consonant spreading rules in which the output is a consonant with a minor articulation (e.g. palatalization, velarization, etc.), the speading feature also maintains its original vocoidal constriction status, as characterized by (122c). We might also expect to find cases in which a consonantal feature spreads to the CONS plane of a vocoid, as shown in (122d). In chapters VI and VII, I discuss consonant-to-vocoid assimilation in Maltese. In one instance the feature [pharyngeal] spreads from a guttural consonant to a preceding vowel, whereas in another the feature [coronal] spreads from a consonant to a vowel. In the representation of these two spreading rules I claim that the consonantal feature maps directly to the vocoidal plane as shown in (122e). As such, the marked option 'yes' is chosen. Given this representation we would not expect the realization of [pharyngeal] and [coronal] on vowels which result from assimilation to a consonant to differ from those on vowels which are not the result of assimilation. Furthermore, we would predict the features [pharyngeal]$_{VOC}$ and [coronal]$_{VOC}$ acquired from assimilation to pattern with other vocoidal instances of these features. Unfortunately, I do not as of yet have access to phonetic data which could be used to test these hypotheses. Nor have I been able to pinpoint any compelling phonological evidence which would either support or falsify these assumptions. If future research reveals that a given feature which spreads from a consonant to a vowel in these or other cases patterns with consonantal instances of this feature or is realized with greater consonantal stricture than the same feature on a vowel which does not undergo assimilation, we would have good evidence for formulating the spreading rule in line with (122d).

Finally, the configuration in (122f) represents a case in which a vocoidal feature spreads directly to the consonantal plane of a consonant, as in Coronalization to be shown just below. Once again, the marked option (i.e. status change: yes) is chosen. Unless otherwise stipulated in the rule statement it will be assumed that the 'no' option applies. With this background, I return to the analyses of Palatalization and Coronalization.

4. PALATALIZATION

In Palatalization, the feature [coronal] is realized as an i-like articulation on a consonant. Thus, [coronal] retains its vocoid-like status after spreading to the consonantal target. Following from the discussion immediately above, the spreading vocoidal feature does not change its constriction status. Thus, the unmarked option 'no' is selected and the feature [coronal] links to interpolated vocoidal substructure on the consonant, as shown in (123).

(123) Palatalization:
(Constriction Status Change: no)

```
        C           V
        :           :
       Cons        Cons
        |           |
      place       place
  [F] ╱ |           |
     (Voc)         Voc
       |           |
    (place)      place
        └ ─ ─ ─ ─ ┘
              [coronal]
                 |
              ([-ant])
```

As (123) illustrates, the feature [coronal] spreads from the front vowel to an interpolated VOC place node of the consonant. The result is a vocoidal place specification superimposed on the original major articulation of the consonant. Although not crucial to this account, I include the redundant [-anterior] specification on the trigger.

Secondary palatalization, either derived or underlying, is characterized by the vocalic articulator [coronal], a feature shared with front vowels. The fronting of vowels in the environment of palatalized consonants is thus characterized as assimilation to the feature value [coronal] of a palatalized consonant. In Russian, for example, back vowels /a o u/ are fronted to [ae ö ü] between 'soft' palatalized consonants (Jones & Ward 1969).

(124) d'ad'ə   [d'æd'ə]   'uncle'
       t'ot'ə   [t'öt'ə]   'aunt'
       t'ul'   [t'ül']   'tulle'

The representation of Palatalization as spreading the feature [coronal] from a vocoidal trigger to a consonant reflects the observation that front vowels commonly condition Palatalization. An alternative account has been proposed by Lahiri & Evers (1991) who claim that Palatalization involves spreading the feature value [+high]. In their account, the coronality of the palatal glide is assigned by default.

With the feature organization assumed by Lahiri & Evers, spreading [+high] is the only viable means of characterizing Palatalization. Contrary to the model in this work, they propose that [coronal] is arrayed on the same plane regardless of whether or not the articulator is consonantal or vocoidal. As I showed in chapter IV, this is problematic for independent reasons. Lahiri & Evers analyze Coronalization as spreading the feature values [coronal, -anterior] to the target consonant, as I do below (see also Hume 1988, 1990). Given their organization of [coronal] on a single plane, the representation of Palatalization cannot be formulated using the feature [coronal], since it would be indistinguishable from Coronalization. This then leaves them with the only remaining option which is to analyze Palatalization as spreading [+high]. As I will show, however, analyzing Palatalization in this manner is not without problems.

Lahiri & Evers claim that characterizing Palatalization as spreading the feature value [+high] is motivated in part by cases in which Palatalization is triggered by back as well as front high vowels. Citing an example from Clements (1976a), they note that in the standard dialect of Japanese spoken in Tokyo, dental /t/ becomes affricated before the high vowels [i ɯ]. It is significant that the dental is both affricated and changed to palatoalveolar [tʃ] if the vowel is [i]. Before the high back vowel, the affricate remains dental, i.e. [ts].

The first point to be made regarding this evidence is that the change incurred on the consonant in the context of high vowels is not Palatalization, strictly speaking, since Palatalization adds a secondary articulation onto the consonant. In Japanese, the consonant is affricated not palatalized. Moreover, before a high front vowel, the consonant undergoes Coronalization, i.e. /t/ → [tʃ], not Palatalizaton, i.e. /t/ → [tʲ]. Consequently, drawing on Japanese as an argument in support of analyzing Palatalization as spreading [+high] is a non sequitur. Furthermore, despite the fact that in Japanese the vowels involved are both [+high], the affrication of the dental consonant before a high back vowel need not be analyzed as Palatalization or Coronalization since only continuancy is added to the consonant; there is no change in the consonant's place of articulation. The most straightforward account is to attribute affrication before a high back vowel to assimilation to the feature value [+continuant] of the vowel. It is important to keep in mind that such cases are extremely rare; in the unmarked case, Palatalization, properly speaking, is triggered by a front vowel.

Additional motivation for characterizing Palatalization as spreading the feature [+high] in Lahiri & Evers' (1991) account is their claim that [coronal] is the default specification for glides. I would suggest, however, that it is equally plausible to consider [+high] as the default specification since glides, e.g. [j ɥ w], are typically [+high]. Thus, although the place specification of glides may differ, the height specification does not. Consequently, underspecifying glides for the feature value [+high] is well-motivated since this feature specification is completely predictable. Recall also from chapter I that when a coronal consonant alternates with a vowel, the vowel is typically high and front (see e.g. Malay, Romanian, Sunwari). The observation that a coronal vocoid surfaces recurrently as [+high] by default might suggest that in the absence of language-specific rules to the contrary, the feature value [+high] is the universal default value for (at least) [coronal] vocoids, vowels and glides combined.

Perhaps the strongest evidence against an analysis of Palatalization as spreading the feature [+high] comes from the observation that non-high vowels are frequently triggers. In Acadian French, for example, both high and non-high front vowels palatalize a preceding velar consonant. To account for such cases, Lahiri & Evers posit that non-high front vowels are represented phonologically with a preceding onglide. For example, "/e/ would be phonologically /je/" (p.95).

Applying such a proposal to the analysis of Palatalization in Acadian French would require including the ad hoc stipulation that an abstract segment is present underlyingly just in case the output is a palatalized consonant. Assimilation is thus to the height specification of the onglide rather than to some quality of the front vowel itself. Conversely, they propose that in Coronalization the consonant assimilates directly to the place specification of the front vowel. Consequently, although Palatalization and Coronalization in Acadian French, as in many other languages, are both conditioned by the identical environment, in Lahiri & Evers' account we would be forced to posit an additional underlying segment before the front vowel just in case the output is a palatalized consonant, clearly an undesirable move.

In the following section I elaborate on my analysis of Coronalization. As is now evident from the preceding discussion, both Palatalization and Coronalization are characterized as spreading the feature value [coronal].

5. CORONALIZATION

As stated above, the conditioning environment for Coronalization is the same as that for Palatalization in Acadian French (as in many other languages). However, in Coronalization, the target's major articulator changes to [coronal, -anterior]. What is at issue in representing the differences between the two rules does not involve the feature or features that spread, but rather how these features are realized. In the account of Palatalization above, the features [coronal, -anterior] retain their original vocalic status by linking to interpolated vocalic structure on the target. Conversely, in Coronalization the status of these features changes from vocoidal to consonantal. This change in constriction status is expressed by a direct mapping onto the consonantal place node of the consonant, as shown in (125). I assume that the redundant feature value [-anterior] is filled in on the vocoidal trigger at least by the time Coronalization applies.

(125) Coronalization:
Constriction Status Change: yes

```
        C                V
        ⋮                ⋮
       Cons             Cons
        |                |
      place            place
 [F]⊬⁄                   |
       ╲                Voc
        ╲                |
         ╲             place
          ╲              |
           ╲─ ─ ─ ─ [coronal]
                         |
                       [-ant]
```

As shown in (125), the acquired [coronal, -anterior] specification replaces the original major place specification of the target consonant. Thus, in the change from velar to nonanterior coronal, e.g. /ki/ → [t͡ʃi] 'who', [dorsal] is delinked (126a), whereas when the target is an anterior coronal, e.g. /tiɛ̃/ → [t͡ʃɛ̃] 'yours', the original [coronal] node and its specification for [+anterior] delink (127b). It must be assumed that delinking occurs, otherwise the output would be a consonant specified for two major places of articulation, i.e. [coronal, +anterior] + [coronal, -anterior], and [dorsal] + [coronal, -anterior].[3] Recall that a non-syllabic vocoid trigger is not realized phonetically when Coronalization or Palatalization apply. We may thus assume that subsequent to assimilation, the trigger is deleted if non-syllabic.

(126)

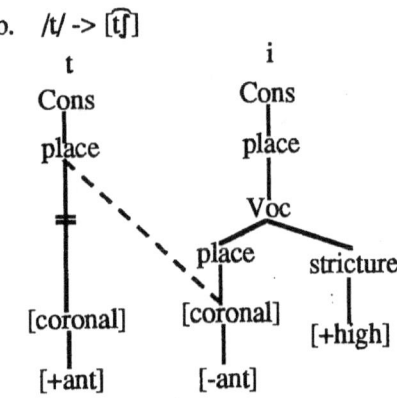

a. /k/ -> [t͡ʃ]

b. /t/ -> [t͡ʃ]

Coronalization, as represented above, is characterized as a direct change rule in which a dental or velar consonant changes into a postalveolar without passing through an intermediate stage of palatalization, as is required in Sagey's model (see also SPE, Clements 1989). In the synchronic phonology of Slovak, for example, positing a succession of stages is unmotivated in this language; there is no evidence suggesting that an intermediate palatalization stage is required (Rubach, forthcoming; p.c.). A velar changes directly into a palato-alveolar in the context of a front vocoid, i.e. /k g x ɣ/ → [t͡ʃ dʒ ʃ ʒ] before /i e æ/ and the palatal glide, as shown in (127) (repeated from chapter I). Unlike Acadian French, Slovak does not have an independent rule of palatalization affecting velars; velars are never palatalized (Rubach, p.c.).

(127)
k → t͡ʃ   vnuk 'grandson'
        vnúk+ik → [vnut͡ʃik] (dimin.)
        vnúk+æ → vnút͡ʃæ → [vnut͡ʃa]⁴ (dimin.)
        t͡ʃlovek 'man'
        t͡ʃlovek+e → [t͡ʃlovet͡ʃe] (voc.)
        t͡ʃlovek+æ → t͡ʃloviet͡ʃæ → [t͡ʃloviet͡ʃa] 'children'
g → d͡ʒ   cveng 'sound'
        cveng+æ+t' → cvend͡ʒæt' → [cvend͡ʒat'] 'to sound'
x → ʃ   strach 'fright'
        strach+i+t' → [staʃit'] 'frighten'
ɣ → ʒ   boh 'god'
        boh+e → [boʒe] (voc.)
        beh 'run' (N)
        beh+æ+t' → beʒæt' → beʒat' 'to run'

Were Coronalization in Slovak accounted for by first palatalizing the velars and then changing these segments into postalveolars we might expect the output to bear secondary palatalization. Dvončová et al. (1969) indicate that the tongue is sometimes raised slightly toward the hard palate in Slovak palato-alveolar affricates. Yet, this is not always the case nor is secondary palatalization contrastive for these segments (see also Rubach, forthcoming, for related discussion). Thus, I assume that Coronalization is best accounted for as a direct-change rule.

In most current work in non-linear phonology it is (at least) implicitly assumed that there is a correlation between the markedness of the rule in question and the complexity involved in representing that rule, i.e. the more complex its representation, the more marked the rule is predicted to be. Along these lines, my representation of Coronalization and Palatalization predicts the former to be more marked for two reasons. First, Coronalization involves a shift in the status of the vowel's place features from vocoidal to consonantal, whereas in Palatalization no change in status is incurred. Second, Coronalization involves two operations, spread and delink, whereas Palatalization requires only one: spread.

Relevant in this respect is the observation of Lucci (1972) concerning the realization of consonants before front vowels in Acadian French. Lucci notes that the palato-alveolar affricate realized by assimilation to a following front vocoid is typical of older speakers and represents the more marked and extreme pronunciation. Younger speakers tend to pronounce the velar and anterior coronal consonants as palatalized consonants, e.g. [k^j, t^j], before a front vocoid. Although both pronunciations are still commonly heard (Cichocki p.c.), the existence of both variants within the speech of Acadians reflects a change in progress (Labov 1966, 1981). Given our predictions concerning the markedness of these two processes, the change from Coronalization to Palatalization may be characterized as a shift towards the more unmarked pronunciation.

6. SUMMARY

The representation of Coronalization proposed above differs significantly from accounts in which front vowels are specified as [-back]. Recall that within Sagey's account (as well as SPE), the fact that a postalveolar coronal is realized before a front vowel can only be indirectly attributed to the vowel, i.e. it is not the direct result of assimilation. Rather, assimilation creates palatalized consonants whereas the realization of the non-anterior coronal is due to additional operations which apply to the output of palatalization. In my analysis, both Coronalization and Palatalization are represented as spreading a single articulator node from the vowel to the consonantal target with no need for formally arbitrary restructuring rules. The change affected in the feature specification of the consonant is thus directly attributable to the vowel, a characterization which correctly reflects their status as natural assimilation processes.

7. [CONTINUANT] AND [STRIDENT]

The characterization of Coronalization as assimilation to the features [coronal, -anterior] of a front vocoid correctly accounts for the observation that the velar and anterior coronal stops of Acadian French are realized as nonanterior coronals. Yet in addition, the stops are realized as affricates, thus acquiring the feature values [+continuant, +strident]. Unlike the features [coronal, -anterior], I assume that these features are not acquired from the vowel itself. This would clearly be impossible for the feature [+strident], since vowels are not strident. With respect to continuancy, although a property of vowels, there are many languages in which the output of Coronalization is a nonstrident noncontinuant consonant. Thus, characterizing Coronalization as assimilation to both the continuancy and place specification of a front vowel is incorrect. In Ngiyambaa, for example, interdental stops, /ḍ ṇ/ are realized as postalveolar stops, [ɟ ɲ] respectively, when immediately preceded by a front vocoid (Donaldson 1980). Note that the phonemic vowel inventory of Ngiyambaa is made up of only three vowels: /i a u/, so the only trigger of Coronalization is /i/, realized phonetically as [i] or [j] depending on syllable position.

(128)

	Root	Suffix (ḍul is the diminutive suffix, ṇa is a present tense inflection)	Gloss
	miri	miri-ɟul	'dog'
	buraaj	buraaj-ɟul	'child'
	ḍari-j	ḍari-ɲa	'disappear'
	wiriN-j	wiri-ɲa	'cook'
cf.	mura	mura-ḍul	'spear'
	baamir	baamir-ḍul	'tall'
	baluur	baluur-ḍul	'frogmouth'
	waṛa	waṛa-ṇa	'stand'

Similar to Acadian French, the high front vowel affects a change in the consonantal target from [+anterior] coronal to [-anterior] coronal. Consistent with the representation of Coronalization further above, I account for the facts in (128) by spreading the feature specification [coronal, -anterior] from the adjacent front vocoid to the CONS place node of the consonant. Once again, the original coronal specification of the consonant is delinked.

(129)

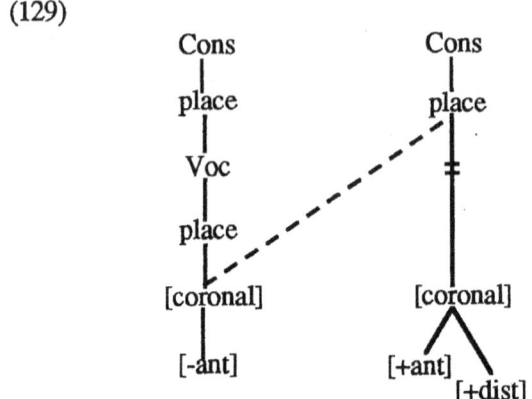

It will be noticed that, unlike Acadian French, the consonant remains a non-continuant (non-strident) stop. Thus, attributing the continuancy (and stridency) of a postalveolar affricate to the front vowel need not be considered a general characteristic of Coronalization. Rather, it is best viewed as the result of redundancy rule assignment determined on a language specific basis (see Lahiri & Evers 1991 for a similar proposal and related discussion; cf. Jacobs 1989, 1991).

8. THE APPARENT DORSALITY OF FRONT VOWELS

Throughout this work I have maintained the view that front vowels are specified for the articulator feature [coronal]. This is in sharp contrast with Sagey (1986), who proposes that all vowels are specified for the tongue body articulator [dorsal], an articulator which also characterizes velar consonants. If it were the case that front vowels were specified as [dorsal], we would predict velar consonants and front vowels (in fact all vowels) to form a natural class. Moreover, we would expect consonant-to-front vowel asssimilation to result in a velar, as opposed to coronal, consonant. As I showed in the preceding chapter, the assimilation of a consonant to a front vowel results in a consonant with either a major or minor specification for [coronal]. In this section, I review two cases in which consonant-to-vowel assimilation appears to result in a velar consonant, thus supporting the view that front vowels are specified as [dorsal]. The languages involved are Pame and Romanian. I show, however, that the evidence is inconclusive.

8.1 Pame

Drawing on data from Gibson (1956) and Gibson & Bartholomew (1979), Sagey (1986:112-113) discusses a rule of palatalization in Pame in which it appears that alveolar stop consonants are realized as velar consonants after [i]. In (130), I provide representative examples following the transcriptions of Gibson, and Gibson & Bartholomew.

(130)   ski- + -táhah?   'soap'   skikyą́han?   'your(sg.) soap'
        ki- + -dóa   'to walk' kigyóa   'you(sg.) walk'
        ki- + -ną̂   'tongue'   kiŋyą̀   'your tongue'

From Gibson's (1956) description, however, it is not entirely evident that the 'velar' consonants in question are in fact velars. First, in her classification of phonemes, she divides consonants into four places of articulation: bilabial, alveolar, velar-palatal and back. I provide Gibson's classification of relevant non-labial sounds in (131) (all symbols are Gibson's).

(131)   Alveolar   Velar-palatal   Back
        t d   k g   ḳ
        c   č
        s   š
        n   ŋ
        l   lʸ
                   y

As illustrated in (131), the sounds which she transcribes as /k g ŋ/ are classified under the same heading as sounds which are normally referred to as postalveolar (palatal or palato-alveolar), i.e. /č š lʸ y/ (lʸ is palatal as opposed to palatalized). Based on this classification, it is unclear whether the author intends all of the sounds included under this heading to be interpreted as 'velar-palatal' or whether some are velar whereas others are palatal. From her further descriptions it would seem that it is the latter that is intended, i.e. they are palatal. Gibson distinguishes between two k's, the first, /k/, which she refers to as *velar-palatal* and the second, /ḵ/, which she classifies as *back*. As she points out, these two sounds are contrastive before /e ɛ/, e.g. [kêič?] 'they [heavy weight things] are on top of' vs. [ḵêi] 'they hunt [for game]'. Thus, their status as independent phonemes appears to be well-motivated. That /k/ is palatal as opposed to velar, however, is suggested by her description. She states (p. 245) that "the spectogram showed the k in kíhwa?a 'you should bring it (sg.)', occurring as a 'front palatal variety'". Furthermore, she states that 'preceded by i, k has palatal fronting whether or not it is followed by y: likyèhe 'he has muscle cramps', šikè? 'adult, elder, chief'." The evidence that the segments which result from assimilation to a front vowel are in fact velars is thus not compelling. Based on Gibson's description, it is reasonable to assume that the 'velars' are in fact palatal consonants. With this classification, the observation that palatal consonants are derived from the alveolar stops (/t d n/) as the result of assimilation is consistent with the effect that assimilation has on the remaining alveolar consonants, i.e. /s c l/, since they are realized as postalveolars, as shown in (132).

(132)

snakạc? + -i 'his wash-tub'   snakàič?   'their wash-tub (dual)'
ni- + sậs   'to play (music)'   nišậs   'you played (sg.)'
sandàl + -i   'soldier'   sandàil^y 'soldiers (dual)'

Thus, the evidence from Pame for the specification of /i/ with both a [dorsal] and a [coronal] component is inconclusive.

8.2   Romanian

In this section I briefly discuss sound shift which occurred in non-standard dialects of Romanian such as that spoken in Transylvania. According to Nandris (1963) (see also Sala 1976), an intrusive consonant optionally developed from the sequence of a labial consonant and high front vocoid i(j). In many cases, the new sequence was eventually reduced with the elimination of the initial labial consonant. In some forms the intrusive consonant was realized as [k g], in others as an anterior or nonanterior coronal, and in others, it surfaced as [h]. Examples are given in (133).

(133)
  pelle > piele > k'ele
  bene > bine > g'ine
  fĕle > fiere > fk'ere
  piept > t'ept
  vitel > d'itel
  vinu > vin > d͡ʒin
  albi > albd' > ald' > ald͡ʒ
  pantofi > pantoh'i

The realization of the labial/front vowel sequence as [k' g'] in pelle > piele > k'ele, bene > bine > g'ine, would appear to support the view that front vowels bear both [coronal] and [dorsal] specifications. One might argue that the [coronal] specification was realized on the derived consonant as palatalization and the vowel's [dorsal] specification surfaced as the consonant's major articulation. The evidence is not strong enough to support this conclusion, however.[5]

First, the realization of the labial/front vowel as [k' g'] occurred in only a small number of forms. Moreover, as Nandris points out, the sequence /pi/, for example, is attested to have at least three different realizations within the same dialect: picior (labial unchanged); pk'ele (<piele) (with an intrusive velar consonant); t'ept (<piept) (with an anterior coronal). These facts suggest that the change from labial to velar before a front vowel was not a regular process. In fact, Nandris claims that many factors contributed to the attested changes, not all of which are phonological, as indicated just below.

"Ces incohérences et divergences de traitements, qui reflètent la déroute où se trouvent les labiales et labio-dentales, révèlent les caractéristiques d'un phénomène en pleine évolution, sur lequel en outre agissent: le roumain commun, l'influence des parlers voisins non-palatalisants, les phénomènes d'analogie, d'assimilation, de dissimilation, etc. " (p.243).

In phonological theory, we seek to develop a formalism which will express common, natural phonological processes in relatively simple terms. Although positing that front vowels are specified for both [coronal] and [dorsal] would allow us to account for the emergence of the palatalized velars in Romanian, there is considerable doubt that first of all, the process was in fact phonological, and second, that it constituted a regular and natural process. As such, I do not take sound shift in Romanian as compelling evidence for the specification of front vowels for articulators other than [coronal].

NOTES

1. In some varieties the low central vowel may follow a palato-alveolar affricate. As I point out further below, however, in these cases the low vowel is derived from an underlying front vowel.

2. Vowel lengthening is the result of an independent rule.

3. To the best of my knowledge, segments characterized with both major [dorsal] and [coronal, -anterior] articulations have not been attested. If this observation is correct, it may be the case that the delinking of [dorsal] in Coronalization is triggered by a more general constraint prohibiting this combination. Why this pair of major articulations would be excluded remains unclear to me at the present time although one might speculate that it is in some way related to the close proximity of the two articulations.

4. Recall from the Introduction, that the low front vowel is backed to [a] by an independent rule after nonlabial consonants. The diminutive suffix that surfaces as [a] in, e.g. vnútʃ+a is the same suffix as in chláp+æ 'man' (dimin.).

5. Stefan Oltean (p.c.), a native speaker and scholar of Romanian, informed me that the sounds transcribed as [k' t'] can both be described as voiceless, palatal plosives. Similarly, he describes the segments [g' d'] as voiced, palatal plosives. To present, I have not been able to confirm this with phonetic data. However, if correct, Romanian would not serve as potential evidence for the specification of front vowels as [dorsal] since palatal consonants are nonanterior coronals.

PART II

MALTESE ARABIC

VI

Maltese Arabic: A Case Study

0. INTRODUCTION

Part II of this work presents a study of consonant/vowel interaction in Maltese Arabic. I focus on the class of triliteral strong verbs and examine the realization of, in particular, the imperfective form of these verbs. In this chapter I examine the typical formation of imperfectives as well as a subset of these verbs which appear exceptional. I will have more to say about this just below. The analyses presented in this chapter provide necessary background for those of the following chapter where I focus more exclusively on coronal vowel and consonant parallelisms in Maltese.

The analyses in this chapter have consequences for various areas of phonological theory. One area concerns the nonlinear representation of consonant/vowel metathesis. Although, in general, the plural imperfective stem is comprised of three adjacent consonants, there are a number of verbs which stand out as exceptional in that they contain a stem vowel. In earlier studies, the presence of this vowel has been attributed to consonant/vowel metathesis (e.g. Brame 1972, Puech 1979, Berrendonner et al. 1983). Underlyingly, the vowel occurs to the right of the medial stem consonant but then by metathesis, it switches positions with this consonant. I show that the traditional view of metathesis is unable to account for the full range of imperfective plurals. The problem, I propose, is associated with the view of metathesis as a one-step operation, frequently expressed by means of linear tranformational notation where two segments simply switch position, e.g. 1 2 3 → 1 3 2. In this chapter I argue that metathesis is rather the product of three elementary operations: delete, insert and associate. The first two characterize independently motivated rules of Maltese: Syncope and Epenthesis, respectively. The third operation, associate, takes the form of a universal association convention which maps a floating melody onto an unspecified slot of the prosodic template. When these three operations are sequenced within a single derivation, the result is metathesis. By analyzing metathesis in these terms, there is no longer a need to rely on a linear transformational notation to represent this process, a formalism which has otherwise been eliminated from phonological theory. Rather, we are able to provide a straightforward account of metathesis by drawing on fundamental operations of nonlinear phonology. Moreover, under the assumption that metathesis involves more than one operation, it elucidates why this process is less common cross-linguistically than, for example, a process such as assimilation which could arguably by viewed as the result of one or at most two operations: spread, delink.

A further implication of this study concerns the representation of total vowel assimilation. In this chapter we will see evidence for the spreading of the entire VOC node of a vowel across intervening consonants, thus providing strong evidence for the VOC node as an independent constituent in feature organization. Furthermore, it shows that with the enriched model of feature organization assumed in this work, total vowel movement across intervening consonants may be analyzed in simple terms without the need to invoke complete consonant/vowel segregation (for a proposal along these lines, see McCarthy 1989).

Finally, the analyses in this chapter also have implications for underspecification theory. As I show, the existence of a given default value need not imply that all surface occurrences of this value are unspecified in underlying representation, thus corroborating evidence discussed in Herzallah (1990) and Hualde (1991). This opposes the view espoused by proponents of Radical Underspecification (see e.g. Archangeli 1984, Archangeli & Pulleyblank 1986). The findings with respect to Maltese suggest that default feature values are independent of the underlying feature specification of a given system, available perhaps universally or on a language-specific basis as a means of filling in unspecified segments.

Maltese Arabic is spoken on the Maltese archipelago situated in the Mediterranean Sea approximately 60 miles south of Sicily and 180 miles east of the Tunisian coast. The two main islands which comprise the archipelago are Malta and Gozo. Although Maltese itself comprises many dialects, I will be focussing on the variety characterized as standard Maltese. My data are drawn from a wide range of sources which include Aquilina (1959), Berrondonner et al. (1983), Borg (1973), Brame (1972, 1973), Bugeja (1984), Busuttil (1981), Butcher (1938), Puech (1978, 1979) and Sutcliffe (1936). These data are consistent with the variety of Maltese spoken by my consultants.[1]

The organization of this chapter is as follows. The first section provides preliminary information concerning the phonemic inventory of Maltese and lays out certain assumptions that will figure into subsequent analyses. In section 2, I present an overview of the problems to be addressed in this chapter with respect to the realization of imperfective triliteral verbs. Section 3 focusses on the typical formation of the imperfective, first measure. In section 4, I motivate the underlying vowel quality of triliteral verbs which serves as a basis for subsequent discussion. The following section begins our examination of plural imperfective verbs, starting with a description of the relevant forms. In section 6, I discuss and motivate consonant/vowel metathesis in certain plural verbs and show how the traditional view of metathesis is unable to account for all verbs. From this point I go on to motivate the rules which I claim result in metathesis. Following this, I show how my proposed analysis accounts not only for the realization of the metathesized vowel but, in addition, that of the imperfective prefix vowel. At the end of the chapter I discuss implications of this study for the representation of total vowel movement and for underspecification theory.

1. PRELIMINARIES

1.1 Phonemic Inventory

In (134) and (136) below, I provide the phonemic inventory of Standard Maltese Arabic. In tables (134b) and (136b), segments are fully specified for place (and vowel height) features. Below each of these tables, the underspecified system assumed in this work is given.

(134) Vowels:[2]

(a) i u
     e o
       a

(b) Fully specified:

	i	e	a	o	u
coronal	+	+	-	-	-
dorsal	-	-	-	+	+
labial	-	-	-	+	+
pharyngeal	-	-	+	-	-
high	+	-	-	-	+

(c) Underspecified:

	i	e	a	o	u
coronal	+	+			
dorsal					
labial				+	+
pharyngeal			+		
high	+	-		-	+

In the underspecified chart in (c), all vowels are specified for at least an articulator feature. Characterizing back rounded vowels as [labial] with [dorsal] assigned by redundancy rule is not crucial. It would be equally feasible to specify them as [dorsal] with [labial] assigned redundantly. Specifying non-low vowels for both place and height assures that all vowels are underlyingly distinct. In addition to the vowels included in the tables above, I recognize an additional vowel which enters into the derivation as an empty V-slot. In the absence of feature-filling assimilaton, this vowel receives the feature values [coronal, +high] by default. Given the presence of these default values it might be argued that these values are completely unspecified in underlying representation. This view is consistent with the theory of Radical Underspecification (see e.g. Archangeli 1984, Archangeli & Pulleyblank 1986). However, as I argue in section 9.2, this approach is problematic in accounting for the realization of the imperfective prefix vowel in a number of verbs. I will leave discussion of this issue until that time. Nonetheless, it is important to point out that the underlying specification of /i/ as both [coronal] and [+high] is crucial. Guttural Assimilation, discussed in section 4, is a bidirectional rule which changes /i/ to [a] when adjacent to a guttural consonant. If /i/ were specified as only [+high] (with [coronal] completely unspecified), Guttural Assimilation would need to be defined on [+high]. Yet, this would incorrectly predict /u/ to be a target, e.g. [jimshu] 'they wipe' *[jimsha]. Similarly, if /i/ were specified as only [coronal] (with height completely unspecified), Guttural Assimilation would need to be defined on [coronal]. If this were the case, we would incorrectly predict /e/ to be a target, e.g. [jeħblu] 'they rave' *[jaħblu].

As a final point, note that the feature [low] is not included in the underspecified system. This is due to the observation that the single height feature [high] is sufficient to contrast all underlying segments. The feature value [-high] is redundant for the vowel /a/ and, as a result, may be assigned by the redundancy rule in (135).

(135)   [pharyngeal]$_{VOC}$ → [-high]

In tables (136 a-c), I provide the phonemic inventory of consonants in Maltese.

(136)   Consonants:

(a)   Labial Labio-   Dental   Palato-   Velar   Pharyngeal   Laryngeal
              dental   alveolar

stops   p b   t d   k g   ʔ
fricatives   f v   s̬ z̬   ʃ [ʒ]*   ħ
affricates   ts dz*   tʃ dʒ
nasals   m   n
liquids   l r

* dz occurs only in a few Italian/Sicilian loanwords
* [ʒ] occurs only before voiced obstruents

(b) Place specification:

	p	b	m	f	v	t	d	s	z	n	l	r	t͡s	d͡z	ʃ	t͡ʃ	d͡ʒ	k	g	ŋ	ħ	ʔ
lab	+	+	+	+	+																	
cor						+	+	+	+	+	+	+	+	+	+	+	+					
ant						+	+	+	+	+	+	+	+	+	−	−	−					
dors																		+	+	+		
phar																					+	+

(c) Underspecified:

	p	b	m	f	v	t	d	s	z	n	l	r	t͡s	d͡z	ʃ	t͡ʃ	d͡ʒ	k	g	ŋ	ħ	ʔ
lab	+	+	+	+	+																	
cor						+	+	+	+	+	+	+	+	+	+	+	+					
ant						+							+	+	−	−	−					
dors																		+	+	+		
phar																					+	+

As shown in (136b), the place features [labial, coronal, dorsal, pharyngeal] in addition to the terminal feature [anterior] are sufficient to distinguish among consonants in Maltese. Following Sagey (1986), I incorporate the view that place articulators for consonants are privative, i.e. they are either present or absent. Thus, fully specified place features for consonants in Maltese appear as in (136b). Underlyingly, the feature [anterior] is only required in cases in which it serves to contrast between sounds: /s/ vs. /ʃ/, and /t͡s d͡z/ vs. /t͡ʃ d͡ʒ/, respectively. For all other coronal consonants, I assume that the feature value [+anterior] is assigned by redundancy rule (see (137)).

(137)   [coronal]$_{CONS}$ → [+anterior]

Let me also point out that Maltese Arabic differs from many other Arabic dialects in that there is no emphatic/non-emphatic contrast among consonants (see e.g. Herzallah 1990 for a discussion of emphasis in Palestinian Arabic). The observation that in Maltese there is only a single series of plain coronal consonants will prove particularly relevant to the analysis of Vowel Coronal Assimilation in chapter VII.

1.2 Morpheme Structure Constraints

As illustrated in (136c) above, all consonants are underlyingly specified for at least a place articulator. Evidence for this underlying place specification comes from Morpheme Structure Constraints in Maltese. Similar to the observations of McCarthy (1986) (see also Greenberg 1950) for Classical Arabic, the distribution of root consonants in Maltese verbs is highly constrained. Root consonants in Maltese can be classified into six major groups according to whether or not they tend to cooccur within a single root: [labial, -son] (p b f), [labial, +son] (m), [coronal, -son] (t d s z t͡s ʃ t͡ʃ d͡ʒ), [coronal, +son] (n l r), [dorsal] (k g) and [pharyngeal] (ħ ʔ). McCarthy found that for Classical Arabic, a root does not generally contain more than one consonant from any class.[3] The constraints on consonant cooccurrence in Maltese seem to be less strict as more than one consonant from the same class may occur within the same root, e.g. √drs 'beat the grain', √d͡ʒbd 'pull', √trt 'insist', √nfr 'grow angry', √ntn 'putrify', √rml 'become a widow(er)', √ʔlʔ 'close', √ħnʔ 'create'. The observed tendency for Maltese is that roots tend not to contain adjacent consonants from the same class.[4] For example, adjacent coronal obstruents rarely co-occur. Likewise, roots with adjacent coronal sonorants are rare. Yet, roots frequently contain coronal obstruents adjacent to coronal sonorants, e.g. √dlm 'grow dark', √srʔ 'steal', √fʃl 'interrupt', √kns 'sweep', √kbrs 'cast', √ʔrtf 'prune', √ʃnʔl 'cause to totter', √dn 'suppose', √rs 'press', √ʃl 'stitch'. The restrictions on consonant sequences in Maltese roots fall out directly from the Obligatory Contour Principle which prohibits adjacent identical melodies (e.g. McCarthy 1981, 1986). The constraint for Maltese can be formulated as in (138).

(138)

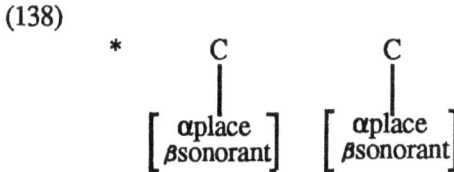

Informally, this states that adjacent homorganic consonants agreeing in their value for the feature [sonorant] are prohibited. Given that this constraint holds on underlying sequences of consonants within the root, it is necessary for root consonants to be specified underlyingly for at least place features and sonorancy.

1.3 Tier Conflation

In McCarthy's (e.g. 1979, 1981) analysis of Classical Arabic, he argues that the consonantal and vocalic melodies of a given stem map onto the prosodic template prior to the phonology. Moreover, the melodies of consonants and vowels are compeletely segregated. As applied to Maltese Arabic, the perfective verb [ʔasam], which is comprised of the consonantism /ʔsm/, the vocalism /a/, and the bisyllabic template CVCVC, would be characterized as in (139).

(139)   ʔsm, a

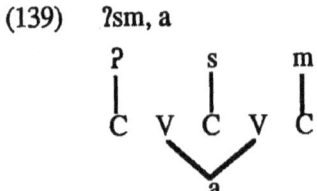

The vowel /a/ is multiply-linked at the root node to both V-slots of the prosodic template. Were, on the other hand, /a/ linked to each V-slot individually as in (140), the configuration would violate the Obligatory Contour Principle, since it contains identical adjacent instances of /a/.

(140)   ʔsm, a

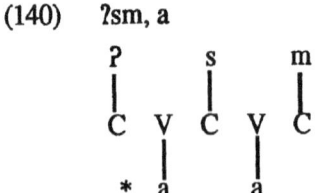

McCarthy (1986), following Younes (1983), motivates a process of general Tier Conflation which conflates the consonantal and vocalic melodies at a specific point in the phonology. The application of general Tier Conflation on the representation of /ʔasam/ is shown in (141).

(141)

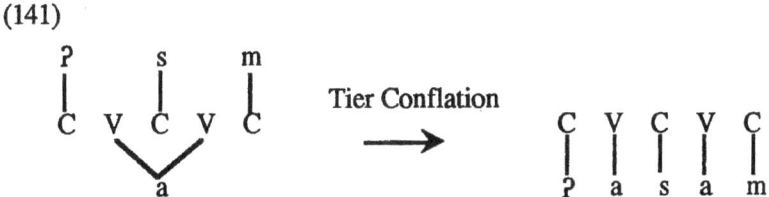

Note that after the application of Tier Conflation the stem vowels are no longer multiply-linked, since, as discussed in chapter IV, the output would otherwise violate the Ordering Constraint. As I show in this chapter (section 9.1), it must be assumed that consonants and vowels are linearly ordered at a relatively early stage in the phonology of Maltese.

2. LAYING OUT THE PROBLEMS

In (142), I present representative imperfective and perfective forms of first measure triliteral strong verbs. The third person masculine singular form of the perfective is given on the right. On the left, we find the corresponding imperfective singular and plural. The imperfective is marked by a CV- prefix added to the stem with plurals bearing the invariable suffix [u]. I have divided the verbs in (142) into eight groups according to vowel quality. In group 1, all vowels surface as [a] and in group 2, [o] always occurs in both perfectives and imperfectives, regardless of the vowel's position. In group 3, all vowels, with the exception of the stem-final vowel, are realized as [i]. Three vowel qualities occur in the verbs of group 4, [a, i, e], depending on the vowel's position. The prefix vowel is invariably [a], the stem-final vowel is [e] and the vowel which occurs in the plural stems in (ii.) is realized as [i]. In group 5, the imperfective prefix vowel consistently occurs as [i] whereas all other vowels are [a]. Similarly, in group 6, the prefix vowel is realized as [i], as is the plural stem vowel in subset (ii.). However, the stem-final vowel is [a] and the stem-initial vowel of the perfective surfaces as [e]. In group 7, all vowels surface as [e] with the exception of the plural stem vowel in certain verbs. Finally, it will be observed that in group 8 all vowels of the imperfective are [o] whereas the vowel quality of the perfective varies.

(142)   Imperfective   Perfective
        3rd p.m.sg.   3rd p.pl.   3rd p.m.sg.
1.i. ja+ʔbad   ja+ʔbd+u   ʔabad   'to catch'
      ja+ʔsam   ja+ʔsm+u   ʔasam   'to break'
      ja+ħbat   ja+ħbt+u   ħabat   'to strike, hit'
  ii. ja+ħrab   ja+ħarb+u   ħarab   'to run away'
      ja+ħlaʔ   ja+ħalʔ+u   ħalaʔ   'to create'
      ja+ħnaʔ⁵   ja+ħanʔ+u   ħanaʔ   'to choke'

2.i. jo+ktor   jo+ktr+u   kotor   'to abound, increase'
      jo+rħos   jo+rħs+u   rohos   'to grow cheap'
      jo+htob   jo+htb+u   hotob   'to propose marriage'
  ii. jo+bloʔ   jo+bolʔ+u   boloʔ   'to be past one's prime'
      jo+frok   jo+fork+u   forok   'to limp'

3.i. ji+bdel   ji+bdl+u   bidel   'to change'
      ji+gdem   ji+gdm+u   gidem   'to bite'
      ji+kʃef   ji+kʃf+u   kiʃef   'to discover'
      ji+nzel   ji+nzl+u   nizel   'to descend'
  ii. ji+fred   ji+fird+u   fired   'to separate'
      ji+dlek   ji+dilk+u   dilek   'to anoint'

4.i. ja+ħdem   ja+ħdm+u   ħadem   'to work'
      ja+ʔbel   ja+ʔbl+u   ʔabel   'to agree'
      ja+ʔfel   ja+ʔfl+u   ʔafel   'to lock'
  ii. ja+ħleb   ja+ħilb+u   ħaleb   'to milk'
      ja+ʔleb   ja+ʔilb+u   ʔaleb   'to overturn'

5.i. ji+lhaʔ   ji+lhʔ+u   lahaʔ   'to reach'
      ji+shaʔ   ji+shʔ+u   sahaʔ   'to pound'
      ji+t͡han   ji+t͡hn+u   t͡han   'to grind'
      ji+t͡ʃhad   ji+t͡ʃhd+u   t͡ʃahad   'to deny'
  ii. ø

Maltese

(142) cont.

	Imperfective 3rd p.m.sg.	3rd p.pl.	Perfective 3rd p.m.sg.	
6.i.	ji+ksaħ	ji+ksħ+u	kesaħ	'to get cold'
	ji+rbaħ	ji+rbħ+u	rebaħ	'to win'
	ji+ftaħ	ji+ftħ+u	fetaħ	'to open'
ii.	ji+flaħ	ji+filħ+u	felaħ	'to be strong'
	ji+sraʔ	ji+sirʔ+u	seraʔ	'to steal'
	ji+tlaʔ	ji+tilʔ+u	telaʔ	'to depart'
7.i.	je+ħbel	je+ħblu	ħebel	'to rave'
	je+ħber	je+ħbru	ħeber	'to predict'
ii.	je+ʔred	je+ʔirdu	ʔered	'to destroy'
	je+ħles	je+ħilsu	ħeles	'to be freed'
	je+ħmez	je+ħemzu/ je+ħimzu	ħemez	'to pin'
8.i.	jo+nfor	jo+nfr+u	nafar	'to expose'
	jo+bzoʔ	jo+bzʔ+u	bezaʔ	'to spit'
	jo+ʔtol	jo+ʔtl+u	ʔatel	'to kill'
ii.	jo+ħrodʒ	jo+ħordʒ+u	ħaredʒ	'to go out'
	jo+ʔmos	jo+ʔoms+u	ʔamas	'to jump'
	jo+brod	jo+bord+u	barad	'to file'

It will be noticed that in certain plural imperfectives a vowel occurs in the stem (subgroup ii.) whereas in the others, the stem is comprised of a three consonant cluster (subgroup i.). Moreover, the quality of this vowel may be [a], [o], [i] or [e]. In a number of verbs, the quality of this vowel is identical to all other vowels of a given class, as seen in groups 1 and 2. In others, however, it is not immediately evident how the quality of this vowel is determined, as in the verbs in group 4 and 6. There are then at least two observations which need to be accounted for with respect to plural imperfectives. First, how do we account for the presence of the plural stem vowel in only a subset of the imperfectives? Second, what are the factors which determine the surface quality of the plural stem vowel? Is it predictable and if so, how?

Consider next the quality of the imperfective prefix vowel. Similar to plural stem vowels, the surface quality of this vowel may be either [a], [o], [i] or [e]. In groups 1, 2 and 7, the quality of this vowel is identical to that of the perfective stem vowels. However, in the remaining groups of verbs this is not the case. Thus, once again we need to determine the factors which account for the quality of the prefix vowel. It is also important to point out that it is only in verbs of the first measure, as above, that the quality of the prefix vowel can differ. In all other measures, as illustrated in (143) below, the vowel is realized systematically as [i][6] (the parenthesized [i] is epenthetic; see discussion of epenthesis, section 8). An adequate account of the realization of the imperfective prefix vowel in first measure verbs should then also be able to account for this asymmetry.

(143)

Measure	Perfective	Imperfective	
First	ja+ʔsam	ʔasam	to break
Fifth	ji+tʔattel	tʔattel	to destroy oneself
Sixth	ji+tbierek	tbierek	to be blessed
Seventh	ji+nʔabad	(i)nʔabad	to be caught
Eighth	ji+rtabat	(i)rtabat	to be bound
Ninth	ji+ḥdaar	ḥdaar	to grow green
Tenth	ji+stenbaḥ	stenbaḥ	to awaken

A final observation concerns the verbs of group 8. It will be noticed that in these verbs the vowels of the imperfective are consistently [o], whereas [o] never occurs in the perfective verb. In most other groups of verbs there appears to be, to a certain degree, some link between the quality of vowels of the perfective and that of the imperfective. This is most readily observed by comparing the stem-final vowel of the perfective with that of the imperfective singular. However, for verbs of group 8 there is no such similarity. Group 8 verbs can also be compared with verbs of group 2 in which the stem vowels of the perfective are [o], as are all vowels of the imperfective. A further problem that must be addressed then is how to account for the vowel qualities in group 8 perfective vs. imperfective verbs.

I have pinpointed a number of observations that need to be addressed. These are summarized in (144) below.

(144) i. How do we account for the presence of the plural stem vowel in only a subset of the imperfectives?
ii. What are the factors which determine the surface quality of the plural stem vowel? Is it predictable and if so, how?
iii. How do we account for the quality of the prefix vowel in first measure verbs?
iv. How do we account for the observation that the vowel quality of the prefix vowel only differs in first measure verbs but is always realized as [i] in verbs of other measures?
v. How do we account for the fact that in group 8 verbs all vowels of the imperfectives are [o] whereas [o] never occurs in the perfective?

As will become evident in the remainder of this chapter (and is perhaps not surprising) all of these problems are closely interrelated. In fact, it is difficult to discuss one without also touching on one or more of the others. As a first step, I will discuss how the imperfective is typically formed. Following this, I motivate the underlying vowel qualities of each of the groups of verbs above. This provides a necessary basis for the analyses which follow.

3. TYPICAL FORMATION OF THE IMPERFECTIVE, FIRST MEASURE TRILITERAL VERB[7]

As seen in the previous discussion, the imperfective of the triliteral verb, first measure, is characterized by a prefix of the form CV- added to the stem. Plural imperfectives also have the invariable suffix [-u]. This is illustrated below for the verb [ʔasam] 'to break'.

(145) Imperfective

3rd masc. sing.	já+ʔsam	3rd plural	já+ʔsm+u
3rd fem. sing.	tá+ʔsam		
2nd singular	tá+ʔsam	2nd plural	tá+ʔsm+u
1st singular	ná+ʔsam	1st plural	ná+ʔsm+u

In the singular, the verb stem has the form -CCVC whereas in the plural, the stem is typically comprised of three adjacent consonants, i.e. -CCC-. Following Aquilina (1959) and Puech (1979), I claim that the imperfective stem of the triliteral strong verb is derived from the canonical form -CVCVC-, a bisyllabic structure corresponding to the third person masculine singular form of the perfective verb, e.g. [ʔasam] 'he broke'. In deriving the singular imperfective, the first stem vowel is deleted and in the plural, both stem vowels delete. Vowel deletion in the imperfective stem falls out of a more general rule of Syncope which is described in its preliminary formulation in (146) (based on Brame 1973).

(146) Syncope (preliminary formulation):
$\breve{V} \rightarrow \emptyset / C\_\_ C V$
A short unstressed vowel in an open syllable deletes in non word-final position.

Note that stress assignment in Maltese is similar to that of most Arabic dialects in that stress generally falls on a final superheavy syllable. If there isn't one, the penultimate syllable is stressed if heavy (or if there are only two syllables), otherwise the antepenult is stressed (see e.g. Brame 1972, 1973).

The application of Syncope in the imperfective is illustrated in (147). Stress falls on the prefix vowel and the first stem vowel is subsequently deleted. The output of cycle 1 gives the form of the singular imperfective. With the addition of the suffix -u in cycle 2, the context for Syncope is once more defined and the second stem vowel deletes. Assuming that Syncope is cyclic is based on the observation that it only applies in derived environments.

(147)
1. Input	CV+CVCVC
Stress	CÝCVCVC
Syncope	CÝCCVC
2. Input	CÝCCVC+u
Syncope	CÝCCCu

Maltese

Independent evidence for Syncope comes from the observation that this rule also accounts for perfective verb forms of the first measure, for example. This is illustrated in (148) below where I give the perfective of the verb [ʔasam]. Once again, I assume that the verb stem in all forms is derived from a bisyllabic canonical structure which corresponds to the form of the third person masculine singular perfective.

(148)　Perfective, first measure triliteral verb

ʔásam	→	[ʔásam]	'he broke'
ʔásam+et	→	[ʔásmet]	'she broke'
ʔasám+t	→	[ʔsámt]	'I, you (sg.) broke'
ʔásam+u	→	[ʔásmu]	'they broke'
ʔasám+na	→	[ʔsámna]	'you (pl.) broke'
ʔasám+tu	→	[ʔsámtu]	'we broke'

4.　UNDERLYING VOCALISM OF THE STEM

In this section I focus on the vowel quality of perfective and imperfective verbs. Although in some verbs the surface quality of vowels may differ, I claim that each stem has a vocalism of a single quality, /i/, /e/, /o/ or /a/, in underlying representation. As we will see in subsequent sections, this claim is of particular importance in accounting for the realization of the imperfective prefix vowel and the stem vowel which occurs in certain imperfective plural verbs. The analyses in this section owe much to the insights of Berrendonner et al. (1983) who were the first, I believe, to suggest that each stem is associated with a single vowel quality in UR.

The verbs listed in (149) are representative of two groups of verbs in which no vowel alternations occur. In other words, the surface quality of all vowels is always identical. These involve verbs given in (149a) in which all vowels have the quality [a] and those in (149b) in which the vowel quality is [o] (excepting, of course, the imperfective plural suffix which is invariably [u]).

(149) Imperfective   Perfective
       3rd p.m.sg.   3rd p pl.   3rd p.m.sg.
 a.i. ja+ʔbad   ja+ʔbd+u   ʔabad   'to catch'
       ja+ʔsam   ja+ʔsm+u   ʔasam   'to break'
       ja+ħbat   ja+ħbt+u   ħabat   'to strike, hit'
  ii. ja+ħrab   ja+ħarb+u   ħarab   'to run away'
       ja+ħlaʔ   ja+ħalʔ+u   ħalaʔ   'to create'
       ja+ħnaʔ   ja+ħanʔ+u   ħanaʔ   'to choke'
 b.i. jo+ktor   jo+ktr+u   kotor   'to abound, increase'
       jo+rħos   jo+rħs+u   roħos   'to grow cheap'
       jo+ħtob   jo+ħtb+u   ħotob   'to propose marriage'
  ii. jo+frok   jo+fork+u   forok   'to limp'
       jo+bloʔ   jo+bolʔ+u   boloʔ   'to be past one's prime'

Note that in all cases the imperfective prefix vowel is identical in quality to the stem vowel, when there is one. Also, in plural imperfectives in which there is a stem vowel (group ii. in each case), the quality of this vowel is also either [a] or [o], depending on the class. Given that there are no vowel alternations in either of these classes, we may assume, in accordance with the null hypothesis, that there is a vocalism of a single quality in underlying representation. In group a. it is /a/ and in group b. it is /o/.

Consider next the verbs in (150).

(150) Imperfective   Perfective
       3rd p.m.sg.   3rd p.pl.   3rd p.m.sg.
   i. ji+bdel   ji+bdl+u   bidel   'to change'
       ji+gdem   ji+gdm+u   gidem   'to bite'
       ji+kʃef   ji+kʃf+u   kiʃef   'to discover'
       ji+nzel   ji+nzl+u   nizel   'to descend'
  ii. ji+fred   ji+fird+u   fired   'to separate'
       ji+dlek   ji+dilk+u   dilek   'to anoint'

As can be seen, with the exception of the stem-final vowel, the surface quality of all vowels is [i]. There is strong evidence to suggest, however, that the stem-final vowel is /i/ underlyingly (Brame 1972, 1973; Puech 1979; Berrendonner et al. 1983). When the stem-final vowel is followed by a single word-final consonant, as it is in the forms above, it is realized as [e]. Otherwise, it surfaces as [i]. We see this alternation in the perfective, e.g. bidel 'he changed', bdilt 'I, you (sg.) changed'. (In [bdilt], the first stem vowel is deleted by the rule of Syncope.) The i~e alternation is evidenced more widely in Maltese as exemplified by the third person feminine suffix.

(151) 3rd pers. fem. suffix [-it] ~ [-et]
       (examples from Brame 1972:26)
       [ħatf+it+kom] 'she grabbed you'   cf.[ħatf+et] 'she grabbed'
       [bezʔ+it+l+ek] 'she spit to you'   cf.[bezʔ+et] 'she spit'

Following Puech (1978), I account for this alternation by the rule of I-lowering given in (152).

(152) I-lowering (Puech 1978, see also Brame 1972)
       i → e / __C#
       The vowel /i/ is realized as [e] before a single word-final consonant.

Given that this alternation exists, positing /i/ as the underlying quality of the final stem vowel is well-motivated. With this being the case, it is possible to posit a single underlying vocalism /i/ for verbs of this class. It is important to emphasis that, consistent with the verbs in (149a & b), the imperfective prefix vowel and the plural stem vowel in (150) are identical in quality to the underlying vocalism.

I turn now to verbs in which the vowel sequence of perfectives is [a-e], as represented by the examples in (153).

(153)   Imperfective   Perfective
         3rd p.m.sg.   3rd p.pl.   3rd p.m.sg.
    i.   ja+ħdem   ja+ħdm+u   ħadem   'to work'
         ja+ʔbel   ja+ʔbl+u   ʔabel   'to agree'
         ja+ʔfel   ja+ʔfl+u   ʔafel   'to lock'
    ii. ja+ħleb   ja+ħilb+u   ħaleb   'to milk'
         ja+ʔleb   ja+ʔilb+u   ʔaleb   'to overturn'

In these verbs, surface vowel qualities may be [a], [e] or [i]. In each case, the imperfective prefix vowel is [a], the plural stem vowel is [i] and the stem-final vowel is [e]. Although on the surface the vowel qualities differ, I argue that, like the previous groups of verbs, there is a vocalism of a single quality underlyingly, that being /i/. First, identical to the verbs discussed immediately above, the final stem vowel shows i~e alternations, e.g. ħadem 'he worked', ħdimt 'I, you (sg.) worked'. By positing /i/ as the underlying quality of the second stem vowel, this alternation is accounted for by the independently motivated rule of I-lowering given in (152). However, this still leaves the first stem vowel of the perfective and the prefix vowel which surface as [a]. Were we to assume that the underlying quality of these vowels was /a/, this group of verbs would stand out as exceptional when compared to the three previous groups in that there is not a single underlying vocalism. As is evident, this alone is not sufficient motivation for rejecting /a-i/ as the underlying vocalism in these verbs. However, there is independent evidence which suggests that surface [a]'s are also /i/ underlyingly.

It will be noticed that in each verb in (153), the stem-initial consonant is a guttural, [ħ ʔ]. McCarthy (1989) and Herzallah (1990) claim, based on a wide range of evidence, that these sounds are members of a natural class which we may characterize by the articulator [pharyngeal]. In Herzallah's study of Palestinian Arabic, she provides strong evidence that the vowel [a] is also [pharyngeal]. Given the common place specification of these sounds, I propose that Maltese [a] acquires its quality as the result of assimilation to an adjacent guttural consonant.

The question then is: what is the underlying quality of the vowel which undergoes assimilation? Relevant in this respect is the observation that although [e, o, a] may occur adjacent to a guttural consonant in underived verb forms,[8] e.g. ħebel 'he raved', boloʔ 'he was past his prime', ħabat 'he struck', [i] is excluded. Positing /i/ as the underlying vowel quality is then a potential candidate. Further evidence for this comes from an examination of the verbs in (154).

(154)

	Imperfective		Perfective	
	3rd p.m.sg.	3rd p.pl.	3rd p.m.sg.	
	ji+lħaʔ	ji+lħʔ+u	laħaʔ	'to reach'
	ji+sħaʔ	ji+sħʔ+u	saħaʔ	'to pound'
	ji+tħan	ji+tħn+u	taħan	'to grind'
	ji+tʃħad	ji+tʃħd+u	tʃaħad	'to deny'

Maltese 171

As can be seen, the imperfective prefix vowel in each of these verbs surfaces as [i], despite the fact that all stem vowels are [a]. Recall that in the first three groups of verbs (149a,b & 150), the surface quality of the prefix vowel is identical to that of the underlying vocalism of the stem. Given this, we might expect the underlying vocalism of the verbs in (154) to be /i/. Yet, doing so is potentially problematic since the surface quality of the stem vowels is [a]. This problem is only apparent, however. Note that in each of these verbs there is a guttural consonant in at least medial position. By assuming that the underlying quality of the stem vowels is /i/, the realization of these vowels as [a] can be accounted for by assimilation to an adjacent guttural consonant. Along these lines, we correctly predict the prefix vowel to surface as [i], identical in quality to the underlying vocalism. I state the rule of Guttural Assimilation in (155), using the rule formalism of Archangeli & Pulleyblank (1986) as a model.

(155) Guttural Assimilation:
       Operation: spread [pharyngeal]
       Trigger: [pharyngeal]$_{CONS}$
       Target: [coronal, +high]
       Direction: bidirectional
       Locality: skeletal tier adjacency
       Constriction status change: yes

Guttural Assimilation applies to change the place specification of the vowel target from /i/ to [a]. As shown in (156), this is represented as spreading the feature [pharyngeal] from the consonant to the vocoidal place node of the vowel, replacing the original [coronal] place specification of the target.

(156) Guttural Assimilation

```
        C                V         (mirror image)
        |                |
       Root             Root
        |                |
       Cons             Cons
        |                |
       place            place
                         |
                         Voc
                ___place___
               /           \
              /          stricture
      [pharyngeal]  ⊧       |
               |         [+high]
           [coronal]
```

By spreading [pharyngeal] directly to the vocoidal place node rather than to the consonantal place node, the prediction is that we would not expect there to be any difference in the phonetic realization or the phonological patterning of a vowel [a] which results from Guttural Assimilation, and surface instances of [a] which are not the result of assimilation. At present I have not found any evidence which would support a difference between the two types of [a]. If future research indicates that the [pharyngeal] specification of [a] resulting from assimilation patterns with consonantal instances of [pharyngeal] or is realized with consonant-like constriction, we would have evidence for linking [pharyngeal] of [a] to the consonantal place node. As such, assimilation would involve spreading the [pharyngeal] node from the consonant directly to place$_{CONS}$ of the vowel.

In the preliminaries I stated that the underlying feature value [-high] is redundant for [a] and expressed this in the redundancy rule repeated in (157). To account for the change in vowel height of the vowel /i/ after Guttural Assimilation has applied, I assume that the feature value [+high] is changed to [-high] in a structure preserving manner, consistent with the redundancy rule in (157).[9]

(157)   Redundancy rule:
        [pharyngeal]$_{VOC}$ —> [-high]

With the rule of Guttural Assimilation, we may posit /i/ as the underlying vocalism for the verbs in (154), e.g. [jilħaʔ] / [jilħʔu] / [laħaʔ] 'he reaches / they reach / he reached'. Similar to the verbs in (149a,b, 150), the quality of the prefix vowel is identical to that of the underlying vocalism. Yet, for the prefix vowel to surface as [i] in (154) Guttural Assimilation must apply after the prefix vowel has acquired its quality from the stem vocalism. Were this not the case, we would incorrectly predict the prefix vowel to surface as [a]. For our present purposes, I will assume that the prefix vowel acquires its features by assimilation to the stem vocalism and refer to this rule as Prefix Vowel Assimilation, stated in prose in (158). In section 10 below, I return to the question of how this rule is formally represented.

(158) Prefix Vowel Assimilation (PVA) (preliminary formulation): The imperfective prefix vowel assimilates in quality to the underlying vocalism of the stem.

The partial derivations of the imperfective and perfective of the verb 'to reach' are given in (159).

(159)		j V + l i ħ i ʔ	l i ħ i ʔ
	Prefix Vowel Assim.	j i l i ħ i ʔ	n/a
	Syncope	j i l ħ i ʔ	n/a
	Guttural Assim.	j i l ħ a ʔ	l a ħ a ʔ
		[jilħaʔ]	[laħaʔ]
		'he reaches'	'he reached'

Reconsider now the verbs in (153) above, repeated as (160) below.

(160) Imperfective   Perfective
       3rd p.m.sg.   3rd p.pl.   3rd p.m.sg.

	Imperfective		Perfective	
	3rd p.m.sg.	3rd p.pl.	3rd p.m.sg.	
	ja+ħdem	ja+ħdm+u	ħadem	'to work'
	ja+ʔbel	ja+ʔbl+u	ʔabel	'to agree'
	ja+ʔfel	ja+ʔfl+u	ʔafel	'to lock'
	ja+ħleb	ja+ħilb+u	ħaleb	'to milk'
	ja+ʔleb	ja+ʔilb+u	ʔaleb	'to overturn'

Recall that although positing /i/ as the underlying quality of the stem-final vowel is well-motivated, the prefix vowel and first stem vowel of the perfective both surface as [a]. With the independently motivated rule of Guttural Assimilation, it is now possible to posit /i/ as the single underlying vocalism associated with this class of verbs. As shown in (161) for the verb 'to work', the imperfective prefix vowel first acquires the vowel quality of the underlying vocalism, i.e. /i/. Consistent with the ordering in (159), Syncope then applies to delete the first stem vowel of the imperfective. Guttural Assimilation then applies. This changes the imperfective prefix vowel, as well as the first stem vowel of the perfective to [a]. Note that Guttural Assimilation applies bidirectionally: right to left in the imperfective and left to right in the perfective. The final stem vowel lowers to [e] by the independently motivated rule of I-lowering. (The ordering of Guttural Assimilation before I-lowering is not crucial to this account.)

(161)   jV+ħidim   ħidim
    Prefix Vowel Assim.   jiħidim   n/a
    Syncope   jiħdim   n/a
    Guttural Assim.   jaħdim   ħadim
    I-lowering   jaħdem   ħadem
                               [jaħdem]   [ħadem]
                               'he works'   'he worked'

It will be noticed that the stem vowel which occurs in imperfective plural verbs such as jaħilbu 'they milk', ja?ilbu 'they overturn', surfaces as [i]. Consistent with the verbs in (149a,b & 150), the quality of this vowel is identical to the underlying vocalism of the stem. However, given that Guttural Assimilation applies bidirectionally, we would predict the quality of this vowel to be [a]. This then remains an unresolved problem. I will set aside discussion of this problem for the moment but return to it in sections 6 & 8 where I treat the realization of plural stem vowels in detail. At that time, I will offer a solution to this and other related problems.

Before leaving the discussion of this class of verbs it is important to point out that in order to generate the correct verb forms in (161), Guttural Assimilation must apply after Tier Conflation. Based on McCarthy's (1979, 1981) study of Classical Arabic, in the pre-Tier Conflation stage of the phonology, the vocalism /i/ of 'to work' would be linked to both vowel slots of the perfective in /ħidim/, for example, as shown in (162a). As pointed out in the preliminaries, were /i/ linked to each V-slot separately, as in (162b), the representation would violate the Obligatory Contour Principle.

Maltese 175

(162)

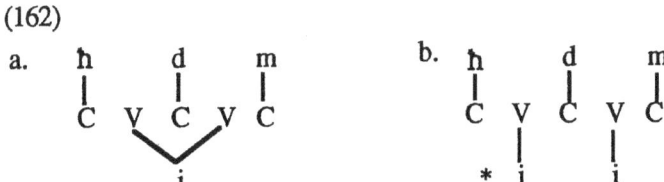

If we were to assume that Guttural Assimilation applied prior to Tier Conflation, as in (163), we would incorrectly predict both stem vowels to surface as [a]. This results from the fact that Guttural Assimilation is defined on /i/, and since /i/ is multiply-linked to both V-slots, both vowels would be affected.

(163)

```
ħ   d   m         ħ   d   m
|   |   |  Guttural  |   |   |
C V C V C   ────→   C V C V C  ──→ *[ħadam]
   \ /              Assimilation   \ /
    i                                a
```

Recall from chapter IV (and section 1.3 above) that after general Tier Conflation has applied, the multiple-linking of non-skeletal adjacent elements is eliminated. Consequently, after Tier Conflation, the representation of the perfective of 'to work' appears as in (164). As shown, Guttural Assimilation will only affect the first stem vowel, as expected. I-lowering is also correctly predicted to apply only to the stem-final vowel.

(164)

```
              Guttural
              Assim.
C V C V C    ────→    C V C V C  ──→ [ħadem]
| | | | |      I-     | | | | |
ħ i d i m   Lowering  ħ a d e m
```

In this section, I have argued that the underlying vocalism of verbs such as [ħadem] and [laħaʔ] is /i/. As a result, verbs of these classes are identical to all other verbs discussed thus far in that there is a vocalism of a single quality associated with the stem underlyingly. Moreover, we are able to account for the quality of the prefix vowel as [i] in, e.g. [jilħaʔ], despite the fact that the stem vowels of both perfective and imperfectives surface as [a]. Guttural Assimilation, applying in the post-Tier Conflation stage of the phonology, correctly predicts the surface quality of the vowels in these and other forms to be [a].

It is important to point out that not all verbs which contain surface instances of [a] adjacent to a guttural consonant have /i/ as the underlying vocalism. I refer, in particular, to the verbs presented above in (149a), some of which are repeated below in (165).

(165) Imperfective   Perfective
       3rd p.m.sg.   3rd p.pl.   3rd p.m.sg.
       ja+ʔbad   ja+ʔbd+u   ʔabad   'to catch'
       ja+ħrab   ja+ħarb+u   ħarab   'to run away'

Positing /i/ as the underlying vocalism for the verbs in (165) is problematic. If we were to assume that the stem vocalism was /i/, Guttural Assimilation would need to apply before Tier Conflation in order for both stem vowels to surface as [a]. This is due to the fact that in many of these verbs there is only a single guttural consonant. In (165), this occurs in stem-initial position. Consequently, unless the vowel /i/ were multiply-linked to both vowel slots, as it would be prior to Tier Conflation, the second stem vowel would not be affected by Guttural Assimilation. Yet, the ordering of Guttural Assimilation before Tier Conflation is precisely the opposite order of that required to account for the vowel alternations in the derivations in (159) and (161) above. It is particularly relevant that, unlike the verbs in (153 (160)) and (154), there are no vowel alternations in the verbs in (149a, 165); all vowels surface consistently as [a] in all positions. It is thus preferable to maintain the null hypothesis and assume that the underlying quality of the vowels in (149a, 165) is identical to their surface quality, i.e. /a/ → [a].

Three groups of verbs remain to be discussed. The first of these is presented in (166).

Maltese

(166)
Imperfective		Perfective	
3rd p.m.sg.	3rd p.pl.	3rd p.m.sg.	
ji+ksaħ	ji+ksħ+u	kesaħ	'to get cold'
ji+rbaħ	ji+rbħ+u	rebaħ	'to win'
ji+ftaħ	ji+ftħ+u	fetaħ	'to open'
ji+flaħ	ji+filħ+u	felaħ	'to be strong'
ji+sraʔ	ji+sirʔ+u	seraʔ	'to steal'
ji+tlaʔ	ji+tilʔ+u	telaʔ	'to depart'

Similar to the verbs in (153 (160)) above, we observe three different surface vowel qualities in these verbs. The prefix vowel and plural imperfective stem vowel surface as [i]. The stem-initial vowel of the perfective is [e] and the stem-final vowel is consistently [a]. Like the previous three classes of verbs, the underlying vocalism of these verbs is also /i/. Motivation for this view comes first, from the fact that both the prefix and plural stem vowels are [i]. Recall from all previous cases that the corresponding vowels are identical to the underlying vocalism of the stem (although the prefix vowel may subsequently undergo Guttural Assimilation, as in the verbs in (153 (160))). By positing underlying /i/ in (166), these verbs pattern with other verbs. Second, it will be observed that the final stem consonant in all verbs in (166) is a guttural consonant. Given the independently motivated rule of Guttural Assimilation, positing /i/ as the underlying quality of the stem-final vowel comes at no extra cost. Remaining to be accounted for is the stem-initial vowel of the perfectives which surfaces as [e]. As observed by Berrendonner et al (1983), in all surface vowel sequences, [a] is only preceded by [e] within the stem; [i] is excluded from this position. I account for this gap by positing /i/ as the underlying quality of the first stem vowel. Due to the effect of a following pharyngeal vowel, the vowel /i/ lowers to [e]. This is stated in the rule of A-assimilation in (167).

(167) A-assimilation:
operation:	spread [-high]
trigger:	[pharyngeal, -high]$_{VOC}$
target:	[coronal, +high]
direction:	right to left
domain:	verb stem

A-assimilation involves spreading the feature value [-high] from the vowel [a] to the Stricture node of the preceding vowel /i/, with the automatic delinking of the original specification [+high] on the target. Limiting the rule's domain to the verb stem excludes the rule from applying to the prefix vowel in forms such as [jisraʔ] 'he steals'. As shown in (168), A-assimilation applies after Guttural Assimilation. The second vowel changes to [a] due to Guttural Assimilation, and the first vowel lowers to [e] due to the effect of the following vowel [a].

(168) /fitiħ/
    Guttural Assim.   fitaħ
    A-Assimilation   fetaħ
    Output   [fetaħ]   'he opened'

By taking into account the rules of Guttural Assimilation and A-assimilation, both stem vowels of the perfective verbs in (166) are treated as underlyingly /i/. Consequently, like all other verbs discussed thus far, the verbs in (166) have a single vocalism in underlying representation. Furthermore, the quality of the imperfective prefix and plural stem vowels is identical to the underlying vocalism, as is the case in verbs discussed thus far.

There is a small number of verbs which have the surface sequence [e-e] in the perfective, and in the imperfective, the prefix vowel is realized as [e]. The exhaustive list of forms accepted by my consultants is given in (169).

(169)

	Imperfective		Perfective	
	3rd p.m.sg.	3rd p.pl.	3rd p.m.sg.	
	je+ħbel	je+ħbl+u	ħebel	'to rave'
	je+ħber	je+ħbr+u	ħeber	'to predict'
	je+ħmez	je+ħemz+u/	ħemez	'to pin'
		je+ħimz+u		
	je+ʔred	je+ʔird+u	ʔered	'to destroy'
	je+ħles	je+ħils+u	ħeles	'to be freed'

Given that the prefix vowel in these verbs is [e], positing underlying /e/ as the vocalic melody of the stem is consistent with the analysis of all other verbs. However, similar to verbs such as [bidel] /bidil/ 'he changed', the final stem vowel alternates with [i] when it is not followed by a single word-final consonant, e.g. ħebel 'he raved', ħbilt 'I/you (sg.) raved' (Puech 1979, Sutcliffe 1936). This then suggests an analysis in which /i/ is assumed to be the underlying vocalic melody of the stem. Yet, positing /i/ as the underlying vocalic melody is problematic. By doing so, some means of accounting for the realization of the first stem vowel and prefix vowel as [e] is needed. It will be noticed that in all of the verbs in (169), the stem-initial consonant is a guttural consonant. One solution would be to attribute the quality of [e] to the stem-initial guttural consonant. This could be done by positing a rule similar to Guttural Assimilation in which the vowel /i/ is realized as [e] when adjacent to a guttural consonant. However, doing so would mean that two rules would exist in the phonology with /i/ as the target and /ħ ʔ/ as the trigger. The only difference between the two would be that in some cases the output is [a] and in others it is [e]. This approach is clearly undesirable since the verbs in (153 (160)) would be phonologically non-distinct from the verbs in (169), e.g. [jaʔbel] 'he agrees' < /jV+ʔibil/ vs. [jehbel] 'he predicts' < /jV+ħibil/. In other words, there would be no way to determine in a principled manner what the output of assimilation to a guttural consonant would be.

Alternatively, analyzing these verbs with underlying /e/ is to be preferred for a number of reasons. It provides a straightforward account of the realization of the prefix vowel as [e] since this vowel would be identical to the underlying vocalic melody of the stem, as in other verbs. Furthermore, there would be no ambiguity concerning what the output of assimilation to a guttural consonant would be; in all cases the vowel would be predictably [a]. I account for the realization of the final stem vowel as [i] in this small class of verbs by the rule of E-raising in (170).

(170) E-raising
e —> i / XC __ CC
where X is either C or V

Including the X variable in (170) excludes the rule from applying to the prefix vowel in forms such as [jeʔred], or to the stem-initial vowel in forms such as [ʔerdet]. The rule also applies to the plural stem vowel in [jeʔirdu], for example. It will be noticed in (169) that the plural imperfective of 'to pin' is either [jeħimzu] or [jeħemzu]. In

Sutcliffe (1936), the form with [e] is given. However, for my consultants, there was hesitation concerning the quality of this vowel. In some instances, the form with [i] was given, and in others, the form with [e] was elicited. The realization of the vowel as [e] is consistent with the general pattern observed for other verbs in that the imperfective plural stem vowel is identical to the underlying vocalism of the stem. The realization of the vowel as [i], on the other hand, is to be expected given the existence of the rule of E-raising. I assume then that at least for this verb, the rule of E-raising applies optionally.

The final group of verbs to be discussed are those which appeared as group 8 in (149), repeated as (171) below.

(171) jo+nfor   jo+nfr+u   nafar   'to expose'
      jo+bzoʔ   jo+bzʔ+u   bezaʔ   'to spit'
      jo+ʔtol   jo+ʔtl+u   ʔatel   'to kill'
      jo+ɦrodʒ   jo+ɦordʒ+u   ɦaredʒ   'to go out'
      jo+ʔmos   jo+ʔoms+u   ʔamas   'to jump'
      jo+brod   jo+bord+u   barad   'to file'

The verbs in (171) are representative of a relatively large number of verbs in which the stem vowel of the perfective differs from that of the imperfective; the stem vowel of the imperfective is [o] regardless of the quality of the perfective stem vowels. This occurs in verbs which have the perfective vowel sequences [a-a], [a-e] and [e-a] (verbs with the sequence [i-e] will be discussed in chapter VII). No examples of verbs with the sequence [e-e] were found although this gap may be due to the simple fact that there are very few verbs with [e-e] to begin with.

There does not appear to be any single property common to all verbs in which the vowels of the perfective alternate with [o] in the imperfective which would distinguish them from verbs not evidencing this alternation. To illustrate, consider the near-minimal pairs listed in (172). Verbs which retain their original vowel quality are given on the left and those which change their stem vowel to [o] appear on the right.

(172) cf.
ʔasam	jaʔsam	'to break'	ʔamas	joʔmos	'to jump'
ħataf	jaħtaf	'to snatch'	ħatab	joħtob	'to enquire'
ħatar	jaħtar	'to elect'	ʔatar	joʔtor	'to fall in drops'
fetaħ	jiftaħ	'to open'	fetaʔ	joftoʔ	'to unstitch'
ʔafel	jaʔfel	'to lock'	ʔatel	joʔtol	'to kill'

It might be the case that an indepth study of the historical sources of the verbs evidencing the alternation would elucidate the original conditioning factor. From a synchronic point of view, however, predicting which verbs are realized with [o] in the imperfective is not possible. Consequently, given the unpredictability of the verbs in which the vowel of the imperfective stem changes to [o], I assume that these verbs are lexically marked to this effect. The rule of Imperfective Vowel Change given in (173) accounts for this change.

(173) Imperfective Vowel Change:

$V \rightarrow o\ /\ \_\_]_{\text{imperfective}}$

We obtain the least complex analysis by applying Imperfective Vowel Change at the beginning of the formation of the imperfective. The partial derivation of [jobsor] 'he predicts' (cf. [basar] 'he predicted') in (174) serves example.

(174)   jV+basar
  Imperfective Vowel Change   jVbosor
  Prefix Vowel Assimilation   jobosor
  Syncope   jobsor
  Output   [jobsor] 'he predicts'
                                    cf. [basar] 'he predicted'

4.1 Summary

To summarize, I have shown that for all triliteral strong verbs of the first measure, a given imperfective stem is associated with a single vocalism in underlying representation. Furthermore, the imperfective prefix vowel as well as the plural imperfective stem vowel are typically identical to the underlying quality of the imperfective stem's vocalism.

5. PLURAL IMPERFECTIVES: DESCRIPTION

As shown in section 3 above, the typical formation of the imperfective plural, first measure triliteral verb, typically results in a stem comprised of only three consonants, as illustrated in (175).

(175)

Imperfective		Perfective	
3rd p.pl.	3rd p.m.sg.	3rd p.m.sg.	
ja+ħbt+u	ja+ħbat	ħabat	to strike
jo+ktr+u	jo+ktor	kotor	to abound
ji+bdl+u	ji+bdel	bidel	to change
ji+lħʔ+u	ji+lħaʔ	laħaʔ	to reach
je+ħbl+u	je+ħbel	ħebel	to rave

However, in verbs in which the medial root consonant is a sonorant, i.e. [m n l r], a vowel occurs to the consonant's left (see (176)). As motivated in section 4, the quality of this vowel is typically identical to the underlying vocalism of the stem, indicated on the right.

(176)

Imperfective		Perfective	Stem V	
3rd p.pl.	3rd p.m.sg.	3rd p.m.sg.		
jo+korb+u	jo+krob	korob	/o/	to groan
ji+ʃorb+u	ji+ʃrob[10]	ʃorob	/o/	to drink
je+ħemz+u	je+ħmez	ħemez	/e/	to pin
ja+ħart+u	ja+ħrat	ħarat	/a/	to plough
ji+tilf+u	ji+tlef	tilef	/i/	to lose
ja+ħilb+u	ja+ħleb	ħaleb	/i/	to milk
ji+filħ+u	ji+flaħ	felaħ	/i/	to be strong

In earlier analyses, the occurrence of the plural stem vowel is accounted for by a rule of consonant/vowel metathesis (e.g. Brame 1972, Puech 1979, Berrondonner et al. 1983). In other words, the vowel which occurs to the left of the medial sonorant consonant in the plural stem originates to the immediate right of the consonant in underlying representation. As the result of metathesis, the linear ordering of the consonant and vowel switches. Berrondonner et al. (1983) make use of the following transformational notation to describe this.

(177) Metathesis:
V C R V C V → 1 2 4 3 5 6
1 2 3 4 5 6   (where R = nasal or liquid)

Consonant/vowel metathesis provides a straightforward account of why Guttural Assimilation fails to affect the plural stem vowel in certain verbs, e.g.[jaħilbu] 'they milk', a problem pointed out above in section 4. At the point in the derivation when Guttural Assimilation applies, metathesis has not yet occurred and, as a result, the stem vowel is not adjacent to a guttural consonant (Puech 1979). I will go into more detail concerning this further below. However, as I will show, this analysis is unable to account for the full range of plural imperfectives. As noted in the introduction, I propose that the problem is associated with the view of metathesis as a one-step operation. Alternatively, I argue that metathesis is the product of three rules: Syncope, Epenthesis and Vocalic Mapping, as will be discussed below.

My analysis of consonant/vowel metathesis in Maltese is similar in some ways to that proposed by Kenstowicz (1981) for Palestinian Arabic. Although the data in the two languages differ in many respects, metathesis is shown to be descriptively inadequate in both analyses. Kenstowicz rejects the metathesis approach since, as he states, "metathesis merely duplicates the work of syncope and epenthesis" (p.460). Although he incorporates syncope and epenthesis into his analysis, Kenstowicz nonetheless assumes that metathesis continues to exist in phonology as an independent one-step operation. The reason for this duplication, I propose, stems from the fact that consonant/vowel metathesis is in fact the product of more than one operation. By analyzing metathesis in this way, it is unnecessary to maintain the traditional one-step approach to metathesis as well.

Two of the rules involved in producing metathesis, i.e. Syncope and Vocalic Mapping, are also shown to be instrumental in accounting for the realization of the imperfective prefix vowel, thus resulting in a more unified analysis. Moreover, as I will show, by incorporating these two rules into the analysis of the prefix vowel, we are able to elucidate why it is only in the first measure that the quality of the prefix vowel differs. It will be recalled that in all other measures, this vowel always surfaces as [i].

The organization of the remainder of this chapter is as follows. I begin by motivating the view that some form of consonant/vowel metathesis is involved in the derivation of these verbs. Following this I show that the traditional view of metathesis is unable to account for the full range of verbs. The next section focusses on the three independent rules which I claim result in metathesis. Next, I illustrate how Syncope and Vocalic Mapping figure into the analysis of the imperfective prefix vowel. At the end of this chapter I discuss implications that this analysis has for the representation of total vowel assimilation and for underspecification theory.

6. METATHESIS

6.1 Motivating Metathesis

In accounting for the occurrence of the plural stem vowel in verbs such as (176) above, the null hypothesis is to assume that this vowel originates to the left of the medial sonorant consonant. However, this approach is problematic. In order to maintain this approach, it must be assumed that the first stem vowel does not undergo Syncope. Recall that in the typical formation of the plural imperfective, both stem vowels delete resulting in a three consonant cluster, e.g. [jaḥbtu] 'they strike'. Thus, we might reformulate the rule of Syncope such that it applies just in case the medial stem consonant is [-sonorant], as stated in (178).

(178)   Syncope II:
        $V \rightarrow \emptyset / C \_\_ C_1 V$
        Condition: if C_1 is a medial stem consonant then it must be [-sonorant]

The revised formulation of Syncope is incorporated into the derivation of [jokorbu] in (179). As can be seen, the first stem vowel will fail to delete since it is followed by a medial sonorant consonant. With the addition of the plural suffix, however, the final stem vowel does delete. Thus, by blocking Syncope from applying just in case the medial consonant is [+sonorant] we are able to derive the correct form of [jokorbu].

Maltese 185

(179) jV+korob
Prefix Vowel Assim. jokorob
Syncope -blocked-

Input jokorob+u
Syncope jokorbu
[jokorbu] 'they groan'

There are two principal weaknesses associated with this analysis. First, we are required to include the seemingly arbitrary stipulation that the rule applies just in case the medial consonant is [-sonorant]. Moreover, the analysis is unable to account for the surface quality of the stem vowel in all plural verbs. The verb [jaħilbu] 'they milk', for example, is derived from underlying /jV+ħilib+u/. As shown in section 4, the realization of the prefix vowel as [a] is due to Guttural Assimilation: the prefix vowel assimilates to the underlying vocalism /i/ then undergoes Guttural Assimilation and surfaces as [a]. If we were to assume that the first stem vowel of the plural imperfective did not undergo Syncope, as in (180) below, this vowel would also be expected to undergo Guttural Assimilation. This is because both the prefix vowel and the stem vowel would be adjacent to the stem-initial guttural consonant.

(180) jV+ħilib
Prefix Vowel Assim. jiħilib
Syncope -blocked-

Input jiħilib+u
Syncope jiħilbu
Guttural Assimilation jaħalbu
 *[jaħalbu]
 ([jaħilbu] 'they milk')

Note that restricting the directionality of Guttural Assimilation to apply from right to left is not a possible solution since, it will be recalled, Guttural Assimilation applies from left to right, e.g. [ħaleb] < /ħilib/ 'he milked'. (The final stem vowel is realized as [e] by I-lowering.) Consequently, it cannot be assumed that the plural stem vowel is to the left of the medial sonorant consonant when Guttural Assimilation applies.

As pointed out by Puech (1979), the quality of the stem vowel in verbs such as [jaḥilbu] 'they milk' is correctly accounted for if we assume that the plural stem vowel originates to the right of the medial consonant, but then undergoes metathesis after the application of Guttural Assimilation. I follow the essentials of Puech's analysis to illustrate this point. In order for the second stem vowel to resist deletion, the rule of Syncope must be revised as in (181).

(181) Syncope III:
$V \rightarrow \emptyset / C_1 \_\_ C V$
Condition: if C_1 is a medial stem consonant then it must be [-sonorant]

Although the rule's revision is trivial, it nonetheless blocks Syncope from applying to the second stem vowel if preceded by a sonorant consonant. The derivation of 'they milk' incorporating this revision is given in (182).

(182)
Input	jV+ḥilib
Prefix Vowel Assim.	jiḥilib
Syncope	jiḥlibu
---	---
Input	jiḥlib+u
Syncope	-blocked-
Guttural Assimilation	jaḥlibu
Metathesis	jaḥilbu
Output	[jaḥilbu]
	'they milk'

In this analysis, the first stem vowel deletes, yet Syncope fails to apply to the second vowel since it is preceded by [l]. Guttural Assimilation changes only the prefix vowel to [a]. Metathesis then applies and the medial consonant and following vowel switch positions. Through the crucial ordering of Guttural Assimilation before Metathesis, the plural stem vowel is correctly realized as [i]. If the ordering were reversed, we would predict the stem vowel as well as the prefix vowel to surface as [a], identical to the output in (182).

I would suggest that the view that the plural stem vowel originates to the right of the medial consonant is the correct approach. In other words, consonant/vowel metathesis is involved. Any analysis in which the stem vowel were to remain to the left of the medial consonant throughout the derivation would run into problems for precisely the reasons cited with respect to the verb [jaħilbu]. There are, nonetheless, problems associated with the approach exemplified in (183) in which the stem vowel remains to the right of the medial consonant. First, we are once again required to formulate Syncope in such a way as to include the ad hoc stipulation that it applies just in case the medial consonant is [-sonorant]. More importantly though, there are a number of verbs that the analysis in (182) will not account for. Consider the verb [jifilħu] < /jV+filiħ+u/ 'they are strong' (cf. [jiflaħ] 'he is strong'), for example. Identical to the verb [jaħilbu], the metathesized vowel surfaces as [i]. However, as illustrated in column I in (183), applying Guttural Assimilation before Metathesis as was required in (182) causes the metathesized vowel in the verb 'to be strong' to surface incorrectly as [a]. The ordering needed to obtain the correct result is given in column II.

(183)

	I.	II.	
Input	jV+filiħ	jV+filiħ	Input
Prefix Vowel Assim.	jifiliħ	jifiliħ	Prefix Vowel Assim.
Syncope	jVfliħ	jVfliħ	Syncope
Input	jifliħ+u	jifliħ+u	Input
Syncope	-blocked-	-blocked-	Syncope
Guttural Assim.	jiflaħu	jifilħu	**Metathesis**
Metathesis	jifalħu	n/a	**Guttural Assim.**
Output	*[jifalħu]	[jifilħu]	Output

In order to obtain the correct output in (183), Metathesis must apply before Guttural Assimilation. In other words, the vowel first shifts to the left of the medial consonant and then Guttural Assimilation fails to apply since the context of the rule is not met, i.e. /i/ is no longer adjacent to a guttural consonant. Note that Guttural Assimilation does apply stem-internally in the singular imperfective of this verb, i.e. [jiflaħ] 'he is strong'. For verbs such as [jifilħu] then, it is clear that Metathesis must apply before Guttural Assimilation, the exact opposite ordering from that needed to obtain the correct result in (182).

The problem then is this: in order to account for forms such as 'to be strong' in (183), Guttural Assimilation cannot apply when the stem vowel is still to the right of the medial consonant, in other words, Metathesis has to precede Guttural Assimilation. Yet, for verbs such as 'to milk' in (182), Guttural Assimilation cannot apply when the stem vowel is already to the left of the medial consonant. In other words, Metathesis has to follow Guttural Assimilation. Thus, in order to account for all forms correctly, Guttural Assimilation needs to apply *after* the time that the second stem vowel has left its position to the right of the medial consonant so that the final stem vowel in [jifilħu] < /jV+filiħ+u/ will not be affected, but *before* the final stem vowel resurfaces to the left of the medial consonant, so that the metathesized vowel in [jaħilbu] will not be affected. Put another way, when Guttural Assimilation applies, the plural stem vowel cannot be "visible" to the rule. In this way, the vowel will retain its underlying quality when it surfaces to the left of the medial consonant.

Given the common view of metathesis as a one-step operation, accounting for the realization of the plural stem vowel in all verbs is impossible. In order to do so, metathesis in Maltese must be viewed as the *product* of more than one operation. These include delete, insert and associate. The first two are operations involved in independently motivated rules of Maltese phonology: Syncope and Epenthesis, respectively. The third operation, associate, takes the form of Vocalic Mapping, a universal association convention. Before elaborating further on each of these rules, the question of why a vowel should occur in these plural imperfectives must be addressed. As I show in the following section, the reason relates directly to the language's syllable structure conditions.

6.2   Syllable Structure Conditions

The occurrence of a vowel before a medial sonorant consonant in plural imperfectives is a direct consequence of the language's syllable structure conditions and not limited to just these forms. In general, word-internal sequences of the form CRC, where R indicates a sonorant consonant ([m,n,l,r]) do not occur in Maltese (Aquilina 1959, Brame 1972, Puech 1979, Sutcliffe 1936). In addition to the plural imperfectives seen above, we also observe that in, for example, the plural of certain nouns the vowel [i] is realized before a sonorant consonant when this consonant would otherwise occur medially between two consonants, e.g. frieʃ 'mattress'/ifirʃa 'mattresses', znied 'flint'/izinda 'flints', cf. lsien 'language'/ilsna 'languages'.

Moreover, my examination of initial consonant clusters in Maltese reveals that in all instances in which a sonorant consonant is followed by a [+consonantal] segment, the consonant cluster is preceded by a vowel. In other words, there are no word-initial consonant clusters beginning with a sonorant consonant. This is seen, for example, in nouns with the definite article prefix given in (184). Before nouns beginning with a consonant, the prefix surfaces as [il-] whereas before vowel-initial nouns, its form is [l-].[11]

(184)   il+belt   'the city'
         il+fellus   'the chicken'
         il+ʔattus   'the cat'
         il+ħitan   'the walls'
         il+moʔdief   'the oar'
   cf.   l+abt   'the arm-pit'
         l+omm   'the mother'

As a further example, in verbal nouns an initial sonorant consonant is preceded by the vowel [i]. In the forms on the right, the vowel does not occur since the initial consonant is non-sonorant.

(185)
  a.   irbiit   'act of tying'   cf. ʔtiil   'act of killing'
       infiiʔ   'act of paying'   tliib   'act of praying'
       (examples from Brame 1972:34-35)

A similar situation arises with respect to word-final consonant clusters. My examination of final consonant clusters in Maltese indicates that sonorant consonants rarely occur as the final member of a complex coda. This observation is based on over 31,000 words in the Maltese lexicon of Busuttil (1981). Numerous examples of final consonant clusters comprised of two non-sonorants (continuant or non-continuant) occur, e.g. irmosk 'trash', ʔabd 'ready money', dalwaʔt 'soon, now'. Final geminates also frequently occur, e.g. boll 'sting ray', bonn 'swelling in the groin', daʔʔ 'he played, sounded' (cf. daʔ 'he tasted, experienced'). Moreover, many examples with sonorant consonants followed by obstruents can be found, e.g. bint 'daughter', dars 'dental', kelb 'dog'. However, only five words were found which contained a sonorant consonant as the final member of a consonant cluster. In each case, the final consonant is a nasal and the preceding consonant is a liquid, i.e. buʔarn 'horned beetle' (ʔarn 'horn'), skalm 'oar peg', sorm 'backside, rear', infern 'hell, infernal'.

Dating at least as far back as Sievers (1881), Jespersen (1904), it has been observed that the sequencing of segments within a syllable is associated with the sonority of the segments involved. The most sonorous segments are vowels, followed in decreasing sonority by glides, liquids, nasals, fricatives and stops. Cross-linguistically, recurrent syllable patterns emerge which show sonority generally rising toward the syllable peak and then falling away from the peak. The sequencing of segments within the syllable observed above for Maltese may be properly accounted for by Jespersen's (1904, 1950) Sonority Principle.

(186) Sonority Principle (Jesperson 1950:131)
Between a given sound and the peak are only found sounds of the same, or a higher, sonority class.

The Sonority Principle expresses the observation that as you move out from the syllable peak, sonority cannot increase. It may, on the other hand, decrease or alternatively, remain relatively constant. It is then not surprising that complex codas comprised of an obstruent followed by a sonorant consonant do not occur in Maltese. Similarly, complex onsets made up of a sonorant consonant followed by an obstruent are also correctly predicted to be absent. Moreover, the observation that word-internal sequences of CRC (where R is a nasal or liquid) do not occur in Maltese can be viewed as a consequence of the Sonority Principle. A medial sonorant consonant is more sonorous than both a preceding and following nonsonorant consonant. As I show in the following section, when such sequences do arise, epenthesis applies to allow for the syllabification of all consonants.

Maltese   *191*

6.3   Epenthesis

As observed in the forms in (184) and (185) just above, the vowel [i] precedes a word-initial sonorant consonant which would otherwise form a complex onset with a following consonant of lesser sonority. Without this vowel, the sonorant consonant is unsyllabifiable given the Sonority Principle in (186). I would suggest that the initial vowel is inserted by epenthesis in order to provide a nucleus for an unsyllabifiable consonant (see (187)).

(187)   Epenthesis: ø → V̲ /__ C'
         (where V̲ characterizes an empty V-slot and C' an
         unsyllabifiable consonant)

Informally stated, a V-slot is inserted before an unsyllabifiable consonant. In the absence of feature filling assimilation rules, this vowel receives the feature values [+coronal, +high] and surfaces as [i] by default. Sutcliffe (1936) observes that a vowel is not required before a word-initial sonorant consonant when the preceding word ends in a vowel (see (188) below) suggesting that epenthesis is a phrase-level rule. I assume then that epenthesis is post-lexical since it applies both within and across word boundaries.

(188)   ma kenuʃ in?as minn tmenin bitʃtʃa li ndʒiebu
         'the pieces brought were not less than eighty'
         (Sutcliffe 1936:16)

Sutcliffe (1936) also notes that in certain words, a medial sonorant consonant need not be preceded by a vowel. Interestingly, in each of these cases, the medial sonorant is adjacent to a sonorant consonant, e.g. yilmħu 'they perceive', iħmla 'stacks of wheat', imarmru 'they murmur', izmna 'times'. The non-application of epenthesis in these cases is consistent with the Sonority Principle since the medial consonant is syllabifiable in all forms. In the first three examples, the nasal is able to form a consonant cluster with an adjacent [l] or [r]. In the last example, [m] is able to syllabify with the following syllable forming the complex onset [mn] since [m] is of the same relative sonority as the following [n].[12]

In this section I have shown that epenthesis is independently motivated in Maltese as a means of providing a nucleus for an unsyllabifiable consonant. In the following section I discuss the role of epenthesis in accounting for metathesis in plural imperfectives.

6.4 Syncope and Vocalic Mapping

I noted above that earlier analyses of the plural imperfective have attributed the position of the stem-initial vowel to consonant/vowel metathesis (see e.g. Puech 1979). Puech claims that the second stem vowel of the plural fails to undergo Syncope since the medial root consonant is [+sonorant]. The medial consonant and following vowel then undergo metathesis (see (182)). However, I have shown that this account is unable to account for the quality of the stem vowel in all verbs. Contrary to this approach, I would suggest that Syncope applies to all verbs, including those in which the medial consonant is [+sonorant]. Consequently, it is unnecessary to include the ad hoc stipulation that Syncope fails to apply just in case the medial consonant is [+sonorant]. By applying Syncope to all verbs, a medial sonorant consonant will be left in an unsyllabifiable position due to the language's syllable structure conditions. Epenthesis then applies to insert a V-slot to the left of the medial consonant. By Epenthesis, the medial consonant is thus able to syllabify as the coda of the newly-formed syllable. Within this approach the fact that a vowel occurs to the left of the medial sonorant falls out directly from the language's syllable structure conditions, in addition to the independently motivated rules of Syncope and Epenthesis. A full derivation illustrating the application of these rules will be given below.

Yet, it is still necessary to account for how the epenthetic vowel acquires its quality in plural imperfectives. I claimed above that in the absence of feature-filling assimilation, the epenthetic vowel surfaces as [i] by default. This was seen in the forms in (184) and (185) in which the epenthetic vowel is realized as [i] (see also discussion of the imperfective prefix vowel below). Given that the plural stem vowel is [i] in certain verbs, e.g. [jaħilbu], it might be argued that the plural stem vowel is simply a default vowel. However, attributing the quality of this vowel to default assignment fails since we would expect the stem vowel in the plural forms on the left in (189) to be [i] as well.

(189) | jo+korb+u | 'they groan' | jo+krob | 'he groans' |
| --- | --- | --- | --- |
| | ji+solħ+u | 'they skin' | ji+sloħ | 'he skins' |
| | je+ħemz+u | 'they pin' | je+ħmez | 'he pins' |
| | ja+ħarb+u | 'they run away' | ja+ħrab | 'he runs away' |

Rather, as shown above, the quality of the metathesized vowel is typically identical to the underlying vocalism of the stem. This then raises the question: if the final stem vowel is deleted, how does the quality of this vowel surface on the metathesized (epenthetic) vowel?

It is generally assumed that when a vowel deletes, the features which characterize that vowel also delete. Yet, for the epenthetic vowel to surface as a copy of the syncopated vowel in plural imperfectives, the stem's vocalism cannot delete. Of relevance to this point is the observation that in Maltese, Syncope need only be defined on the skeletal tier, reference to the specific quality of the vowel is unnecessary. Thus, when Syncope applies, the vowel slot deletes, whereas the vocalic melody remains afloat until there is a melody-bearing unit for it to map onto. This is reminiscent of the notion of 'stability' in tonal phenomena. It has been observed that when a vowel is deleted, the tone that was previously associated with the vowel does not delete. Instead, it links up to the nearest tone-bearing unit. Given the common view that segmental features, like tones, are autosegments, it is not surprising that the features which comprise the vocalic melody behave in a manner similar to tones.

One might suppose that the reason the melody does not delete along with the V-slot is because it is a morpheme in and of itself which "belongs" to a given verb stem whether or not it is mapped onto a melody-bearing unit. The unassociated melody that remains after Syncope is thus assuming, to a certain degree, the same status that it had prior to the phonology. Let me be more explicit. Recall that in Maltese, triliteral verbs of the first measure are associated with a consonantism, e.g. √ʃrb 'drink', and a single vocalism, e.g. /o/. These elements map onto the prosodic template prior to the phonology, as illustrated in (190) below.

(190) ʃrb, o

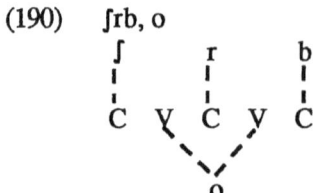

Without a template to map onto, the melodies remain unassociated, or floating. Thus, when the V-slot is deleted as a result of Syncope, we might suppose that the melody resumes the unassociated status that it had prior to the phonology.[13]

Consider now the features that make up a stem's vocalism in Maltese and thus the ones which I claim are not deleted. Only the features that distinguish one vowel from others in the system crucially characterize the vocalism. These refer to place of articulation and height since all other features, e.g. [+sonorant, -consonantal, +continuant, +voice] are redundant. In the model of feature organization employed in this work, the place and height features of a vowel form a constituent dominated by the constriction node VOC. Consequently, when Syncope applies, the VOC node and the features that it dominates remain afloat. I reformulate the rule of Syncope in (191) below (irrelevant structure has been omitted).

(191) Syncope (final version):

$$\begin{array}{ccc} C & \tilde{V} & C & V \\ | & \not| & | & | \\ [\,] & Voc & [\,] & [\,] \end{array} \rightarrow \begin{array}{ccc} C & & C & V \\ | & & | & | \\ [\,] & Voc' & [\,] & [\,] \end{array}$$

Informally stated, the V-slot and noncontrastive features of an unstressed vowel in a non-final open syllable delete. The VOC node remains afloat and will remain as such unless there is an empty V-slot available for it to map onto. Recall that in imperfective plurals with a medial sonorant consonant, Epenthesis provides precisely this. Consequently, by universal association conventions (Haraguchi 1977, Clements & Ford 1979, Pulleyblank 1986), the floating vocalic melody will map onto the epenthetic V-slot in a feature-filling manner. For concreteness, I refer to the association of the floating VOC node to an empty V-slot as Vocalic Mapping and represent it as in (192).

(192) Vocalic Mapping:

A floating vocalic melody maps onto an unspecified V-slot (where VOC' indicates an unassociated vocalic melody and V̲ an empty V-slot).

As I will show in the formal analysis in section 8 below, by incorporating Syncope, Epenthesis and Vocalic Mapping into the analysis of metathesis, we are able to account for the observation that it is the underlying quality of the stem vowel which surfaces in plural imperfective verbs. However, before doing so, it is important to point out that the application of two of these rules extends in a simple way to the realization of the imperfective prefix vowel.

7. THE REALIZATION OF THE IMPERFECTIVE PREFIX VOWEL

In section 4 above, it was shown that the imperfective prefix vowel in verbs of the first measure is typically identical in quality to the underlying vocalism of the stem.[14] One of the initial observations made in this chapter was that it is only in the first measure that the quality of the prefix vowel differs, i.e. it can be realized as /i/, /e/, /o/, /a/. In all other measures which contain a prefix vowel, this vowel always surfaces as [i], regardless of the quality of following vowels. This is illustrated in (193) below in which perfective and imperfective forms of representative fifth through tenth measure verbs are compared with [ja?sam] 'he broke' of the first measure (the parenthesized [i] is epenthetic).

(193)

Measure	Perfective	Imperfective	
First	ʔasam	ja+ʔsam	to break
Fifth	tʔattel	ji+tʔattel	to destroy oneself
Sixth	tbierek	ji+tbierek	to be blessed
Seventh	(i)nʔabad	ji+nʔabad	to be caught
Eighth	(i)rtabat	ji+rtabat	to be bound
Ninth	ħdaar	ji+ħdaar	to grow green
Tenth	stenbaħ	ji+stenbaħ	to awaken

Two properties of first measure verbs have been observed which distinguish them from verbs of other measures. First, it is only in the first measure that the quality of the prefix vowel may differ, and second, it is only in the first measure that stem vowels undergo Syncope. I would suggest that these observations receive a straightforward account given my claim that the melody of a syncopated vowel remains afloat; only a floating melody maps to the prefix vowel. Unlike the plural imperfectives discussed above, the V-slot onto which the melody maps is not provided by epenthesis. Rather, we may assume that the prefix vowel enters into the derivation as an empty V-slot. This is a reasonable proposal given that in the absence of feature-filling assimilation, the prefix vowel surfaces as [i], identical to the language's epenthetic vowel. Since the feature values [+coronal, +high] are already independently motivated as default values for vowels, incorporating them into the analysis of the prefix vowel comes at no extra cost.

Accounting for the realization of the imperfective prefix vowel by Syncope and Vocalic Mapping is advantageous for a number of reasons. First, it accounts for the asymmetry observed between verbs of the first measure and those of other measures. Second, it obviates the need to posit that an additional rule, e.g. Prefix Vowel Assimilation, is responsible for deriving the quality of this vowel. Third, the quality of the imperfective prefix vowel and that of the imperfective plural stem vowel can be accounted for by the same operations, thus resulting in a more unified analysis. In the following section, I provide full derivations illustrating how the proposals in this and preceding sections allow for the realization of both the prefix and metathesized vowels.

8. A NONLINEAR ACCOUNT OF METATHESIS

8.1 Analysis

In the preceding sections I have motivated three independent rules: Syncope, Epenthesis and Vocalic Mapping. The first two are independently motivated rules of Maltese, and the latter a universal association convention. As illustrated in the derivation of [jaħarbu] 'they run away' in (194), the application of all three rules results in metathesis, whereas Syncope and Vocalic Mapping together account for the realization of the prefix vowel.

(194)
Lexical
Input jV́+ħarab
Syncope jV+ħ rab
 a'
Vocalic Mapping jV+ħ rab
 ˋa'

Input jáħrab+u
Syncope jáħr bu
 a'
Vocalic Mapping n/a

Post-lexical
Epenthesis jaħVr bu
 a'
Vocalic Mapping jaħVr bu
 ˋa'
Output [jaħarbu]
 'they run away'

As shown in this derivation, Syncope applies first to delink the vocalic melody from superordinate structure of the first stem vowel. By Vocalic Mapping, the floating melody maps leftward onto the empty V-slot of the prefix. With the addition of the plural suffix, Syncope applies to the second stem vowel. Yet, since there is no empty slot at this point in the derivation, the melody remains afloat. Note that due to the second application of Syncope the medial sonorant consonant is in an unsyllabifiable position. Thus, in the post-lexical component an empty V-slot is inserted to the left of the sonorant consonant by the rule of Epenthesis. At this point, the floating melody is able to map onto the V-slot by Vocalic Mapping.

Although not evident in the above derivation, I assume that general Tier Conflation occurs prior to Syncope. The verbs for which this assumption is particularly crucial will be discussed just below. It is nonetheless important to point out now that even though the consonantal and vocalic melodies are conflated in (194), spreading the vocalic features of /a/ across the intervening consonant /ħ/ will not result in crossed association lines. It will be recalled from chapter IV that the transparency of an intervening consonant to rules of vowel assimilation is expressed in our model by the partial segregation of consonant and vowel place features, as shown below (irrelevant structure is omitted).

(195)

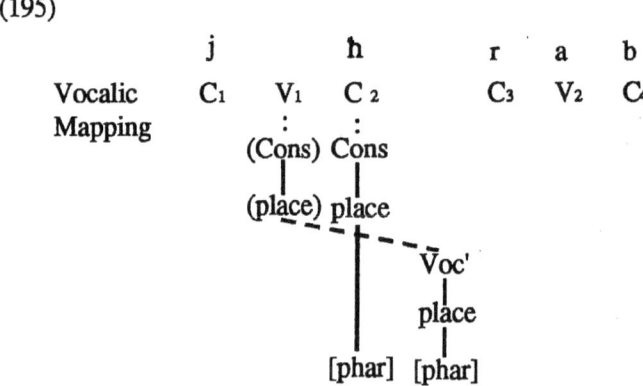

The immediate output of Vocalic Mapping in (195) will be as in (196).

Maltese

(196)

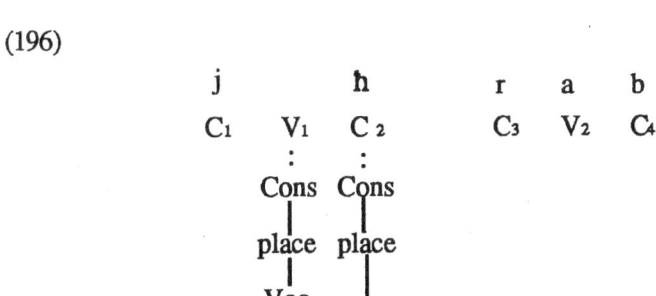

Recall from chapter IV that all instances of a given place feature are arrayed on the same tier. Thus, the output of assimilation shown in (196) results in a configuration in which $[phar]_{CONS}$ precedes $[phar]_{VOC}$ whereas the reverse ordering obtains for the segments (or skeletal slots) to which each of these features (indirectly) link, i.e. $V_1 < C_2$. This then violates the Ordering Constraint. In chapter IV I proposed that violations such as this are eliminated by Cloning. The formulation of Cloning as it pertains to the representation in (196) is stated in (197).

(197) Cloning
    i. Associate, in accordance with general well-formedness conditions, a copy of $[phar]_{VOC}$ to the VOC place node of V_1
    ii. Delink the association line from the VOC place node of V_1 to the original $[phar]_{VOC}$

By applying Cloning to (196), the representation will no longer violate the Ordering Constraint, as shown in (198).

(198)

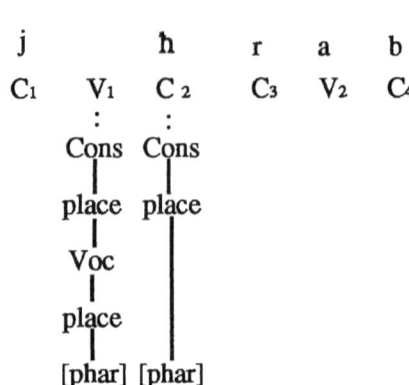

The test cases for the analysis of metathesis proposed above are verbs in which Guttural Assimilation also applies. Recall that accounting for the realization of the metathesized vowel in all plural imperfectives was shown to be problematic for an analysis in which metathesis is viewed as a one-step process. Within this approach, Guttural Assimilation would need to apply before metathesis in a form such as [jaħilbu], yet after metathesis in order to obtain the correct form in [jifilħu]. In (199) below, I provide the derivations of these two verbs within the view of metathesis as the product of more than one operation.

It will be observed in (199) that the rule of Guttural Assimilation is considered to be a postcyclic lexical rule. Motivation for this comes first from the observation that Guttural Assimilation applies in both derived and non-derived environments. For example, in [laħaʔ] 'he reached' < /liħiʔ/, Guttural Assimilation applies within the stem. Conversely, in [ja+ħdem] 'he works' < /jV+ħidim/, the rule applies to the prefix vowel in the derived imperfective verb (note that I-lowering changes the last stem vowel to [e]). Since GA applies in both derived and non-derived environments, the rule is best treated as postcyclic. Moreover, nominals do not appear to be affected by this rule, e.g. riħa 'smell', riħi 'relaxation', tberbiʔ 'lavishness' (cf. tberbaʔ 'to lavish'). I am not aware of any cases in which the rule applies across word boundaries.

(199)

Lexical Input	jV́+ħilib	jV́+filiħ
Syncope	jV+ħ lib	jV+f liħ
	i'	i'
Vocalic Mapping	jV+ħ lib	jV+f liħ
	i'	i'

Input	jiħlib+u	jifliħ+u
Syncope	jiħl bu	jifl ħu
	i'	i'

Postcyclic

Guttural Assimilation	jaħl bu	-n/a-
	i'	

Post-lexical

Epenthesis	jaħVl bu	jifVl ħu
	i'	i'
Vocalic Mapping	jaħVl bu	jifVl ħu
	i'	i'
Output	[jaħilbu]	[jifilħu]
	'they milk'	'they are strong'

The derivation in (199) is identical to that in (194) except that Guttural Assimilation applies in the postcyclic component. This changes the prefix vowel of the first verb, its only target, from /i/ to [a]. After Guttural Assimilation, Epenthesis inserts an empty V-slot to the left of the sonorant consonant and the floating melody maps onto this available slot. This predicts the correct output in all forms. Note that all rules are intrinsically ordered as a result of their stratal assignments. By viewing metathesis as the product of more than one operation, we are able to account for the full range of plural imperfective verbs. Central to this account is the view that Syncope does not delete the vocalic constituent of the vowel. Rather, it remains afloat. Not only does this account for the failure of Guttural Assimilation to apply to the plural stem vowel, it also extends in a simple way to the realization of the prefix vowel.

8.2   Summary and Implications

Consonant/vowel metathesis has traditionally been treated as a one-step process in which the linear ordering of segments in a string switches. Although great advancements have been made to eliminate linear notation in processes such as assimilation and dissimilation, the formal mechanisms used to represent metathesis in nonlinear phonology have changed little. Many current analyses of metathesis continue to make use of a linear transformational notation and treat it as a one-step operation. As I have shown for Maltese, this view of metathesis is unsatisfactory. Alternatively, I have suggested that C/V metathesis is the product of three elementary operations: delete (Syncope), insert (Epenthesis) and associate (Vocalic Mapping). Positing an additional rule of metathesis simply duplicates rules which are already independently motivated in the phonology (Kenstowicz 1981). This approach is advantageous for a number of reasons. For example, it provides a straightforward account of the seemingly complex and poorly understood process of metathesis by drawing on elementary operations of nonlinear phonology. Moreover, under the assumption that metathesis involves more than one operation, it elucidates why this process is less common cross-linguistically than, for example, processes such as assimilation which could arguably by viewed as the result of one or at most two operations: spread, delink.

9.   FURTHER IMPLICATIONS

9.1   Tier Conflation and Total Vowel Assimilation

McCarthy (1989) suggests that total vowel movement across an intervening consonant as in consonant/vowel metathesis implies the complete segregation of consonant and vowel melodies. In other words, vowel movement would need to apply in the pre-Tier Conflation stage of the phonology. In the derivations above, I have implicitly assumed that Tier Conflation applies at a relatively early stage in the phonology. Moreover, total vowel assimilation occurs across intervening consonants even after Tier Conflation has applied. In this section, I will briefly make explicit my assumptions concerning approximately when in the derivation Tier Conflation applies.

Maltese

In section 4 above, it was argued that general Tier Conflation must apply prior to the application of Guttural Assimilation. If this were not the case, we would predict both vowels of verbs such as [ħadem] < /ħidim/ 'he worked' to surface as [a]. Invoking Tier Conflation prior to the application of Guttural Assimilation would require conflation to occur at least by the postcyclic lexical level. Since Vocalic Mapping may apply after Guttural Assimilation, as seen above, is cannot be assumed that consonant and vowel melodies are completely segregated when total vowel assimilation occurs.

In the derivations above, I have assumed that Tier Conflation actually applies prior to the postcyclic component. To illustrate why this is so I first outline the problems associated with assuming that Tier Conflation applies in the postcyclic component just prior to Guttural Assimilaton. The derivation of [jaħilbu] in (200) serves to illustrate. As will be observed, both V-slots of the stem are multiply-linked to a single instance of /i/. Note that Vocalic Mapping, as formulated above, will not be applicable since the vocalic melody will always be associated to a V-slot during the derivation. For the sake of argument I will assume that this is not problematic and simply spread the vowel features of an associated melody, which I refer to as Vowel Assimilation.

204 The Interaction of Front Vowels and Coronal Consonants

(200) Tier Conflation applying in the postcyclic component

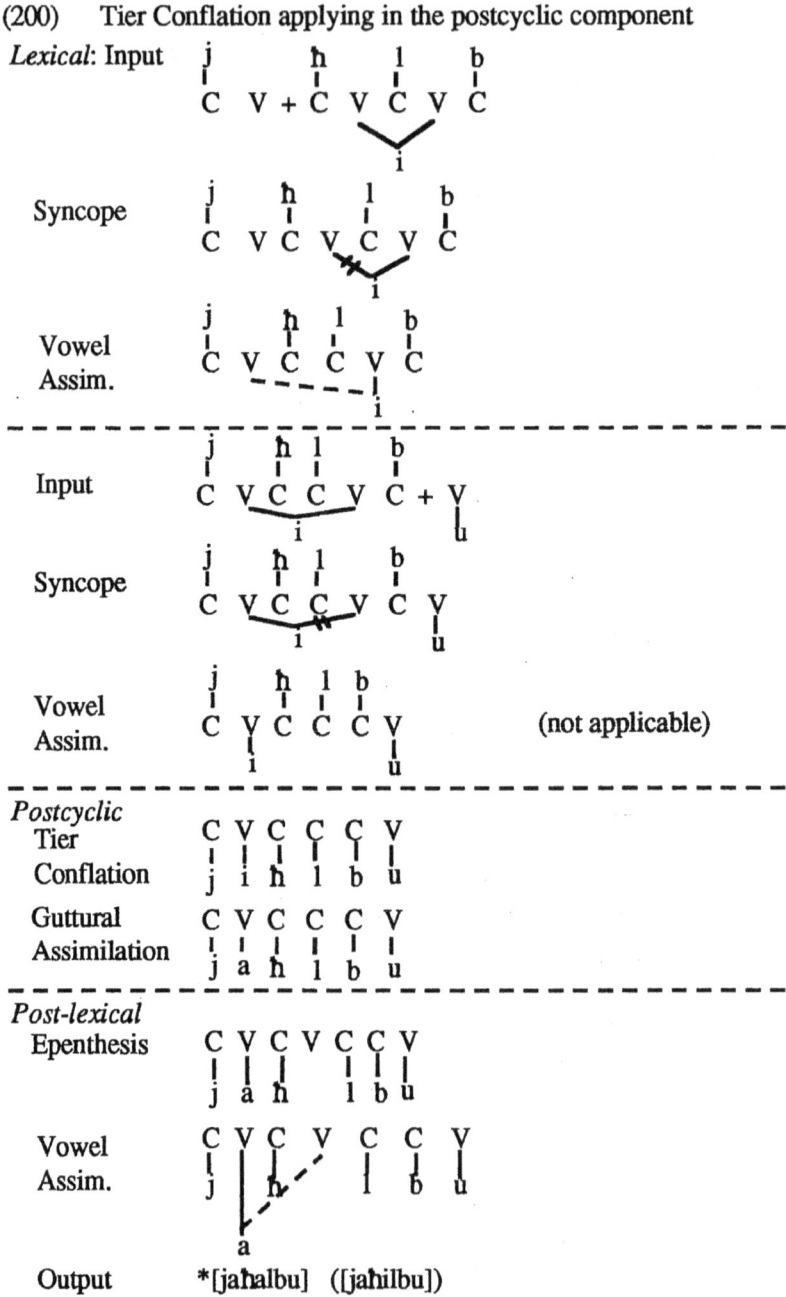

Maltese

In the derivation in (200) above, Syncope applies first to delink the vocalic melody from the stem-initial V-slot. Following this, vowel assimilation applies and, as a result, the melody is multiply-linked to both the V-slot of the prefix and to that of the final stem vowel. With the second application of Syncope the melody becomes dissociated from the second stem vowel. This leaves the melody linked only to the V-slot of the prefix. It is this association which proves problematic, as will be seen. Tier Conflation applies in the postcyclic component prior to Guttural Assimilation, as independently required. With the application of Guttural Assimilation, the prefix vowel changes to [a]. But note that it is now this vowel quality that will map onto the V-slot provided by Epenthesis. As shown by the output, assuming that Tier Conflation applies this late in the derivation predicts the incorrect form of the verb.

In order to generate the correct output, it must be assumed that Tier Conflation applies at a point before the second application of Syncope. In this way, the vowel melody will split creating two instances of /i/, one linked to the V-slot of the prefix vowel and the other linked to the V-slot of the final stem vowel. When Syncope applies to the stem-final vowel, the melody will remain afloat, and consequently, be unaffected by the rule of Guttural Assimilation. Consistent with the derivations in (194) and (199) above, the floating melody of the syncopated stem-final vowel can then spread across the intervening consonant to the epenthetic V-slot and be correctly realized as [i]. For simplicity, I assume that Tier Conflation applies prior to the first application of Syncope.

As I have shown above, total vowel assimilation is able to apply in the post-Tier Conflation stage of the phonology. By drawing on an enriched model of feature organization in which place of articulation in consonants and vowels is partially segregated, we are able to account for total vowel spreading without invoking complete planar segregation.

9.2 Default Rules and Underspecification

I claim above that [i] is the default vowel in Maltese. Specifically, the feature values [+coronal, +high] are assigned to an empty V-slot in the absence of feature-filling assimilation rules. This was shown to be the case both with respect to the imperfective prefix vowel and the epenthetic vowel. Proponents of Radical Underspecification propose that the presence of a default rule requires that all segments of that language are unspecified for this feature value in underlying representation (see e.g. Archangeli 1984, Archangeli & Pulleyblank 1986). Contrary to this view, I argue that in Maltese, instances of /i/ which occur (at least) within the stem, e.g. [bidel] < /bidil/ 'he changed', can not be completely unspecified for the default values [+coronal, +high]. Consequently, there are underlying /i/'s specified for the feature values [+coronal, +high], as well as empty V-slots which may acquire these same features by default assignment. In this section I show why this assumption is crucial.

Consider first the consequences of assuming that all surface instances of [i] are empty V-slots underlyingly. Within this approach, verb stems which I have claimed have /i/ vocalism would simply contain V-slots in UR. For some verbs, this assumption is not problematic. For example, the underlying form of the singular imperfective of the verb [jibdel] would be as in (201a), in which all vowels are completely unspecified for features.

(201) a.　　　　　　C V + C V C V C
　　　　　　　　　 | | | |
　　　　　　　　　 j   b   d   l

b.　　　　　　　　 C V   C   C V C
　　Syncope　　　 | | | |
　　　　　　　　　 j   b   d   l

c.　　　　　　　　 C V   C   C V C
　　I-lowering　　| | | : |
　　　　　　　　　 j   b   d e l

d.　　　　　　　　 C V   C   C V C
　　Default　　　 | : | | | |
　　Assignment　 j i   b   d e l

In (201) above, Syncope deletes the stem-initial V-slot as in b). Note that since the V-slot has no features linked to it, nothing will remain afloat when Syncope applies. The second stem vowel surfaces as [e]. There are two means of deriving the quality of this vowel. Either the rule of I-lowering could be reformulated so that it targets an empty V-slot, i.e. $\underline{V} \rightarrow e/\_\_ C\#$, as shown above, or alternatively, the default

Maltese 207

rules assigning the feature values [+coronal, +high] could apply first, followed by I-lowering, in its orginal formulation, i.e. i → e/ __ C#. Either account will give the correct output. The prefix vowel surfaces as [i] by default assignment.

A similar scenario obtains for first measure verbs in which Guttural Assimilation applies. Recall from the earlier discussion that the rule of Guttural Assimilation is stated such that /i/ changes to [a] when adjacent to a guttural consonant. An alternative solution, which incorporates the view that all surface [i]'s are empty V-slots underlyingly, is to redefine Guttural Assimilation so that its target is an unspecified V-slot, as stated in (202).

(202)   V → a % __ ħ, ʔ
An empty V-slot is realized as [a] when adjacent to a guttural consonant. (% indicates 'mirror image')

By incorporating these revisions, the derivation of the singular imperfective of [jilħaʔ] will be as in (203) below.

(203)   Input   C V + C V C V C
                         | | | |
                         j   l   ħ   ʔ
                         C V   C   C V C
        Syncope | | | |
                         j   l   ħ   ʔ
                         C V   C   C V C
        Guttural | | | : |
        Assimilation   j   l   ħ a ʔ
                         C V   C   C V C
        Default | : | | | |
        Assignment   j i   l   ħ a ʔ

This derivation is similar to the preceding one except that the stem-final V-slot changes to [a] by Guttural Assimilation. Default Assignment will fill in features on the prefix vowel, correctly predicting its surface quality to be [i].

The revised formulation of Guttural Assimilation in (202) predicts that the rule will apply to any empty V-slot adjacent to a guttural consonant. Although this predicts the correct output above, it generates the incorrect forms of, for example, ninth measure verbs such as [ji?raas] 'he becomes embittered', [jiħdaar] 'it grows green'. Recall that in measures other than the first, the prefix vowel is always realized as [i] regardless of the stem's vocalism. To illustrate, I give the derivation of the verb [jiħdaar]. Verbs of the ninth measure are derived from a stem of the form CCVVC, which again corresponds to the third person masculine singular perfective form of the verb. Consistent with the derivation in (203), we may assume first, that the prefix vowel starts out as an empty V-slot and second, that Guttural Assimilation targets an empty V-slot.

(204)

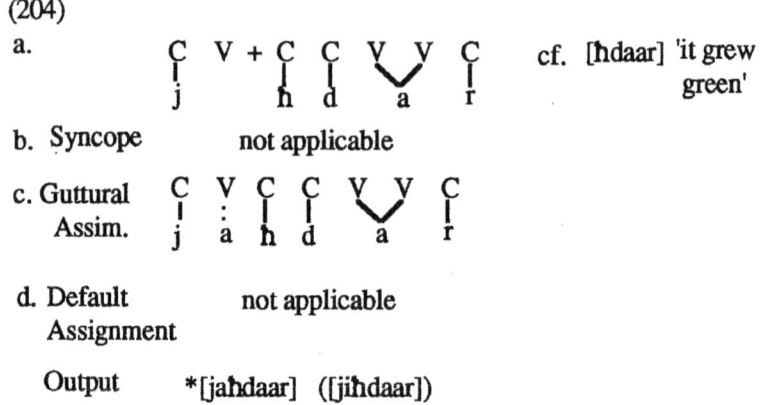

a.   cf. [ħdaar] 'it grew green'

b. Syncope   not applicable

c. Guttural Assim.

d. Default Assignment   not applicable

Output   *[jaħdaar] ([jiħdaar])

Syncope is not applicable since the context for the rule is not met. Note that by defining Guttural Assimilation on an empty V-slot, the prefix vowel will be incorrectly realized as [a] since the stem-initial consonant is guttural.

An alternative approach is to assign the default features [+coronal, +high] before the application of Guttural Assimilation. This is not unlike an approach in which all surface instances of [i] are underlyingly specified for place and height, as assumed in the works of Brame (1972) and Puech (1979). However, this approach is shown to be equally problematic as is illustrated by comparing the derivations of [jiħdaar] < /jV+ħdaar/ 'it grew green' and [jaħdem] < /jV+ħidim/ 'he works'.

Maltese

(205)

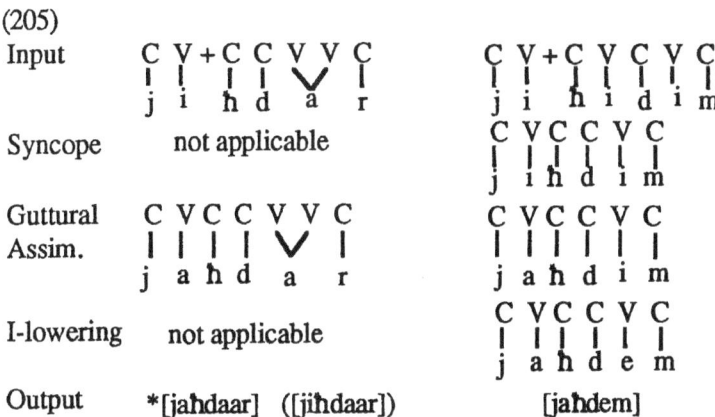

As these derivations reveal, assuming that the prefix vowel enters into the derivation specified as /i/ incorrectly predicts the prefix vowel of [jiħdaar] to be [a]. Consequently, specifying both the prefix and stem vowels as /i/ is just as unsatisfactory as assuming that they all start out as unspecified V-slots. In order to generate the correct output in all forms we must be able to distinguish among those vowels which undergo Guttural Assimilation and those that do not, despite the fact that they are adjacent to a guttural consonant.

This distinction, I would suggest, can be captured in simple terms by assuming that the occurrence of a given default feature does not entail that all segments are unspecified for this feature underlyingly. In this way, we distinguish between underlying instances of /i/ which are specified for place and height features underlyingly, and vowels which enter into the derivation as empty V-slots. By maintaining this distinction, we are able to account for the correct quality of vowels as illustrated by comparing the (partial) representations of [jiħdaar] in (206a) and [jaħdem] in (206b) just below.

(206)

	a.	b.
Input	CV+CCVVC | | | ∨ | j ḥ d a r	CV+CVCVC | | | | | | j ḥ i d i m
Syncope	---	CVC CVC | | | | | | j ḥ d i m i'
Vocalic Mapping	---	CVC CVC | \ | | | | j ḥ d i m i'
Guttural Assim.	---	CVC CVC | | | | | | j a ḥ d i m
I-lowering	---	CVC CVC | | | | | | j a ḥ d e m
Default Assignment	CVC CVVC | : | | ∨ | j i ḥ d a r	---
Output	[jiḥdaar]	[jaḥdem]

In each of the derivations, the prefix vowel enters into the derivation as an empty V-slot. Conversely, stem-internal vowels are specified. The context for Syncope is only met in the verb in (b). By this rule, the stem-initial V-slot is deleted while leaving the vocalic melody afloat. With the application of Vocalic Mapping, the floating melody maps onto the empty V-slot of the prefix. In (a), the prefix remains unspecified for features since Vocalic Mapping is not applicable. Recall that only a floating melody can link onto an unspecified V-slot. At this point, Guttural Assimilation, whose target is /i/, will only affect the prefix vowel of verb (b) thus changing it to [a]. In (a) the vowel still remains unspecified and is ultimately assigned the feature values [+coronal, +high] by default. By incorporating the underlying distinction between the unspecified prefix vowel and the specified stem vowels, we predict the correct output in each form.

As I have shown, the existence of a given default value need not imply that all surface occurrences of this value are unspecified in underlying representation. This corroborates earlier evidence discussed in Herzallah (1990) and Hualde (1991). These findings suggest that default feature values are independent of the underlying feature specification of a given system, available perhaps universally or on a language-specific basis as a means of filling in unspecified segments. Maltese

NOTES

1. Several people associated with the Permanent Mission of Malta to the United Nations graciously served as consultants. I am particularly grateful to Mr. Michael Bartolo, Mr. Tony Borġ and Mr. George Vella and, in particular, Mr. Anton Mifsud-Bonnici.

2. In addition to the vowels in (134a), Maltese also includes the diphthong [iə] (orthographically ie) in its vowel inventory (see e.g. Aquilina 1959).

3. Note that in McCarthy's account of Arabic, all labial consonants are grouped together in a single class.

4. This observation reflects a strong tendency in the sequencing of root consonants in Maltese. Among approximately 300 triliteral strong verbs, there are 9 exceptions: √str 'cover, veil', √tsl 'arrive', √fsd 'cause to bleed', √ħsd 'reap', √nsdʒ 'weave', √mʃt 'comb', √lhʔ 'reach', √shʔ 'pound', √hʔr 'oppress' (based on my examination of the lexicons of Bugeja 1982 and Busuttil 1981).

5. This also appears as [joħ noʔ/joħonʔu]. See discussion of Imperfective Vowel Change further below.

6. The fourth measure is obsolete in Maltese. In verbs of the second and third measures, there is no prefix vowel. These latter measures will be discussed in chapter VII.

7. There are certains verbs in which one of the root consonants is orthographically 'h' or 'għ'. I have not included this class of verbs in the discussion in this chapter since, although they pattern in a manner similar to triliteral strong verbs, there are certain significant differences. In particular, the orthographic consonant is generally not realized phonetically. Providing an full analysis of these verbs is beyond the scope of this work. However, I refer the reader to the insightful discussions in, most notably, Brame (1972) and Puech (1979).

8. [u] does not occur in verb stems of the first measure.

9. The change from [+high] to [-high] can be achieved in several ways, the choice of which is not crucial to this analysis. We might suppose, for example, that there is a constraint which prohibits the feature combination *[pharyngeal, +high]. In order to repair

representations bearing this combination, one might posit a further feature-changing rule of the form [pharyngeal]$_{VOC}$ → [-high]. Alternatively, we could assume that the redundancy rule in (157) itself applies in a feature-changing manner, thus obviating the need to posit the additional negative constraint in the grammar (for related discussion, see Mohanan 1991).

10. The realization of the prefix vowel as [i] in this and other cases is discussed in detail in chapter VII.

11. The definite article assimilates completely to a following coronal consonant (see e.g. Comrie 1980).

12. Epenthesis also applies before a word-initial geminate consonant, as illustrated in (i) below. As will be discussed in chapter VII, the geminate consonant is formed by complete assimilation of the imperfective prefix consonant to a following coronal obstruent.

(i) Triliteral verbs
a. Second binyan

	Perfective	Imperfective	Gloss
	daħħak	iddaħħak	to amuse
	ʃemmeʃ	iʃʃemmeʃ	to sun
cf.	fettaħħ	tfettaħħ	to open
	naʔʔas	tnaʔʔas	to lessen

I assume that the initial [i] in these forms is also the result of the epenthesis rule in (187). However, unlike the forms in (184) and (185) above, the initial segment cannot be considered unsyllabifiable as a consequence of the Sonority Principle. Rather, I would suggest that it is unsyllabifiable since word-initial geminate consonants are not permitted in Maltese. Consequently, in cases in which a word-initial geminate consonant is created by morpheme concatenation, epenthesis applies to create a nucleus for the initial consonant.

13. One might also assume that there is a special principle in Maltese which overrules the more general convention which typically deletes a vocalic melody in syncope rules. For example, we might suppose that in Maltese conventions cannot totally delete morphemes.

14. The only examples in which this is not the case is when the vocalism /i/ is subsequently changed to [a] by Guttural Assimilation.

VII

Coronal Vowel and Consonant Parallelisms in Maltese Arabic

0. INTRODUCTION

In Maltese Arabic, the imperfective form of the triliteral verb is formed by the addition of a prefix CV- to the verb stem. As was shown in the preceding chapter, the quality of this vowel is typically identical to the underlying vocalism of the imperfective stem. However, in verbs which begin with a stem-initial coronal obstruent, the prefix vowel is systematically realized as [i]. It is the exceptional realization of the prefix vowel in these verbs which serves as the basis for discussion in this chapter. I argue that the patterning of the front vowel [i] and coronal obstruents in these cases is most insightfully viewed as a consequence of the fact that these sounds are members of the natural class of coronal sounds. The occurrence of [i] in these forms is analyzed as the result of Vowel Coronal Assimilation, a vowel-to-consonant assimilation rule in which the prefix vowel acquires the place specification [coronal] from a following coronal obstruent. The realization of [i] before coronal obstruents parallels in many ways the realization of [a] which under certain circumstances surfaces as the result of assimilation to the place of articulation of an adjacent guttural consonant.

The second and third person feminine imperfective consonant prefix also assimilates to a stem-initial coronal obstruent. In the default case, this consonant surfaces as [t]. In the latter part of this chapter, I discuss the rule of Consonant Coronal Assimilation which accounts for this assimilation. As will become evident, there are a number of striking parallelisms between Consonant Coronal Assimilation and Vowel Coronal Assimilation. Due to these similarities, I claim that the two rules can be amalgamated into a single rule of Coronal Assimilation, thus providing a simpler and more insightful analysis. Clearly, this is only feasible within a feature theory in which front vowels and coronal consonants are considered to be members of the same natural class.

Further parallelisms are drawn between the default consonant [t] and the default vowel [i] in Maltese. In addition to surfacing as the language's epenthetic segments, these sounds are also the realizations of the imperfective prefix segments in the default case. It is proposed that default assignment for place of articulation in Maltese reduces to a single default rule which assigns the feature [coronal] regardless of whether the segment in question is a consonant or vowel. By positing a single default rule we recognize the non-arbitrary relationship between these segments.

The organization of this chapter is as follows. In the first section, I discuss the realization of the prefix vowel before stem-initial coronal obstruents. In the following section, I show why assuming that the quality of this vowel is the result of default assignment is problematic. Next, I motivate the rule of Vowel Coronal Assimilation. The following section focusses on the rule of Consonant Coronal Assimilation and the default consonant in Maltese. In the final section, I discuss the parallelisms between the rules of Consonant and Vowel Coronal Assimilation and between the realizations of the default consonant and vowel in Maltese.

1. THE REALIZATION OF THE IMPERFECTIVE PREFIX VOWEL BEFORE STEM-INITIAL CORONAL OBSTRUENTS

1.1 Description

In the preceding chapter I showed that the imperfective prefix vowel of the first measure strong verb is typically identical to the underlying vocalism of the stem. This generalization holds regardless of whether or not the stem vowel of the imperfective differs from that of the perfective. There are a number of verbs which prove exceptional to this generalization. Representative examples are provided in (207).

(207) Perfect   Imperfective sing.
      daħal   jidħol   'to enter'
      dalam   jidlam   'to grow dark'
      talab   jitlob   'to pray'
      tebaħ   jitboħ   'to cook'
      siket   jiskot   'to be silent'
      seħet   jisħet   'to curse'
      zelaʔ   jizloʔ   'to slip'
      dʒabar   jidʒbor   'to collect'
      ʃorob   jiʃrob   'to drink'

The verbs in (207) are exceptions to the general formation of the imperfective prefix vowel since unlike the verbs discussed in chapter VI, the prefix vowel is not identical to the stem vocalism of the imperfective. Rather, it systematically surfaces as [i]. This was first observed, I believe, by Brame (1972) (see also Puech 1978). Common to all these verbs is the presence of a stem-initial coronal obstruent, anterior or non-anterior. In fact, in all strong verbs of the first measure which begin with a coronal obstruent, the prefix vowel is realized as [i].[1]

The majority of verbs in (207) occur with [o] as the vowel of the imperfective stem, either with /o/ in UR, e.g. [jiʃrob]/[ʃorob], or /o/ acquired as a result of Imperfective Vowel Change, e.g. [jitlob]/[talab]. The lack of examples with /a/ in the imperfective stem is due to the fact that many verbs with /a/ in the perfective stem change the stem vowels to [o] in the imperfective. This frequently occurs in verbs in which all three of the root consonants are nonguttural although, as discussed in chapter VI, even in verbs with guttural consonants, the stem vowel frequently (and unpredictably) changes to [o] in the imperfective. The quality of the stem vowels in (207) is also limited due to the fact that verbs which have /i/ as the underlying stem vocalism have not been included, e.g. [yisraʔ] < /jV+siriʔ/ 'he steals' ([seraʔ] 'he stole'), [jidneb] < /jV+dinib/ 'he sins' ([dineb] 'he sinned'). In these verbs the realization of the prefix vowel as [i] is to be expected as it is identical to the underlying vocalic melody. Thus, the clearest examples illustrating the exceptional realization of the prefix vowel before coronal obstruents are those in which the stem vowel of the imperfective is [o].

In (208) below, I compare verbs such as those given in (207) with verbs in which the stem-initial consonant is not a coronal obstruent. In the examples in (208b) the prefix vowel is identical to the imperfective stem vowel as expected, whereas in the verbs in (a), the prefix vowel is always [i]. The realization of the prefix vowel as [i] in the examples in (208a) is thus clearly related to the presence of a stem-initial coronal obstruent.

(208)a.   b.

Imperf.	Perf.		Imperf.	Perf.	
jidhol	dahal	'to enter'	jolʔot	laʔat	'to hit'
jitboʔ	tebaʔ	'to shut'	jolfoʔ	lefaʔ	'to sob'
jisboʔ	sebaʔ	'to exceed'	jonfoʔ	nefaʔ	'to spend'
jisrom	saram	'to puzzle'	jobrom	baram	'to twist'
jiskot	siket	'to be silent'	joʔtol	ʔatel	'to kill'
jizloʔ	zelaʔ	'to slip'	johloʔ	holoʔ	'to make trouble'
jiʃrob	ʃorob	'to drink'	joktor	kotor	'to abound'
jidʒbor	dʒabar	'to collect'	jobsor	basar	'to predict'

1.2 Default Assignment

The most obvious means of accounting for the occurrence of [i] in the verbs in (207, 208a) is to attribute the quality of the prefix vowel to default, given my claim that the default vowel in Maltese is [i]. However, as I show in this section, attributing the entire quality of the prefix vowel to default is problematic.

Recall from the preceding chapter that in first measure verbs the imperfective stem vocalism maps onto the V-slot of the prefix by Vocalic Mapping. In order to attribute the quality of the prefix vowel in the above verbs to default, one might suppose that Vocalic Mapping fails to apply, blocked by an intervening coronal obstruent. The prefix vowel would then be assigned the feature values [coronal, +high] by default. As discussed in chapters III and IV, the selective opacity of segments is generally attributed to the Line-Crossing Prohibition. It was shown, for example, that vowel harmony is blocked in Turkish just in case a palatalized velar or lateral consonant intervenes between the rule's target and trigger. The opacity of these segments is accounted for in simple terms given the consonant's specification for secondary

Coronal Vowel and Consonant Parallelisms in Maltese

vowel features. In a similar manner, we might suppose that coronal obstruents in Maltese are specified for some value of the feature or node that spreads from the imperfective stem vowel. As a result of this specification, spreading the vowel features across an intervening coronal obstruent would result in crossed association lines. However, as I will show, this approach is problematic for a number of reasons.

First, consider the verbs [jidlam] < /jV+dalam/, [jiʃrob] < /jV+ʃorob] and [jisħet] < /jV+seħet/. In order to invoke the No Line-Crossing principle coronal obstruents must block the features which spread from /a/, /o/ and /e/ to the prefix vowel. I assume that /a/ is specified underlyingly as [pharyngeal], /o/ as [labial, -high] (contrasting with /u/ which is [labial, +high]), and /e/ as [coronal, -high] (contrasting with /i/ which is [coronal, +high]). Vocalic Mapping, i.e. the mapping of unassociated features onto an empty vowel slot, may thus be defined on the VOC node since this single node dominates all relevant features that spread from the vowels. Hence, in order for coronal obstruents to block the spreading of vowel features, coronal obstruents, to the exclusion of all other consonants, must be specified for a VOC node, as shown in (209) (I include the V-slot of the vowel trigger for clarity).

(209)

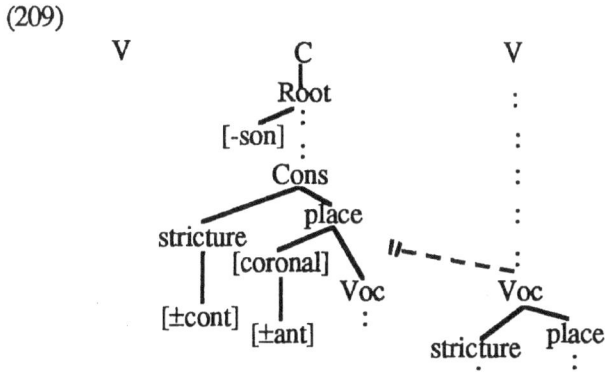

This characterization of coronal obstruents is problematic, however. As seen in the consonantal inventory of Maltese in chapter VI, section 1.1, the language has only a single set of plain coronal consonants. Thus, specifying coronals, both anterior and non-anterior, for vocalic features is unmotivated.

Let me point out that the problem is not associated with any particular model of feature organization. Consider, for example, the feature organization proposed in Sagey (1986). Within this model, we may assume that /a/ is specified as [+low], /o/ as [+round,-high] and /e/ as [-back,-high]. A single spreading rule can be defined on the Place node as illustrated in (210) below, since this is the nearest superordinate node which dominates all spreading features. Since coronal obstruents are also specified for a Place node, they would naturally block the spreading of the Place node from the vowels. Yet, as is evident, coronal obstruents are not the only consonants specified with a Place node in Maltese. All consonants would then be predicted to be opaque.

(210) Feature Organization (based on Sagey 1986):

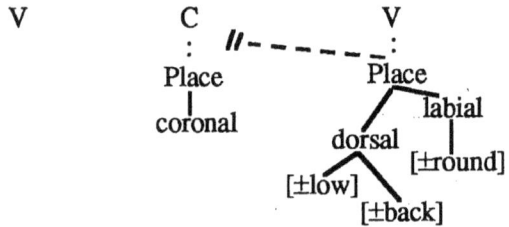

An alternative in Sagey's framework is to define spreading on the dorsal node as shown in (211). This can be accomplished by specifying /o/ as [+back] instead of [+round], a revision which does not appear to be problematic. In this view, dorsal consonants are predicted to be opaque. This is incorrect, however, as evidenced by verbs such as [joktor] /jV+kotor/ 'it increases', [jikʃef] /jV+kiʃif/ 'he discovers'. Moreover, in order for coronal obstruents, both anterior and non-anterior, to block the spreading of dorsal, they too must be specified with a dorsal node.

(211)

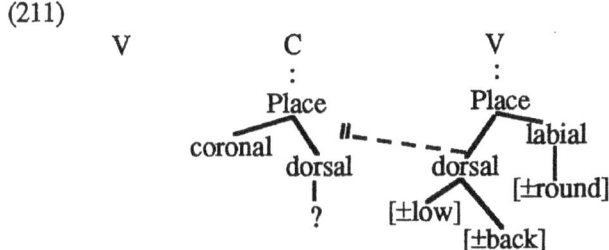

Since dorsal dominates the vocalic features [high, back, low], we must assume once again that coronals are specified for a secondary (vocalic) articulation. The problem then is that in order to invoke No Line-Crossing coronal obstruents, to the exclusion of all other consonants, must be specified for vocalic features, a specification which is otherwise unmotivated in the phonology.

Vowel harmony in Maltese provides independent evidence that coronal obstruents cannot be specified for secondary vocalic features. Vowel harmony is triggered by /o/ and affects, for example, the vowel of the the 2nd person singular suffix which shows the alternation [-ik] ~ [-ek] ~ [-ok]. As illustrated in (212a) through (212c), the suffixal vowel surfaces as [o] when preceded by /o/ in the stem, otherwise (d-f) it surfaces as [e] (from /i/ as the result of I-lowering) (for related discussion see Puech 1978, 1979).

(212)
a.	ʃorob	jiʃrob	jiʃroblok
	'he drank'	'he drinks'	'he drinks for you'
b.	tebaħ	jitboħ	jitboħlok
	'he cooked'	'he cooks'	'he cooks for you'
c.	tines	jitnos	jitnoslok
	'he cried'	'he cries'	'he cries to you'
d.	gideb	jigdeb	jigdiblek
	'he lied'	'he lies'	'he lies to you'
e.	daħak	jidħak	jidħaklek
	'he laughed'	'he laughs'	'he laughs to you'
f.	siredʒ	jisredʒ	jisridʒlek
	'he fried'	'he fries'	'he fries for you'

I assume (although not crucially) that the suffixal vowel enters into the derivation as /i/. Vowel harmony, triggered only by a preceding /o/, involves spreading the VOC node of /o/ dominating the features [labial, -high] to the following suffix vowel. When the preceding vowel is not /o/, no harmony occurs and the suffixal vowel surfaces as [e] when followed by a single word-final consonant (see I-lowering, chapter VI, section 4), otherwise it surfaces as [i].

As evidenced by the form [jitnoslok] in c), vowel harmony spreads rightward across an intervening coronal obstruent (in this case [s]) to change the suffixal vowel to [o]. Note, however, that the imperfective prefix vowel is realized as [i] since it is immediately followed by a coronal obstruent. Thus, although the features of /o/ are able to spread rightward as the result of Vowel Harmony, they do not spread leftward by Vocalic Mapping. If we were to propose that coronal obstruents were specified for secondary features we would not expect this asymmetry to exist. Rather, we would predict the spreading of vowel features to be blocked regardless of whether spreading occurs from right-to-left or left-to-right. Or, we would have to specify only the stem-initial coronal obstruent for secondary features while leaving the stem-final obstruent unspecified for these features, clearly an arbitrary move.[2]

The behaviour of coronal sonorants provides additional evidence against an analysis based on invoking No Line-Crossing. It will be recalled that Vocalic Mapping applies as expected when the stem-initial consonant is a coronal sonorant, e.g. [jol?ot] 'he hits', [jorhos] 'it grows cheap'. If coronal obstruents are specified in such a way as to block the spreading of vocalic features, we might expect coronal sonorants to be opaque as well. This follows from the common assumption that coronal obstruents and sonorants both share a common place specification. Note that underspecifying coronal sonorants for place features is not a viable means of accounting for this asymmetry. As was discussed in chapter IV (section 1.2), Morpheme Structure Constraints in Maltese require coronal sonorants to be specified for, at least, place of articulation in underlying representation.

Based on the arguments above, I conclude that drawing on the opacity of coronal obstruents in order to account for cases in which the prefix vowel surfaces as [i] before coronal obstruents is problematic.

1.3 Vowel Coronal Assimilation

It is nonetheless apparent that the realization of [i] in the verbs in (207) is directly related to the presence of a stem-initial coronal obstruent. The affinity evidenced between front vowels such as [i] and coronal consonants is not limited to Maltese but rather recurs across languages, as illustrated in previous chapters. Given that this affinity exists, the quality of frontness of the prefix vowel [i] in Maltese can be attributed to that of the following coronal obstruent. This is reminiscent of the rule of Guttural Assimilation discussed in chapter VI. Recall that /i/ is realized as [a] when adjacent to a guttural consonant. The naturalness of this rule stems from the fact that the output of assimilation and the rule's trigger both share the common place specification [pharyngeal]. However, attributing the quality of the vowel [i] to that of an adjacent coronal consonant is problematic in standard feature theory. To illustrate, consider the linear rule in (213) which describes this process: the prefix vowel surfaces as [-back, +high] before a coronal obstruent.

(213)   V → [-back, +high] /__ [coronal, -sonorant]

As stated, the relationship between [i] and coronals is an arbitrary one; there is nothing in the feature specification of coronals that would predict the vowel to surface as [i]. Given that the affinity between front vowels and coronal consonants exists, we have evidence that our classification of the two classes of sounds is unsuccessful since it does not reveal why the statement in (213) is more natural than the one expressed below in (214), where the vowel surfaces as [+back] before a coronal consonant.

(214)   V → [+back, +high]/__ [coronal, -sonorant]

However, by incorporating the view that front vowels and coronal consonants are members of the natural class [coronal], the patterning of [i] and coronal obstruents does not represent an arbitrary relationship. Instead, the fact that [i] surfaces before a coronal consonant in Maltese is an expected parallelism. As seen in the case of Guttural Assimilation, parallelisms such as this are given a straightforward account. Attributing some feature of a given segment to that of an adjacent segment suggests assimilation. Thus, by incorporating these two insights, first, that front vowels and coronals are specified as [coronal], and secondly, that assimilation is involved, the forms evidencing this parallelism can be accounted for by the assimilation of the prefix vowel to the coronality of a following coronal obstruent. I refer to this process as Vowel Coronal Assimilation and give its formal representation in (215).

(215) Vowel Coronal Assimilation:

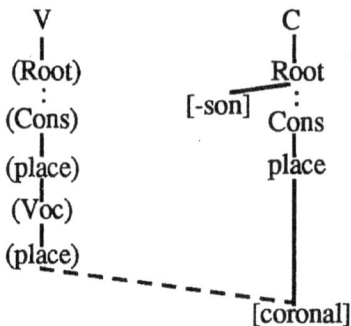

As illustrated in (215), the feature [coronal] spreads from the consonant to an interpolated VOC place on the preceding vowel slot (interpolated nodes are parenthesized). It will be noticed that the output of (215) is a vowel specified only for the place feature [coronal], height remains unspecified. Since [+high] is already independently motivated as the default value for vowel height in Maltese, it is (correctly) predicted that the output will be the high front vowel [i]. Thus, although the vowel's height is assigned by default, the vowel's place specification is acquired by assimilation.

As evident in the representation in (215), Vowel Coronal Assimilation (VCA) is a feature-filling rule. If we are correct in assuming, following Kiparsky (1985), that the unmarked type of assimilation rule is feature-filling (see also Herzallah 1990 for strong evidence in support of this view), treating VCA as such is to be preferred. Positing that VCA is feature-filling also provides a straightforward account of its failure to apply, for example, to stem-internal [a] and [o] in [jaʔbad] 'he catches' and [jobroʃ] 'he scratches'. Since /a/ and /o/ are specified for place of articulation in underlying

Coronal Vowel and Consonant Parallelisms in Maltese 223

representation, [pharyngeal] in the case of /a/ and [labial] in the case of /o/, VCA will not apply.

Moreover, treating VCA as a feature-filling rule results in a less complex analysis. If we were to assume that VCA were a feature-changing rule, it would be required to apply after the features of the stem vowel had mapped onto the vowel slot of the prefix, i.e. after the application of Vocalic Mapping. Thus, both Vocalic Mapping and VCA would need to apply, the first in a feature-filling manner and the second, in a feature-changing manner. So, for example, we would have the change V→a→[i] in deriving [jidlam] (/jV+dalam/), V→o→[i] for [jiʃrob] (/jV+ʃorob/), and V→e→[i] for [jisħet] (/jV+seħet/). A simpler analysis is one in which both processes are feature-filling, as shown in (216).

(216)

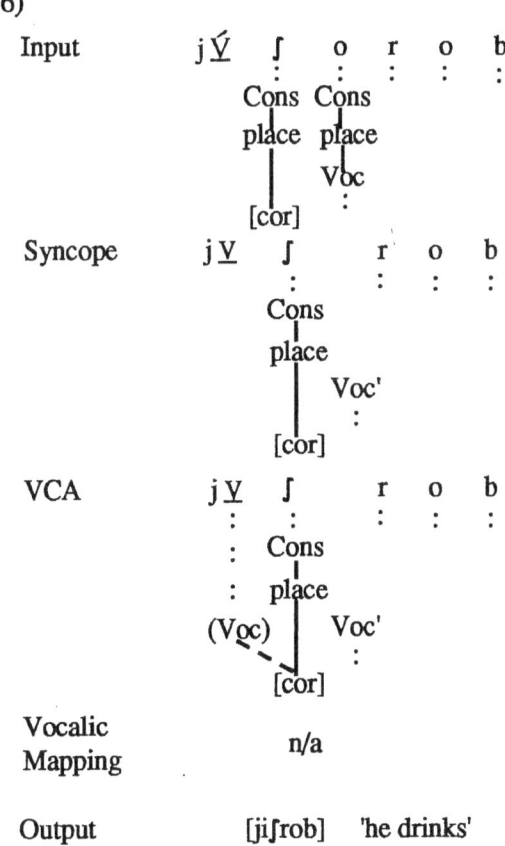

Output   [jiʃrob]   'he drinks'

Identical to the derivations presented in chapter VI, the V-slot of the stem-initial vowel deletes as the result of Syncope. However, there are two potential means of filling in the feature content of the prefix vowel, either by Vocalic Mapping or by Vowel Coronal Assimilation, both of which are feature-filling processes. In order to obtain the correct result, Vowel Coronal Assimilation must apply prior to Vocalic Mapping. Although this could be accomplished by extrinsic ordering, I would suggest that a more preferable solution comes from the observation that the two rules are in an elsewhere relationship. The Elsewhere Condition as formulated by Kiparsky (1982) is as follows:

(217) Elsewhere Condition:
Rules A, B in the same component apply disjunctively to a form φ if and only if
(i) The structural description of A (the special rule) properly includes the structural description of B (the general rule).
(ii) The result of applying A to φ is distinct from the result of applying B to φ.
In that case, A is applied first, and if it takes effect, then B is not applied.

Both Vowel Coronal Assimilation and Vocalic Mapping target an empty V-slot. However, the output of the two rules differ. By the former, the output is [coronal], unspecified for height, whereas by the latter, the output is [o], [a], [e] or [i]. Context-sensitive rules are necessarily in an elsewhere relationship with context-free rules. Consequently, Vowel Coronal Assimilation, the context-sensitive rule, constitutes the special rule, and Vocalic Mapping is the general rule, since it is context-free. Consequently, by the Elsewhere Condition, Vowel Coronal Assimilation is expected to take precedence over Vocalic Mapping, thus deriving the correct result.(Although not explicit in the derivation, I assume that the default rule assigning [+high] applies at some point in the derivation to provide the vowel with its height specification.)

Vowel Coronal Assimilation is characterized as spreading the feature value [coronal] from the consonant onto the vowel. As discussed in chapter III, I assume that the articulator [coronal] dominates the terminal feature [anterior]. Furthermore, although front vowels are

Coronal Vowel and Consonant Parallelisms in Maltese 225

[-anterior], this value is non-contrastive. It is thus absent underlyingly and assigned by the redundancy rule in (218).

(218) [+coronal]_VOC → [-anterior]

For consonants, the feature [anterior] serves to contrast anterior and non-anterior consonants, and must be present in underlying representation to contrast, for example, /s/ ([+coronal, +anterior]) with /ʃ/ ([+coronal, -anterior]). Consequently, when the prefix vowel assimilates to the place specification of a coronal consonant, it will also acquire the consonant's specification for the feature [anterior]. Assimilation to /ʃ/ in [jiʃrob] 'he drinks', for example, will involve spreading both the place articulator [coronal] and its terminal feature [-anterior]. Conversely, assimilation to /s/ in [jisrom] 'he puzzles' will involve spreading both [coronal] and [+anterior]. As a result, the output of assimilation to /s/ will result in the derived /i/ specified as [+anterior] whereas to /ʃ/, /i/ will be specified as [-anterior], as shown in (219a, b), respectively.

(219)

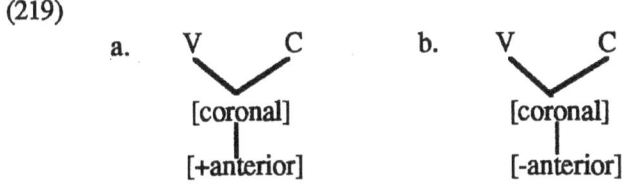

If the vowel were to retain these values for [anterior] we would predict the phonetic realization of [i] before [ʃ] to differ from that of [i] before [s]. In other words, we would expect [i] to have a more anterior articulation before [s] than before [ʃ]. In addition, [i] derived from assimilation to /s/ would be expected to differ from instances of [i] not resulting from assimilation. In these latter cases, [i] would surface as [-anterior] due to the application of redundancy rule. Unfortunately, I do not, as of yet, have access to acoustic or articulatory data which could be used to test these hypotheses. If it is the case that the front vowel is articulated in the non-anterior coronal region regardless of the consonant to which it assimilates, the representation in (219a) would need to be adjusted. Note that simply changing the value of [+anterior] on the vowel in (219a) to [-anterior] would be unsatisfactory given the multiple-linked structure resulting from assimilation. If we were to do this, both consonant and vowel would end up bearing the feature value [-anterior] which would incorrectly predict that the consonant, e.g. /s/, surfaces as a postalveolar coronal. An alternative solution would be invoke Cloning, as suggested in chapter IV. In this way, the [coronal, +anterior] specification would be cloned resulting in the single linking of this specification to each segment. By phonological rule, the [+anterior] specification of the vowel could then be changed to [-anterior] without affecting the feature specification of the consonant. I leave these issues open for further consideration.

1.4 Summary

The quality of the imperfective prefix vowel of first measure triliteral verbs is typically identical to that of the underlying vocalic melody of the verb stem. However, verbs with a stem-initial coronal obstruent are systematically preceded by an [i] prefix vowel. I have argued that the simplest and most insightful account of these forms draws from the proposal that front vowels and coronal consonants are members of the same natural class. The parallelism between these sounds receives a natural account in nonlinear phonology by attributing the place specification of the prefix vowel to assimilation. Vowel Coronal Assimilation is represented as a feature-filling rule in which the articulator feature [coronal] spreads from the consonant onto the empty V-slot of the prefix.

In the following section, I discuss the behaviour of the imperfective prefix consonant of second and third person feminine verbs. In the first measure this consonant is realized as [t]. In certain other measures this consonant undergoes assimilation to a stem-initial coronal obstruent in a way similar to that observed for the imperfective prefix vowel. There are a number of striking parallelisms between the behaviour of the prefix consonant and vowel, and by extension, the language's default consonant and vowel. As I argue below, these parallelisms provide independent support for the rule of Vowel Coronal Assimilation, and for the view that [i] is coronal.

2. CONSONANT CORONAL ASSIMILATION

It will be recalled that the imperfective of the strong triliteral verb, first measure, is characterized by a prefix of the form CV-. In the second person and third person feminine, the prefix consonant surfaces invariably as [t], e.g. [taʔtel] 'you (sg.) kill' ([ʔatel] 'he killed'). In the 5th through 10th measure, the imperfective prefix consonant is also [t] and is followed by the prefix vowel [i], as illustrated in (220).

(220)	Perfective 3rd. p.m.sg.	Imperfective 2nd p./3rd p.f.sg.	
Fifth measure	tʔattel	titʔattel	to destroy oneself
Sixth measure	tbierek	titbierek	to be blessed
Seventh measure	inʔatel	tinʔatel	to be killed
Eighth measure	irtabat	tirtabat	to be bound
Ninth measure	ḣdaːr	tiḣdaːr	to grow green
Tenth measure	stenbaḣ	tistenbaḣ	to awaken

Verbs of the second and third measure differ from those above in that there is no prefix vowel[3]; the prefix consonant occurs directly adjacent to the stem-initial consonant. As in the other measures above, the prefix consonant is typically realized as [t] as illustrated in the forms in (221).

(221)	Perfective	Imperfective	
Second measure	naʔʔas	tnaʔʔas	'to lessen'
	kattar	tkattar	'to multiply'
Third measure	bierek	tbierek	'to bless'
	ḣaːres	tḣaːres	'to observe'

Before stems beginning with a coronal obstruent, however, the prefix consonant assimilates completely to the initial consonant. Representative examples are given in (222). Note that the vowel [i] which precedes the geminate consonant is epenthetic (see chapter VI).

(222)		Perfective	Imperfective	
Second measure		daħħak	iddaħħak	'to amuse'
		sallab	issallab	'to crucify'
		ʃemmeʃ	iʃʃemmeʃ	'to sun'
		dʒedded	idʒdʒedded	'to renew'
Third measure		dierek	iddierek	'to rise early'
		siefer	issiefer	'to depart'
		dʒieled	idʒdʒieled	'to incite'

The complete assimilation of a consonant to a following coronal obstruent is not restricted to the imperfective verbs illustrated in (222) above. This is also evidenced, for example, in perfective verbs of the fifth and sixth measures. These verbs are the reflexive or passive forms of corresponding second and third measure verbs and are formed by prefixing /t/ to the stem of a second and third measure verb, respectively, as illustrated in (223a). As can be seen in (223b), the reflexive/passive prefix also assimilates completely to a following coronal obstruent.

(223) Perfective

a) Second measure		Fifth measure	
nizzel	'to bring down'	tnizzel	'to be brought down'
ressaʔ	'to cause to approach'	tressaʔ	'to be brought near'
kabbar	'to enlarge'	tkabbar	'to grow proud'

Third measure		Sixth measure	
fieraʔ	'to separate' (trans.)	tfieraʔ	'to separate' (intrans.)
haːres	'to observe'	thaːres	'to be observed'

b) Second measure		Fifth measure	
daħħak	'to amuse'	iddaħħak	'to amuse oneself'
tarraʃ	'to deafen'	ittarraʃ	'to become deaf'
tʃaħħad	'to deny'	itʃtʃaħħad	'to deny oneself'

Third measure		Sixth measure	
sieħeb	'to unite'	issieħeb	'to associate together'
ʃierek	'to take into partnership'	iʃʃierek	'to enter into partnership with'

The realization of the reflexive/passive prefix consonant is identical to that of the imperfective prefix consonant in (221) and (222). Both are realized as [t] except when followed by a coronal obstruent, in which case the prefix undergoes total assimilation. Due to this symmetry, it is reasonable to assume that both prefixes have the same underlying representation. Moreover, a single analysis should be able to account for the realization of both prefixes.

A further observation concerning the reflexive/passive marker is that in certain measures it occurs to the right of the first root consonant as exemplified by the verbs of the eighth measure, the reflexive or passive form of the corresponding first measure verb, as shown in (224).

(224) Perfective   Perfective
       First measure   Eighth measure
  baram   'to twist'   btaram   'to be twisted'
  nefaʔ   'to spend'   intefaʔ   'to be spent'
  rabat   'to bind'   irtabat   'to be bound'
  sabar   'to bear with   stabar   'to have patience'
           patience'
  ʃeħet   'to throw'   ʃteħet   'to throw oneself down'

As evidenced by the forms in (224), the infix is invariably realized as [t]. This is the case even when the infix is adjacent to a coronal obstruent, e.g. [stabar], [ʃteħet]. Note, however, that in these instances, the infix [t] occurs to the right of the coronal obstruent. In this position, no assimilation occurs. On the other hand, in the verbs in (222) and (223b) above, the prefix consonant occurs to the left of the coronal and assimilation occurs. Given that the infix in (224) and the prefix in (223) are both the reflexive/passive marker, and furthermore, that in certain environments they both surface as [t], it is a reasonable to assume that both have the same underlying form. I claim then that the imperfective prefix consonant in (221,222), the reflexive/passive marker in (223) and the reflexive/passive infix in (224) are represented in a uniform manner underlyingly. For clarity, I will use the term *t-affix* when referring to these elements as a group. Individually, I will continue to use the terms *imperfective prefix consonant* to characterize the segment in (221,222), *reflexive/passive prefix* for the segment in

(223), and *reflexive/passive infix* for the segment which occurs in (224).

As observed above, assimilation only applies when the t-affix occurs to the left of a coronal obstruent. Otherwise, the segment surfaces as [t]. These observations are given a straightforward account by assuming first, that the rule of assimilation is defined such that it applies only from right to left, and second, that the affix enters into the derivation unspecified for features. I elaborate on these points just below. The rule of Consonant Coronal Assimilation which, I propose, accounts for the complete assimilation of the t-affix to a following coronal obstruent is given in (225) (C̲ characterizes a consonant unspecified for features).

(225) Consonant Coronal Assimilation (CCA)
     operation: spread Root node
     trigger: [coronal, -sonorant]
     target: C̲
     direction: right to left
     condition: skeletal tier adjacency

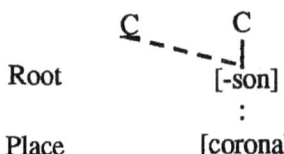

Root

Place

Informally stated, the root node of a coronal obstruent spreads to a preceding C-slot. The output is a geminate consonant identical in quality to the rule's trigger. Assimilation will not apply to the t-infix in the verbs in (224). This follows first from the claim that the stem-initial coronal obstruent in e.g. [stabar] is specified for features and is thus not a potential target (see chapter VI for evidence from Morpheme Structure Constraints that root consonants must be specified for at least place features in UR). Moreover, the t-infix enters into the derivation as an empty C-slot and is therefore not a potential trigger of assimilation. In the absence of assimilation rules, the affix in all cases surfaces as [t] by default.

I have proposed that the t-affix enters into the derivation unspecified for features and that in the absence of feature-filling assimilation, it surfaces as [t] by default. With respect to place of articulation, the t-affix receives the feature values [coronal, +anterior] by default. Further evidence for positing these feature values as the language's default values for consonants comes from the observation that the epenthetic consonant surfaces predictably as [t] in Maltese. For example, in forming the possessive of nouns, the pronominal suffix [i] is typically added to the noun stem, e.g. [difer] 'nail'/[difr+i][4] 'my nail', [isem] 'name'/[ism+i] 'my name'. However, for nouns stems ending in final [a], the suffix [i] is preceded by [t], e.g. [saħħa] 'health'/[saħħti] 'my health', [mara] 'woman'/ [marti] 'my wife' (Sutcliffe 1936).

The presence of [t] in these forms is best considered the result of epenthesis. As I show in (226), adding [t] to the stem in (a) creates the context for Syncope. As a result, the unstressed stem-final vowel deletes, in a manner identical to that in (b).

(226) a. mara + i   b. isem+i
t-epenthesis   marati   n/a
Syncope   marti   ismi
               [marti]   [ismi]

An alternative account is to suppose that the suffix is underlyingly /-ti/ with the /t/ deleting when the stem-final segment is a consonant, as shown below.

(227) a. difer+ti   b. isem+ti
t-deletion   diferi   isemi
Syncope   difri   ismi

However, there is no independent motivation for positing a rule of t-deletion. Postvocalic sequences of [mt] and [rt] are well-formed in the language, e.g. tartet 'she insisted', ort 'garden', imtaʔʔab 'pierced', imtedd 'to lie down'. On the other hand, a survey of Bugeja's (1984) lexicon of over 8,000 words reveals that there are no forms which contain adjacent instances of the vowels [ai]. The vowel [a] followed by the palatal glide is equally rare with only two reported forms, dayaj 'blasphemer', ħaj 'alive'. T-epenthesis can thus be seen as a strategy in Maltese to avoid an otherwise highly marked vowel sequence. The predictability of [t] as the epenthetic consonant in these forms (as opposed to e.g. [p] or [k]) follows from the assumption that the default place features for consonants in Maltese are [coronal, +anterior].

Consonant epenthesis also occurs in certain verbs of the seventh measure which, like the eighth measure, is most commonly used as the passive form of the first measure. In general, seventh measure verbs are formed by prefixing [n] to the verb stem as illustrated in (228). (Again, epenthetic [i] occurs word-initially. See chapter VI, section 6.3.)

(228) . *First measure*   *Seventh measure*
    bidel   'to change'   inbidel 'to be changed'
    daħal   'to enter'   indaħal 'to interfere'
    kiteb   'to write'   inkiteb 'to subscribe'
    ʔabad 'to catch'   inʔabad 'to be caught'

In verbs in which the stem-initial consonant is sonorant, i.e. [m l r] (no forms with initial [n] were found), the consonant [t] systematically occurs between the prefix [n] and the following sonorant consonant. Representative examples are given in (229).

(229)   Seventh measure   First measure
       intlaħaʔ   'to be reached'   laħaʔ   'to reach'
       intmesaħ 'to be wiped'   mesaħ 'to wipe'
       intrabat   'to be tied'   rabat   'to tie'

Sutcliffe (1936:93) notes that "the addition of the letter t is not purely arbitrary...l,m,r are letters with which n tends to assimilate" (p.93). Sutcliffe's remark refers to the observation that a nasal prefix consonant generally undergoes complete assimilation to a following sonorant consonant, as illustrated in (230). The prefix in these verbs characterizes the first person imperfective. (Note once again that the initial [i] is epenthetic.)

(230)   irross < n+ross   'I press'
       irrid < n+riːd   'I wish/want'
       illum < n+luːm   'I chide'
       illaʔʔam < n+laʔʔam 'I inoculate'
       immut < n+muːt   'I die'
       immur < n+muːr   'I go'

In roots beginning with a non-sonorant consonant, the prefix consonant is realized as [n], e.g. inħobb < n+ħobb 'I love', inberbaʔ < n+berbaʔ 'I squander away'. Sonorant Assimilation is formally stated in (231) below.

(231) Sonorant Assimilation:
    operation: spread Root
    trigger: [+cons, +son]
    target: Root
                     [+nasal]
    direction: right to left
    locality   skeletal tier adjacency

I assume that the target of Sonorant Assimilation is a consonant specified only as [+nasal]. Similar to Consonant Coronal Assimilation, the target is unspecified for place and acquires the place specification [coronal, +anterior] by default. There are several reasons why underspecifying the prefix consonant in this case is to be preferred. First, given that the features [coronal, +anterior] are already independently motivated as the default features for consonants in Maltese, underspecifying the nasal prefix comes at no extra cost. Second, the underspecification of /n/, the 1st person imperfective prefix, is consistent with the underspecification of /t/, the 2nd and 3rd person feminine imperfective prefix. Third, the underspecification of the nasal prefix provides a straightforward account for why Sonorant Assimilation fails to apply in forms with an /m/ prefix such as, [imleff] < m+leff 'a child's cloak', [imnaʔʔas] < m+naʔʔas 'diminished'. I assume that the prefix /m/ is underlyingly specified for [labial] place. Thus, Sonorant Assimilation, a feature-filling rule, will not apply since the target is already specified for place features.

During this brief aside, I have motivated the rule of Sonorant Assimilation which applies in a feature-filling manner provided that the target and trigger are adjacent on the skeletal tier. Let us return now to the verbs of the seventh measure in which the consonant [t] intervenes between the prefix [n] and the stem-initial sonorant consonant. Characteristic of this measure is the fact that Sonorant Assimilation is prohibited from applying. This is achieved by inserting [t] between the two sonorant consonants since by intervening between the target and trigger, the adjacency condition is not met. Note that representing epenthetic [t] underlyingly as simply a C-slot is sufficient to block Sonorant Assimilation from applying; specification for place features is not required. The surface quality of the epenthetic consonant (as well as that of the nasal target of Sonorant Assimilation) is nonetheless predictable given my claim that the default place features for consonants in Maltese are [coronal, +anterior].

In the above discussion, I have motivated [t] as the epenthetic consonant in Maltese. I have also proposed that the t-affix enters into the derivation as a C-slot unspecified for features. Coronal obstruents trigger the rule of Consonant Coronal Assimilation, a feature-filling operation applying from right to left. In the absence of assimilation, the t-affix receives the feature values [coronal, +anterior] by default, the same features assigned to the epenthetic consonant.

3. CORONAL VOWEL/CONSONANT PARALLELISMS

In the preceding sections I have identified two processes triggered by a stem-initial coronal obstruent. The first involves the assimilation of the imperfective prefix vowel to the place of articulation of a following coronal obstruent. In the second, the t-affix undergoes complete assimilation to a following coronal obstruent. Due to the overwhelming parallelisms between Vowel Coronal Assimilation (VCA) and Consonant Coronal Assimilation (CCA), I propose that these two rules are subclasses of a single rule which I refer to as Coronal Assimilation. Moreover, I suggest that due to the similarities between /t/ and /i/ as general default segments in Maltese, there is a single default feature for place in Maltese, that being [coronal]. I begin by discussing the latter proposal.

3.1 Default Segments

In the absence of feature-filling assimilation, the epenthetic vowel as well as the imperfective prefix vowel receive the default feature values [coronal, +high] and thus surface as [i]. Similarly, in the absence of assimilation rules the t-affix is assigned the default feature values [coronal, +anterior] and surfaces as [t] (see also the 1st person imperfective prefix [n]). As I showed in the previous section, this is the same quality attributed to the language's epenthetic consonant. Thus, for both consonants and vowels in Maltese, the default place feature is [coronal]. Recognizing [coronal] as the default value for place in consonants is consistent with the earlier proposals of, e.g. Kean (1976), Paradis & Prunet (1989), Avery & Rice (1989), in which [coronal] is considered the unmarked place specification for consonants. I propose, however, that [coronal] can be extended to include not only consonants but vowels as well. As such, we are able formulate a single default rule for place in Maltese.

(232) Place → [coronal]

This opposes an SPE-based feature approach in which vowels would be characterized by the feature [-back] and consonants by the feature [coronal]. In this approach, the relationship between the default consonant and vowel is an arbitrary one. Conversely, by positing a single default rule we recognize the non-arbitrary relationship between these segments. Moreover, including a single default rule results in a simpler grammar in that reference to only a single default feature for place is needed regardless of whether the segment in question is a consonant or a vowel.

Within the natural class of coronal sounds in Maltese, the unmarked consonant is an anterior coronal and for vowels it is the high front vowel [i]. The relevant default and redundancy rules are thus as in (233).

(233)
$[coronal]_{CONS}$ → [+anterior]
$[coronal]_{VOC}$ → [-anterior]
$stricture_{VOC}$ → [+high]

Despite the existence of these default rules, underspecifying all surface instances of, e.g. [t] and [i] for these features is not feasible. As discussed in chapter VI, root consonants and vowels must be underlyingly specified for features. It will be recalled that the need to distinguish between an unspecified V-slot and the specified vocalic root melody /i/ is associated with the rule of Guttural Assimilation. Guttural Assimilation changes /i/ to [a] when adjacent to a guttural consonant and applies both stem-internally and across a morpheme boundary. In [jaħleb] < /jV+ħilib/, for example, the vocalic melody /i/ maps onto the V-slot of the prefix and then undergoes Guttural Assimilation. Conversely, in verbs such as [jiħmaar] < /jV+ħmaar/

Guttural Assimilation fails to apply to the prefix vowel. I proposed that the failure of Guttural Assimilation to apply in the latter case is explained by positing that the prefix vowel enters into the derivation unspecified for features and surfaces as [i] by default. Since an empty V-slot is not a target for Guttural Assimilation, the rule does not apply to forms like [jiħmaar]. The disadvantage of assuming that stem-internal instances of /i/ are unspecified for features is that the explanation for the asymmetrical behaviour of Guttural Assimilation in cases like the ones just cited would be lost. Positing two /i/s in UR, one specified for place (and height) and the other unspecified, is then crucial in accounting for the realization of the prefix vowel in all imperfective verbs.

Similarly, I have proposed that there are two /t/s in underlying representation: the t-affix which enters into the derivation as an unspecified C-slot, and the root consonant /t/ which is specified for features. Positing that the latter /t/ also receives its features by default is problematic for the Root Structure Constraints discussed in chapter VI. Recall that adjacent homorganic consonants agreeing in their value for [sonorant] tend not to cooccur within a root. If we were to assume that the root consonant /t/ were unspecified for place features in UR, there would be nothing to prevent it from cooccurring with all consonants, coronal obstruents included. Moreover, underspecifying the t-affix was shown to be necessary to account for the asymmetrical behaviour of affixes with respect to the rule of Consonant Coronal Assimilation. When the affix occurs to the right of a coronal obstruent no assimilation occurs. Conversely, when located to the left of the coronal obstruent, the affix undergoes total assimilation. A straightforward account of this asymmetry is given under the assumption that Coronal Consonant Assimilation is directional applying from right to left and furthermore, that the affix is unspecified for features in underlying representation. Distinguishing between two /t/s is therefore also necessary in the underlying system of Maltese.

As discussed in chapter VI, these findings provide strong counterevidence to the view that the existence of a given default rule necessarily entails the complete underspecification of this default value on all segments in underlying representation. Instead, default features can be considered to be independent of the underlying feature specification of a given system, available either universally or on a language-specific basis as a means of filling in unspecified values on segments.

3.2 Coronal Assimilation

In addition to the parallelisms between the default consonant and vowel in Maltese, there are a number of similarities between the rules of Vowel and Consonant Coronal Assimilation. I repeat the two rules below for reference (irrelevant structure has been omitted).

(234)a.
Consonant Coronal Assimilation
Trigger: [coronal, -sonorant]
Target: C
Direction: right to left
Locality: skeletal tier
Operation: spread root

b.
Vowel Coronal Assimilation
Trigger: [coronal, -sonorant]
Target: V
Direction: right to left
Locality: skeletal tier
Operation: spread [coronal]

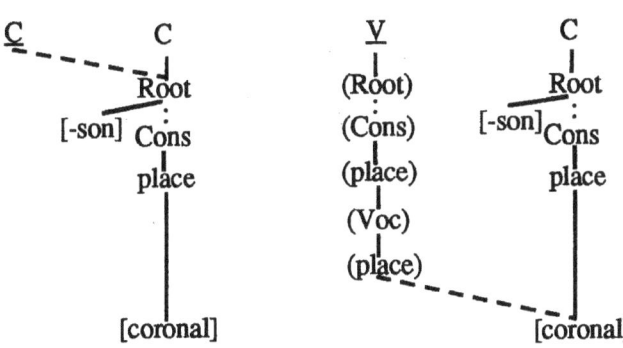

First, in both rules the trigger is a coronal obstruent. Reference to the feature specification [-sonorant] in the description of the rules assures that only a subset of the entire class of coronal consonants acts as triggers. The distinct patterning of coronal obstruents to the exclusion of sonorants is not limited to these rules. As discussed in the preceding chapter, Morpheme Structure Constraints in Maltese indicate that coronal obstruents pattern differently from their sonorant counterparts in the sequencing of consonants within the root. In this case, the underlying specification of [sonorant] is independently required to distinguish between the two sets of consonants.

Second, both Vowel Coronal Assimilation and Consonant Coronal Assimilation are feature-filling operations. Given my claim that the prefix consonant enters into the derivation unspecified for features, feature-filling assimilation is the only option for CCA. For VCA, on the other hand, viewing this as a feature-filling process is motivated on the basis of simplicity. Ordering VCA after Vocalic Mapping would require the application of two processes, with Vocalic Mapping being a feature-filling rule and VCA, a feature-changing rule. By treating both operations as feature-filling, VCA, will take precedence over Vocalic Mapping by the Elsewhere Condition. Also, with respect to markedness, viewing VCA as a feature-filling operation is to be preferred.

Third, both rules are directional, applying from right to left and fourth, skeletal tier adjacency is a necessary locality condition in both rules. Finally, when assimilation is not an available option for filling in features on the consonant or vowel target, the surface realizations of these segments are identical to the language's epenthetic consonant and vowel, i.e. [t] and [i].

The overwhelming similarities between the two rules suggest that we are dealing with a single rule whose target is an empty slot. It will be noticed, however, that the one difference between the two rules concerns the level at which spreading occurs from the trigger. When the target is an empty C-slot, the entire root node spreads resulting in a geminate consonant whereas when the target is an empty V-slot, the feature [coronal] spreads. Spreading the entire root node of the consonant to the vowel would entail spreading features values such as [-sonorant, -continuant], thus creating an ill-formed vowel. We might suppose then that the rule applies in a structure-preserving manner (Kiparsky 1985),[5] i.e. its application cannot create a segment which is not part of the language's phonemic inventory. Along these lines, spreading from the consonant to the vowel cannot occur from a level higher than the place node, given the proposal that [-continuant] links to the stricture node of the consonant. Thus, defining spreading on the articulator [coronal] is consistent with the structure-preserving nature of the rule.[6] Coronal Vowel and Consonant Assimilation can therefore be considered subclasses of a single rule with the particular

Coronal Vowel and Consonant Parallelisms in Maltese 239

subclassification defined in terms of the level from which spreading occurs. This is formally stated in (235).

(235) Coronal Assimilation
 Trigger: [coronal, -sonorant]
 Target: X̠, where X̠ is C̠ or V̠
 Direction: right to left
 Locality: skeletal tier adjacency
 Operation: a. spread [coronal] if V̠
  b. otherwise, spread root

As formulated in (235), the trigger of Coronal Assimilation is a coronal obstruent and the target is an empty slot. I characterize the empty skeletal slot by the variable X̠, referring to either C̠ or V̠. The operation defined in the rule divides into two subclasses as is required to maintain the structure-preserving nature of the rule. When the target is an empty V-slot, the operation is defined on the articulator node [coronal] whereas when the target is an empty C-slot total assimilation is possible.

Coronal Assimilation provides a unified account of the realization of the imperfective consonant and vowel prefix before coronal obstruents in Maltese. By doing so we recognize the symmetrical patterning of these two segments, a parallelism which we would expect given that these sounds are members of the same natural class.

A final comment is in order concerning the application of Coronal Assimilation and its potential interaction with the default rule assigning the place specification [coronal]. Both rules assign (at least) the feature value [coronal] to an empty slot. Archangeli & Pulleyblank (1986) propose that a default rule is activated when reference to the specific default feature value is referred to. This is formally stated as the Redundancy Rule Ordering Constraint in (236).

(236) Redundancy Rule Ordering Constraint (Archangeli & Pulleyblank 1986:15)
 A default or complement rule assigning [αF], where "α" is "+" or "-", is automatically assigned to the first component in which reference is made to [αF].

Given that the rule of Coronal Assimilation makes specific reference to the feature value [coronal], we might then predict that the default rule assigning the feature value [coronal] would assign this value to the empty consonant and vowel slots. If this were the case, Coronal Assimilation would be unable to apply since the former target of the rule (i.e. the empty slots) would be specified for place.

However, context-free default rules are necessarily in an elsewhere relationship with any context-sensitive rule assigning the same features (see formulation of the Elsewhere Condition in section 1.3 above). Coronal Assimilation, the context-sensitive rule, constitutes the *special* rule while Coronal Default, the *general* rule. Given that the two rules are in an elsewhere relationship it is (correctly) predicted that the rule of Coronal Assimilation will have priority over Coronal Default.

4. CONCLUSION

The phonology of Maltese evidences numerous parallelisms between, in particular, the high front vowel and coronal consonants. These include the realization of the imperfective prefix vowel as [i] before coronal obstruents, the patterning of the prefix [i] and [t] in the formation of the imperfective prefix and the surfacing of [t] and [i] as the language's default segments. I have proposed that these parallelisms are a natural consequence of the fact that front vowels and coronal consonants are members of the class [coronal]. By incorporating such an approach into feature theory we are able to account for these parallelisms in a straightforward and non-arbitrary manner.Maltese

NOTES

1. I have found one exception to this generalizaton. The imperfective of [tarat] 'he insisted' occurs as either [jitrot] or [jotrot] 'he insists'. My consultants indicated a clear preference for the imperfective prefix vowel [i], however.

2. In previous accounts of the formation of the imperfective (e.g. Brame 1972, Puech 1978, 1979), it is assumed that the realization of the prefix vowel as [o] in certain verbs (see chapter VI) is due to the same rule of vowel harmony which propagates rightward affecting the

suffixal vowel of, for example, the 2nd person singular suffix as shown in (212). Since only /o/ is a trigger of vowel harmony, the realization of the prefix vowel as [o] before an /o/-stem verb in these accounts must be treated exceptionally from the way in which the prefix vowel is realized before all other stems. By doing this we are also losing the insight that the prefix vowel is typically identical in quality to that of the underlying stem vocalism, whereas the suffix vowels (as in (212)) are not. My analysis has the advantage of treating the realization of the prefix vowel in a uniform manner regardless of the quality of the following vowel. The vocalic melody of the stem vowel spreads to the empty V-slot of the prefix in a feature-filling manner. Since vowel harmony differs from the realization of the prefix vowel in that only /o/ is a trigger, I consider vowel harmony to be an independent rule which spreads only rightward.

3. The absence of the prefix vowel in these verbs is accounted for by the rule of Syncope (see chapter VI).

4. The deletion of the stem-final vowel is due to the rule of Syncope.

5. Spreading the entire root node to the vowel could occur, however, if it is assumed that redundancy rules apply in a feature-changing manner (see e.g. Mohanan 1991 for discussion). Along these lines Coronal Assimilation could be stated as a single rule spreading the root node with the values of e.g. [sonorant] and [continuant] changing (when relevant) in a structure preserving manner to turn the output into a well-formed vowel.

6. It is equally feasible to define spreading from the consonant to the vowel on the place node. Nothing hinges on whether it is place or [coronal] that spreads.

VIII

Conclusion

In this work I have examined a range of phenomena involving front vocoids and coronal consonants. These include, among others, consonant-to-vowel assimilation, vowel-to-consonant assimilation, dissimilation and default assignment. By specifying front vocoids and coronal consonants with a common place articulator, I have shown that the affinity evidenced between these two groups of sounds is treated in a natural and non-arbitrary manner.

In chapter II, I showed that the phonologically salient feature for classifying front vowels and coronal consonants is [coronal]. This feature is redefined as an articulation implemented by raising the tip, blade and/or front of the tongue, a reinterpretation which is independently needed in order to recognize palatal consonants as coronal sounds. Front vowels are natural members of this new class of coronal sounds as they are articulated with the front of the tongue raised to a greater degree than their noncoronal counterparts.

An equally important aspect of this work concerns the formal representation of consonants and vowels, and their interaction in nonlinear theory. With respect to feature organization, I incorporate a slightly modified version of the Unified Features model of Clements (1990c). Like Clements, I assume the partial segregation of consonant and vowel features. However, I argue that all instances of a given place feature are arrayed on the same tier. The single-tier hypothesis is advantageous as it allows OCP-related phenomena such as dissimilation to be accounted for in simple terms without increasing the power of the OCP.

In the study of Maltese Arabic in the second part of this work a number of significant points were brought out. For example, I showed that metathesis is best viewed as the product of three independent rules: Syncope, Epenthesis and Vocalic Mapping. By breaking metathesis down in these terms we are able to provide a straightforward account of metathesis by drawing on elementary operations of nonlinear phonology, i.e. delink, insert and associate. In addition, several parallelisms were observed between front vowels and coronal consonants in this language. For example, in the imperfective of triliteral verbs, the prefix consonant and vowel both undergo assimilation to an adjacent coronal obstruent. Moreover, it is proposed, based on a range of evidence, that there is a single default rule assigning place of articulation in Maltese, i.e. place → [coronal]. This applies regardless of whether the segment in question is a consonant or vowel.

A number of issues have emerged from this work which warrant futher consideration. First, I have posited the universal repair convention, Cloning, which serves to eliminate violations of the Ordering Constraint. It was suggested at that time that this convention may be independently required in phonological theory. A more indepth investigation into this issue is clearly warranted.

A second issue concerns the underspecification of default values. In chapters VI and VII, I showed that the existence of a given default value need not imply that all surface occurrences of this value are unspecified in underlying representation. This corroborates earlier evidence discussed in Herzallah (1990) and Hualde (1991). These findings suggest that default feature values are independent of the underlying feature specification of a given system. The extent to which this proposal holds true for other languages is an issue well worth pursuing as it has important implications for the role of default rules and underspecification in phonological theory.

As noted above, in my analysis of Maltese in chapter VII, [coronal] is shown to be the default place feature not only for consonants but for vowels as well. The observation that both the default consonant and vowel surface as coronal sounds is treated as a natural consequence of the fact that these segments are members of the same natural class. This proposal raises a number of questions. First, does the default place feature for consonants parallel that of vowels in a wide range of languages? If future research reveals the relatedness of consonant and vowel default features in other languages, we have additional evidence for the unified classification of consonantal and vocoidal place features. Second, it has been proposed by a number of researchers that [coronal] is the unmarked place of articulation for consonants cross-linguistically (Avery & Rice 1989, Kean 1976, Paradis & Prunet 1989, 1991). In light of the evidence from Maltese, it would appear that the unmarked status of [coronal] extends naturally to front vowels as well.

References

Abondolo, D. 1988. *Hungarian inflectional morphology*. Budapest: Akadémai Kiadó.
Ao, B. 1990. Lip rounding and formant frequencies of the Nantong vowel system. Paper presented at 119th Meeting of the Acoustical Society of America, May 1990, at Pennsylvania State University.
Aquilina, J. 1959. *The structure of Maltese*. Malta: The Royal University of Malta.
------. 1965. *Maltese*. Kent: Hodder and Stoughton.
Archangeli, D. 1984. Underspecification in Yawelmani phonology and morphology. Ph.D. diss., MIT.
Archangeli, D., and D. Pulleyblank. 1986. The content and structure of phonological representations. ms., University of Arizona and University of Southern California.
Avery, P., and Rice, K. 1989. Constraining underspecification. In *Proceedings of NELS 19*, ed. J. Carter and R.-M. Déchaine, 1-15. GLSA, Department of Linguistics, University of Massachusetts, Amherst.
Bell, M. 1867. *Visible speech*. London: Simpkin and Marshall.
Berrendonner, A., M. Le Guern, and G. Puech. 1983. *Principes de grammaire polylectale*. Lyon: Presses universitaires de Lyon.
Bgazba, X.S. 1964. *Bzybskij dialekt abxazskogo jazyka*. Tbilisi.
Bhat, D.N.S. 1978. A general study of palatalization. In *Universals of human language*, ed. J. Greenberg. Vol. 2. Stanford: Stanford University Press.
Blumstein, S., and K. Stevens. 1979. Acoustic invariance in speech production: Evidence from measurements of the spectral characteristics of stop consonants. *Journal of the Acoustical Society of America* 66 (4): 1001-1017.
Bolla, K. 1980. *A phonetic conspectus of Hungarian: The articulatory and acoustic features of Hungarian speech sounds*. Budapest: A Magyar Tudományos Akadémia Nyelvtudományi Intézete.

------. 1981. *A conspectus of Russian speech sounds*. Budapest: Akadémiai Kiadó.
Booij, G. 1984. Neutral vowels and the autosegmental analysis of Hungarian vowel harmony. *Linguistics* 22: 629-641.
Borg, A. 1973. The segmental phonemes of Maltese. *Linguistics* 109: 5-11.
Brame, M.K. 1972. On the abstractness of phonology: Maltese ſ. In *Contributions to generative phonology*, ed. M. Brame. Austin: University of Texas Press.
------. 1973. On stress assignment in two Arabic dialects. In *A Festschrift for Morris Halle*, ed. S.R. Anderson and P. Kiparsky, 14-25. New York: Holt, Rinehart and Winston.
Bright, J.O. 1964. The phonology of Smith River Athapaskan (Tolowa). *International Journal of American Linguistics* 30(2): 101-107.
Bright, W. 1965. Luiseño phonemics. *International Journal of American Linguistics* 31(4): 342-345.
------. 1972. The enunciative vowel. *International Journal of Dravidian Linguistics* 1: 26-55.
Broselow, E., and A. Niyondagara. 1989. Feature geometry of Kirundi palatalization. ms., SUNY Stony Brook.
------. 1990. Morphological structure in Kirundi palatalization: Implications for feature geometry. In *Studies in inter-lacustrine Bantu phonology*, ed. F. Katamba. Cologne: Afrikanistische Arbeitspapiere.
Browman, C., and L. Goldstein. 1989. Articulatory gestures as phonological units. *Phonology* 6: 201-251.
Bugeja, P. 1984. *Kelmet il-Malti*. Malta: Gulf Publishing.
Busuttil, E.D. 1981. *Kalepin Malti-Ingliz*. Malta: Union Press.
Butcher, M. 1938. *Elements of Maltese*. London: Oxford University Press.
Catford, J.C. 1977. *Fundamental problems in phonetics*. Bloomington: Indiana University Press.
------. 1988. *A practical introduction to phonetics*. Oxford: Clarendon Press.
Cheng, L. 1989. Feature geometry of vowels and co-occurrence restrictions in Cantonese. ms., MIT.
Chiba, T., and M. Kajiyama. 1941. *The vowel: Its nature and structure*. Tokyo: Tokyo-Kaiseikan Publishing Co.
Chomsky, N. 1981. *Lectures on government and binding*. Dordrecht: Foris.
------. 1986. *Barriers*. Linguistic Inquiry Monograph No.13. Cambridge, MA: MIT Press.

Chomsky, N., and M. Halle. 1968. *The sound pattern of English.* New York: Harper and Row.

Christdas, P. 1988. Tamil morphology and phonology. Ph.D. diss., Cornell University.

Clements, G.N. 1976a. Palatalization: Linking or assimilation? *Chicago Linguistic Society* 12: 96-109.

------. 1976b (1980). *Vowel harmony in nonlinear generative phonology.* Distributed by the Indiana University Linguistics Club.

------. 1977. Neutral vowels in Hungarian vowel harmony: An autosegmental interpretation. *NELS* 7: 49-64.

------. 1985. The geometry of phonological features. *Phonology Yearbook* 2: 225-252.

------. 1987. Phonological feature representation and the description of intrusive stops. *Chicago Linguistic Society*: 29-50.

------. 1988a. The role of the sonority cycle in core syllabification. *Working Papers of the Cornell Phonetics Laboratory* 2: 1-68.

------. 1988b. Toward a substantive theory of feature specification. In *Proceedings of NELS 18*, ed. J. Blevins and J. Carter, 79-93. GLSA, Department of Linguistics, University of Massachusetts, Amherst.

------. 1989. A unified set of features for consonants and vowels. ms., Cornell University.

------. 1990a. The hierarchical representation of vowel height. ms., Cornell University.

------. 1990b. Secondary articulations. ms., Cornell University.

------. 1990c. Place of articulation in consonants and vowels: a unified approach. NELS 21, U.Q.A.M., Montreal, 1990. [In *Working Papers of the Cornell Phonetics Laboratory* no. 5, Cornell University, Ithaca, N.Y., 1991, 77-123]

------. 1992. Phonological primes: gestures or features? *Phonetica* 49: 181-193.

------. 1993. Lieu d'articulation des consonnes et des voyelles: une théorie unifée. In *Architecture des représentations phonologiques*, ed. B. Laks and A. Rialland, 101-145. Collection Sciences du Langage. Paris: CNRS Editions. [Revised French translation of Clements 1990b]

Clements, G.N., and K.C. Ford. 1979. Kikuyu tone shift and its synchronic consequences. *Linguistic Inquiry* 10: 179-210.

Clements, G.N., and S.J. Keyser. 1983. *CV phonology.* Linguistic Inquiry Monograph No. 9. Cambridge, MA: MIT Press.

Clements, G.N., and E. Sezer. 1982. Vowel and consonant disharmony in Turkish. In *The structure of phonological representations II*, ed. H. van der Hulst and N. Smith, 213-255. Dordrecht: Foris.

Cohn, A. 1990. Phonetic and phonological rules of nasalization. Ph.D. diss., UCLA. Distributed as *UCLA Working Papers in Phonetics* 76.

Comrie, B. 1980. The sun letters in Maltese: Between morphophonemics and phonetics. *Studies in the Linguistic Sciences* 10 (2): 25-37.

Cowan, W. 1970. A persistent rule in Maltese. *Canadian Journal of Linguistics*. 15 (2): 122-128.

Diffloth, G. 1984. *The Dvarāvati Old Mon language and Nyah Kur*. Bangkok: Chulalongkorn University Printing House.

Dogil, G. 1990. Hissing and hushing fricatives: A comment on non-anterior spirants in Polish. ms., Universität Bielefeld.

Donaldson, T. 1980. *Ngiyambaa: The language of the Wangaaybuwan*. Cambridge: Cambridge University Press.

Dvončová, J., G. Jenča, and A. Král'. 1969. *Atlas Slovenských Hlások*. Bratislava: Vydavatel'stvo Slovenskej Akadémie Vied.

Fant, G. 1959 (1961). The acoustics of speech. In *Proceedings of the Third International Congress on Acoustics*, ed. L. Cremer. Amsterdam: Elsevier Publishing Co.

------. 1960. *Acoustic theory of speech production*. The Hague: Mouton.

Flikeid, K. 1988. Unity and diversity in Acadian phonology: An overview based on comparisons among the Nova Scotia varieties. *Journal of the Atlantic Provinces Linguistic Association* 10: 64-110.

Foley, W. 1986. *The Papuan languages of New Guinea*. Cambridge; New York: Cambridge University Press.

Foster, M. L. 1969. *The Tarascan language*. University of California Publications in Linguistics 56. Berkeley and Los Angeles: University of California Press.

Friedrich, P. 1975. *A phonology of Tarascan*. The University of Chicago Studies in Anthropology, No. 4. Chicago: Department of Anthropology, The University of Chicago.

Garbell, I. 1965. *The Jewish Neo-Aramaic dialect of Persian Azarbaijan*. The Hague: Mouton.

Gendron, J.-D. 1966. *Tendances phonétiques du français parlé au Canada*. Paris: Klincksieck.

Genetti, C. 1990. Segmental alternations in the Sunwari verb stem: A case for the feature [front]. ms., University of Oregon.

Gerdel, F. 1973. Paez phonemics. *Linguistics* 104: 28-48.

Gerzenstein, A. 1968. *Fonología de la lengua Gününa-Kena*. Buenos Aires: Universidad de Buenos Aires, Centro de Estudios Lingüísticos.

Gibson, L. 1956. Pame (Otami) phonemics and morphophonemics. *International Journal of American Linguistics* 22 (4): 242-265.

Gibson, L., and D. Bartholomew. 1979. Pame noun inflection. *International Journal of American Linguistics* 45 (4): 309-322.

Goldsmith, J. 1976. Autosegmental phonology. Ph.D. diss., MIT. Distributed by the Indiana University Linguistics Club, Bloomington, Indiana.

Goodman, B. 1991. Ponapean labiovelarized labials: Evidence for internal segment stucture. In *Proceedings of NELS 21*, ed. T. Sherer, 111-126. GLSA, Department of Linguistics, University of Massachusetts, Amherst.

Greenberg, J. 1950. The patterning of root morphemes in Semitic. *Word* 6: 162-181.

Halle, M. 1959. *The sound pattern of Russian*. 'S-Gravenhage: Mouton.

------. 1976. Roman Jakobson's contribution to the modern study of speech sounds. In *Sound, sign, and meaning*, ed. L. Matejka. Ann Arbor: The University of Michigan.

------. 1983. On distinctive features and their articulatory implementation. *Natural Language and Linguistic Theory* 1 (1): 91-105.

------. 1989. The intrinsic structure of speech sounds. ms., MIT.

Halle, M., and G.N. Clements. 1983. *Problem book in phonology*. Cambridge, MA: MIT Press.

Halle, M., and K. Stevens. 1979. Some reflections on the theoretical bases of phonetics. In *Frontiers in speech communications research*, ed. B. Lindblom and S. Ohman, 335-349. London: Academic Press.

------. 1989. The postalveolar fricatives of Polish. ms., MIT.

Hammond, M. 1988. On deriving the well-formedness condition. *Linguistic Inquiry* 19: 319-325.

Haraguchi, S. 1977. *The tone pattern of Japanese: An autosegmental theory of tonology*. Tokyo: Kaitakusha.

Harris, J.W. 1969. *Spanish phonology*. Cambridge, MA: MIT Press.

------. 1977. Remarks on diphthongization in Spanish. *Lingua* 41: 261-305.

------. 1983. *Syllable structure and stress in Spanish: A nonlinear analysis*. Cambridge, MA: MIT Press.

------. 1985. Spanish diphthongization and stress: A paradox resolved. *Phonology Yearbook* 2: 31-46.

Harshman, R.A., P. Ladefoged, and L. Goldstein. 1977. Factor analysis of tongue shapes. *Journal of the Acoustical Society of America* 62: 693-707.

Hashimoto, O.-K.Y. 1972. *Phonology of Cantonese*. Cambridge: Cambridge University Press.

Hayes, B. 1986. Inalterability in CV phonology. *Language* 62: 321-351.

------. 1989a. Compensatory lengthening in moraic phonology. *Linguistic Inquiry* 20: 253-306.

------. 1989b. Dipthongisation and coindexing. *Phonology* 7: 31-71.

Herzallah, R. 1990. Aspects of Palestinian Arabic phonology: A nonlinear approach. Ph.D. diss., Cornell University. Distributed as *Working Papers of the Cornell Phonetics Laboratory* No. 4.

Hualde, J. 1988. A lexical phonology of Basque. Ph.D. diss., University of Southern California.

------. 1991. Unspecified and unmarked vowels. *Linguistic Inquiry* 22: 205-209.

Hulst, H. van der. 1985. Vowel harmony in Hungarian: A comparison of segmental and autosegmental analyses. In *Advances in nonlinear phonology*, ed. H. van der Hulst and N. Smith, 267-304. Dordrecht: Foris.

Hume, E. 1988. Polish palatalization: Evidence for the underlying specification of redundant features. ms., Cornell University.

------. 1990. Front vowels, palatal consonants and the rule of umlaut in Korean. In *Proceedings of NELS* 20: 230-243. GLSA, Department of Linguistics, University of Massachusetts, Amherst.

------. 1991a. Consonant/vowel interaction in Maltese: implications for feature theory. In *Proceedings of WECOL 20*, ed. B. Birch et al. California State University, Fresno.

------. 1991b. Metathesis in Maltese: Implications for the strong morphemic plane hypothesis. In *Proceedings of NELS 21*, ed. T. Sherer, 157-172. GLSA, Department of Linguistics, University of Massachusetts, Amherst.

Hyman, L. 1972. *A phonological study of Fe?-fe?-Bemileke*. Studies in African Linguistics, Supplement 4.

------. 1973. The feature [grave] in phonological theory. *Journal of Phonetics* 1: 329-337.

Itô, J., and A. Mester. 1989. Feature predictability and underspecification. Palatal prosody in Japanese mimetics. *Language* 65: 258-293.

Jackson, M. 1988. Phonetic theory and cross-linguistic variation in vowel articulation. *UCLA Working Papers in Phonetics* 71.

------. 1989. Are there cross-linguistic differences in front vowel production? *UCLA Working Papers in Phonetics* 72: 17-38.
Jacobs, H. 1989. Non-linear studies in the historical phonology of French. Ph.D. diss., Nijmegen University.
------. 1991. A nonlinear analysis of the evolution of consonant + yod sequences in Gallo-Romance. *Canadian Journal of Linguistics* 36: 27-64.
Jakobson, R., G. Fant, and M. Halle. 1952. *Preliminaries to speech analysis*. Cambridge: MIT Press.
Jakobson, R., and M. Halle 1971. The revised version of the list of inherent features. *Roman Jakobson: Selected Writings* 1:738-742. The Hague; Paris: Mouton.
Jakobson, R., and L. Waugh. 1987. *The sound shape of language*. Berlin: Mouton. Originally published in 1979.
Janson, T. 1986. Cross-linguistic trends in CV sequences. *Phonology Yearbook* 3: 179-196.
Jespersen, O. 1904. *Lehrbuch der Phonetik*. Leipzig and Berlin.
------. 1950. *English phonetics*. 5th ed. Translated by B. Jürgensen. Copenhagen: Gyldendalske Boghandel.
Jones, D., and D. Ward. 1969. *The phonetics of Russian*. Cambridge: Cambridge University Press.
Kaye, J., and J. Lowenstamm. 1984. De la syllabicité. In *Forme sonore du langage*, ed. F. Dell, D. Hirst and J.-R. Vergnaud, 123-160. Paris: Hermann.
Kean, M.-L. 1976. The theory of markedness in generative grammar. Ph.D. diss., MIT. Distributed in 1980 by Indiana University Linguistics Club, Bloomington, Indiana.
Keating, P. 1988. Palatals as complex segments: X-ray evidence. *UCLA Working Papers in Phonetics* 69: 77-91.
------. 1990. Coronal places of articulation. *UCLA Working Papers in Phonetics* 74: 35-60.
Kenstowicz, M. 1981. Vowel harmony in Palestinian Arabic: A suprasegmental analysis. *Linguistics* 19: 449-465.
Kiparsky, P. 1982. Lexical morphology and phonology. In *Linguistics in the morning calm*, ed. The Linguistic Society of Korea, 3-91. Seoul: Hanshin Publishing Co.
------. 1985. Some consequences of lexical phonology. *Phonology Yearbook* 2: 85-138.
Kirton, J., and B. Charlie. 1978. Seven articulatory positions in Yanyuwa consonants. Pacific Linguistics Series A, No. 51. Canberra: Pacific Linguistics.
Labov, W. 1966. *Social stratification of English in New York City*. Washington: Center for Applied Linguistics.

------. 1981. What can be learned about change in progress from synchronic descriptions? In *Variation Omnibus*, ed. D. Sankoff and H. Cedergren. Edmonton: Linguistic Research.

Ladefoged, P. 1968. *A phonetic study of west African languages*. Cambridge: Cambridge University Press.

------. 1982. *A course in phonetics*. New York: Harcourt Brace Jovanovich. Originally published in 1975.

Ladefoged, P., and P. Bhaskararoa. 1983. Non-quantal aspects of consonant production: A study of retroflex consonants. *Journal of Phonetics* 11: 291-302.

Ladefoged, P., and I. Maddieson. 1986. Some of the sounds of the world's languages. *UCLA Working Papers in Phonetics* 64.

Lahiri, A., and S. Blumstein. 1984. A re-evaluation of the feature coronal. *Journal of Phonetics* 12 (2): 133-146.

Lahiri, A., and V. Evers. 1991. Palatalization and coronality. In C. Paradis and J.-F. Prunet (1991), 79-100.

Lahiri, A., L. Gewirth, and S. Blumstein. 1984. A reconsideration of acoustic invariance for place of articulation in diffuse stop consonants: Evidence from a cross-language study. *Journal of the Acoustical Society of America.* 76 (2): 391-404.

Laughren, M. 1984. Tone in Zulu nouns. In *Autosegmental studies in Bantu tone*, ed. G.N. Clements and J. Goldsmith, 183-234. Dordrecht: Foris.

Laycock, D. 1965. *The Ndu language family* (Sepik District, New Guinea). Pacific Linguistics C1.

Levin, J. 1985. A metrical theory of syllabicity. Ph.D. diss., MIT.

Lewis, G.L. 1967. *Turkish grammar*. Oxford: Clarendon Press.

Lieberman, P., and S. Blumstein. 1988. *Speech physiology, speech perception, and acoustic phonetics*. Cambridge: Cambridge University Press.

Lightner, T. 1965. Segmental phonology of modern standard Russian. Ph.D. diss., MIT.

Lisker, L. 1963. *Introduction to spoken Telugu*. New York: American Council of Learned Societies.

Lombardi, L. 1990. The Nonlinear orgnaization of the affricate. *Natural Language and Linguistic Theory* 8 (3): 375-426.

Lozano, M. 1979. *Stop and spirant alternations: Fortition and spirantization processes in Spanish phonology*. Bloomington: Indiana Linguistics Club.

Lucci, V. 1972. *Phonologie de l'Acadien*. Studia Phonetica 7. Ottawa: Didier.

Lytkin, V.I. 1961. *Komi-yaz'vinskiy dialekt*. Moscow.

Maddieson, I. 1984. *Patterns of sounds*. Cambridge: Cambridge University Press.
Maddieson, I., and K. Precoda. 1990. Preferred syllables. Paper presented at the 120th Meeting of the Acoustical Society of America, at San Diego.
McCarthy, J. 1979. Formal problems in Semitic phonology and morphology. Ph.D. diss., MIT.
------. 1981. A prosodic theory of nonconcatenative morphology. *Linguistic Inquiry* 12: 373-418.
------. 1986. OCP effects: Gemination and antigemination. *Linguistic Inquiry* 17. 207-263.
------. 1988. Feature geometry and dependency: A review. *Phonetica* 43.
------. 1989. Guttural phonology. ms., University of Massachusetts, Amherst.
McCarthy, J., and A. Prince. 1989. Prosodic morphology. ms., University of Massachusetts, Amherst, and Brandeis University, Waltham, MA.
Michailovsky, B. 1975. On some Tibeto-Burman sound changes. In *Proceedings of the First Annual Meeting of the Berkeley Linguistics Society*, ed. C. Cogen et al. Berkeley: University of California at Berkeley.
Mohanan, K. P. 1991. On the bases of radical underspecification. *Natural Language and Linguistic Theory* 9: 285-325.
Morgan, T.A. 1984. Consonant-glide-vowel alternations in Spanish: A case study of syllabic and lexical phonology. Ph.D. diss., University of Texas at Austin.
Morgenstierne, G. 1945. Notes on Burushaski phonology. *Norsk Tidsskrift for Sprogvidenskap* 13: 61-95.
Müller, J. 1848. *The physiology of the senses, voice, and muscular motion with the mental faculties*. Translated by W.Baly. London: Walton and Maberly.
Nandris, O. 1963. *Phonétique historique du roumain*. Paris: Klincksieck.
Ní Chiosáin, M. 1991. Topics in the phonology of Irish. PhD diss., University of Massachusetts, Amherst.
Odden, D. 1978. Further evidence for the feature [grave]. *Linguistic Inquiry* 9: 141-144.
------. 1988. Dissimilation as deletion in Chukchi. ms., Ohio State University.
------. 1991a. Adjacency parameters in phonology. ms., Ohio State University.
------. 1991b. Simplicity and underspecification. Paper presented at the Underspecification Workshop, Ohio State University.

------. 1992. Vowel geometry. *Phonology* 8 (2): 261-290.
O'Grady, C., C.F. Voegelin, and F.M. Voegelin. 1966. Languages of the world: Indo-Pacific fascicle six. *Anthropological Linguistics* 8 (1): 56-67.
Paradis, C. 1988. Towards a theory of constraint violations. *McGill Working Papers in Linguistics* 5 (1): 1-43.
Paradis, C., and J.-F. Prunet. 1989. Markedness and coronal structure. In *Proceedings of NELS 19*, ed. J. Carter and R.-M. Déchaine, 330-344. GLSA, Department of Linguistics, University of Massachusetts, Amherst.
------. eds. 1991. *The special status of coronals*. San Diego: Academic Press.
Perkell, J.S. 1969. *Physiology of speech production*. Research Monograph, No. 53. Cambridge, MA: MIT Press.
Piggott, G. 1988. The parameters of nasalization. ms., McGill University.
Pike, K. 1943. *Phonetics: A critical analysis of phonetic theory and a technic for the practical description of sounds*. Ann Arbor: University of Michigan Press.
Prost, G. 1967. The phonemes of the Chácobo language. *Linguistics* 35: 61-65.
Puech, G. 1978. A cross-dialectal study of vowel harmony in Maltese. *Chicago Linguistic Society* 14: 377-389.
------. 1979. Les Parlers maltais. Ph.D. diss., L'université Lyon II.
Pulleyblank, D. 1986. *Tone in lexical phonology*. Dordrecht: Reidel.
Pulleyblank, E. 1989. Articulator based features of vowels and consonants. ms., University of British Columbia.
Ringen, C. 1975. Vowel harmony: Theoretical implications. Ph.D. diss., Indiana University. Published in 1988, New York: Garland.
------. 1977. Vowel harmony: Implications for the alternation condition. In *Phonologica 1976*, ed. W. Dressler and O. Pfeiffer, 127-132. Innsbruck: Innsbrucker Beiträge zur Sprachwissenschaft.
------. 1988. Transparency in Hungarian vowel harmony. *Phonology* 5: 327-342.
Rubach, J. 1984. *Cyclic and lexical phonology: The structure of Polish*. Dordrecht: Foris.
------. Forthcoming. *The lexical phonology of Slovak*. Oxford: Oxford University Press.
Sagey, E. 1986. The representation of features and relations in nonlinear phonology. Ph.D. diss., MIT.
Sala, M. 1976. *Contributions à la phonétique historique du romain*. Paris: Editions Klincksieck.

Sastry, J. V. 1972. *Telugu phonetic reader*. Mysore State, India: Central Institute of Indian Languages.

Schein, B., and D. Steriade. 1986. On geminates. *Linguistic Inquiry* 17: 691-744.

Selkirk, E. 1988. Dependency, place and the notion 'tier'. Paper presented at the Annual Meeting of the Linguistic Society of America.

Sievers, E. 1881. *Grundzüge der Phonetik*. Leipzig: Breitkopf and Hartel.

Smith, N. 1973. *The acquisition of phonology*. Cambridge: Cambridge University Press.

Staalsen, P. 1966. The phonemes of Iatmul. *Pacific Linguistics* A7: 69-76.

Steriade, D. 1985. A note on coronal. ms., MIT.

------. 1987. Redundant values. In *Parasession on Autosegmental and Metrical Phonology* (Papers from the 23rd Annual Regional Meeting of the Chicago Linguistic Society, part 2), ed. A. Bosch et al., 339-362. Chicago Linguistic Society.

------. 1989. Affricates and the analysis of place features. Paper presented at the Conference on Feature and Underspecification Theories, at MIT.

Stevens, K. 1972. Quantal nature of speech. In *Human communication: A unified view*, ed. E.E. David Jr. and P.B. Denes. New York: McGraw Hill.

Stevens, K., and A. House 1955. Development of a quantitative description of vowel articulation. *Journal of the Acoustical Society of America* 64: 1358-1368.

Stevens, K., and S.J. Keyser. 1989. Primary features and their enhancement in consonants. *Language* 65: 81-106.

Straka, G. 1965. Naissance et disparition des consonnes palatales dans l'évolution du latin au français. *Travaux de linguistique et de littérature* 3: 117-167. Strasbourg: Centre de Philologie et de Littérature Romanes.

Strevens, P. 1967. Spectra of fricative noise in human speech. In *Readings in acoustic phonetics*, ed. I. Lehiste, 202-219. Cambridge: MIT Press.

Sutcliffe, E. 1936. *A grammar of the Maltese language*. London: Oxford University Press.

Swift, L.B. 1963. *A reference grammar of modern Turkish*. Indiana University Publications, Uralic and Altaic Series, Vol. 19. Bloomington: Indiana University.

Tucker, A.N., and A.A. Bryan. 1966. *Linguistic analyses: The non-Bantu languages of north-eastern Africa*. Oxford: Oxford University Press.

Trigo, L. 1991. On pharynx - larynx interactions. *Phonology*. 113-136.

Vago, R. 1976. More evidence for the feature [grave]. *Linguistic Inquiry* 7: 671-674.

------. 1980. *The sound pattern of Hungarian*. Washington: Georgetown University Press.

von Soden, W. 1969. *Grundiss der Akkadischen Grammatik*. Rome: Pontificium Institutum Biblicum.

Wängler, H.-H. 1958. *Atlas Deutscher Sprachlaute*. Berlin: Academie-Verlag.

Westerman, D. 1930. *A study of the Ewe language*. London: Oxford University Press.

Whitney, W.D. 1889. *Sanskrit grammar*. Cambridge, MA: Harvard University Press.

Wierzchowska, B. 1980. *Fonetyka I Fonologia Jezyka Polskiego*. Warsaw: Ossolineum.

Wood, S. 1971. A spectrographic study of allophonic variation and vowel reduction in West Greenlandic Eskimo. *Working Papers* 4: 58-94. Lund: Department of Linguistics.

------. 1979. A radiographic analysis of constriction locations for vowels. *Journal of Phonetics* 7: 25-43.

------. 1982. X-Ray and model studies of vowel articulation. *Working Papers* 23, Lund University, Department of Linguistics.

Yip, M. 1982. Reduplication and CV skeleta in Chinese secret languages. *Linguistic Inquiry* 13: 637-662.

------. 1988. The obligatory contour principle and phonological rules: A loss of identity. *Linguistic Inquiry* 19: 65-100.

Younes, R. 1983. The representation of geminate consonants. ms., University of Texas, Austin.

Zemlin, W. 1968. *Speech and hearing science: Anatomy and physiology*. Englewood Cliffs, NJ: Prentice-Hall.

Index

Abondolo, D., 36
Adjacency, 108, 114-115
Akkadian, 112
Alveopalatal Consonants, 83-85
Ao, B., 103
Aquilina, J., 155, 166, 189
Archangeli, D., 20, 21, 35, 120, 56, 171, 206, 239, 154
Avery, P., 235
Bartholomew, D., 147
Basque, 96-98
Baule, 10
Bell, M., 49
Berrendonner, A., 153, 155, 168, 182
Bgazba, X.S., 88
Bhaskararao, P., 29
Bhat, D.N.S., 125
Blumstein, S., 49, 53, 54, 74
Bolla, K., 33, 34, 40, 41, 42, 43, 44
Booij, G., 77
Borg, A., 155, 153, 155, 166, 168,
Brame, M., 169, 182, 189, 215, 240
Bright, J.O., 114, 123
Bright, W., 73
Broselow, E., 15, 133
Browman, C., 99
Browne, W., 48
Bryan, A.A., 73
Bugeja, P., 155
Busuttil, E.D., 155, 190
Butcher, M., 155

Cantonese, 10, 109
Catford, J.C., 26, 29
Charlie, B., 87
Cheng, L., 10, 15, 92, 109, 123
Chiba, T., 49
Chinese, 83
Chomsky, N., 5, 19, 20, 72, 123, 133
Christdas, P., 21
Cichocki, W., 126, 144
Classical Arabic, 174
Clements, G.N., 5, 7, 11, 12, 14, 15, 17-9, 20, 21, 31, 46, 51, 58, 59, 70, 77-9, 83, 88, 92, 98, 99, 101, 103-5, 109, 112, 115, 117, 138, 142, 194
Cloning, 119, 120, 199
Cohn, A., 119
Coronal:
    phonetics (see ch. II)
    consonants/vowels: feature specification, (see ch. III)
    definition, 15, 25
    feature organization, (see ch. IV)
    sonorant consonants: specification, 86-87
Coronalization, (see Palatalization)

Cross-Plane Interaction, 134-137
Czech, 7
Default Feature: [coronal], 234
Default Rules, 205
Diffloth, G., 13
Diphthongization: Porteño Spanish, 61-63
Dissimilation, 12, 13, 107-114
Dogil, G., 84, 85
Donaldson, T., 145
English: low vowels, 45
Evers, V., 93, 96, 138, 139, 146
Ewe, 31
Fant, G., 5, 31, 45, 47, 49, 52, 72, 74
Fe?fe?-Bamileke, 11
Flikeid, K., 126, 128
Foley, W., 8
Ford, K.C., 20, 194
Foster, M., 74
French: Acadian (see ch. V)
    Canadian French vowels, 41, 43, 44
    sound change, 6
Friedrich, P., 74
Front Vowels: acoustics, 52
    articulatory description, 39-52
Front Vowels and Glides: feature specification, 57-71
Garbell, I., 102
Genetti, C., 14
Gerdel, F., 75, 82
German, 38, 40
Gerzenstein, A., 74
Gewirth, L., 53
Gibson, L., 147, 148
Glide Fronting, 10

Glide Strengthening, 64-68
Goldsmith, J., 20, 79, 104
Goldstein, L., 99
Goodman, B., 15, 99
Greenberg, J., 59
Gününa-Kĕna, 74
Halle, M., 5, 15, 19, 20, 25, 31, 32, 46, 48, 52, 54, 58, 60, 64, 72, 74, 75, 83, 84, 91, 133
Hammond, M., 116, 117, 123
Haraguchi, S., 20, 194
Harris, J., 32, 61-3, 66, 68
Harshman, R.A., 99
Hashimoto, O.-K.Y., 109
Hayes, B., 8
Herzallah, R., 15, 20, 50, 98, 99, 154, 158, 170
House, A., 49
Hualde, J., 20, 96, 122, 154
Hulst, H. van der, 77
Hume, E. V., 15, 89, 92, 99, 127, 133, 138
Hungarian, 32, 33-38, 40, 42, 44, 77-81, 93
Hyman, L., 11, 31, 82
Iatmul, 7
Itô, J., 127
Jackson, M., 48, 51
Jacobs, H., 146
Jakobson, R., 5, 7, 31, 52, 72, 74
Janson, T., 12
Japanese, 138-139
Jasanoff, J., 60
Jespersen, O., 190
Jones, D., 138
Kajiyama, M., 49
Kaye, J., 59

Index

Kean, M.-L., 235
Keating, P., 28, 29, 31, 39, 71, 73, 76, 78
Kenstowicz, M., 183
Keyser, S.J., 59, 86, 88
Kingston, J., 85
Kiparsky, P., 21, 222, 224
Kirton, J., 87
Komi, 75-76
Korean, 12
Labov, W., 144
Ladefoged, P., 27, 29, 38, 53, 73, 75, 83, 84, 87, 88
Lahiri, A., 53, 74, 93, 96, 138, 139, 146
Laughren, M., 117
Levin, J., 9, 88
Lewis, G.L., 78
Lhasa Tibetan, 9
Lieberman, P., 49
Lightner, T., 48
Lisker, L., 73
Lombardi, L., 35
Lowenstamm, J., 59
Lozano, M., 61, 63, 66, 68
Lucci, V., 126, 127, 128, 144
Maddieson, I., 2, 73-5, 83, 84, 87, 88
Major/Minor Articulations, 100, 104
Malay, 13
Maltese, 59, 120, 153-211, 213-240
   Consonant Coronal
      Assimilation, 227-234
   Guttural Assimilation, 170-178, 185, 188, 200, 207, 235
   Morpheme Structure
      Constraints, 159
   Vowel Coronal Assimilation, 221-226
Markedness, 143

McCarthy, J., 17, 20, 88, 98, 107, 112, 119, 123, 125, 154, 159, 160, 170, 174, 202
Mester, A., 127
Metathesis, 153-154, 183-202
Michailovsky, B., 9
Mohanan, K.P., 212, 241
Mon, 13
Morgan, T., 32, 61, 63, 68
Morgenstierne, G., 73
Moroccan Arabic, 8
Müller, J., 49
Nandris, J., 148, 149
Ngwo, 38
Ní Chiosáin, M., 9
Niyondagara, A., 15, 133
No Line-Crossing, 104, 116, 118
Nonlinear Phonology, 20
Nupe, 82
O'Grady, C., 73
Obligatory Contour Principle, 17, 108, 109, 160, 174
Odden, D., 8, 21, 31, 32, 94, 99, 105, 110, 112, 114, 123
Oltean, S., 150
Opacity/Transparency, 104, 107
Ordering Constraint, 117, 199
Ordering Paradox, 115
Paez, 74-75
Palatal Consonants, 31, 73-81
Palatalization, 6, 7, 18, 19, 81, (see ch. V)
Palatalized Consonants, 81-85
Palato-alveolar obstruents, 73-76
Palestinian Arabic, 158, 183
Pame, 147
Paradis, C., 35, 235
Perkell, J.S., 45
Piggott, G., 135
Pike, K., 59

Polish, 42, 83-85
Porteño Spanish, 32, 61-71
Postalveolar Coronal Obstruents:
    feature specification, 72-86
Precoda, K., 12
Prince, A., 88
Prost, G., 73
Prunet, J.-F., 235
Puech, G., 153, 155, 166, 168, 169, 182, 183, 186, 189, 192, 215, 219, 240
Pulleyblank, D., 20, 21, 35, 120, 154, 156, 171, 194, 206, 239
Pulleyblank, E., 70, 92
Retroflex Consonants, 73
Rice, K., 235
Ringen, 77
Romanian, 14, 148
Rubach, J., 84, 142, 143
Russian, 41, 43, 46, 48, 138
Sagey, E., 9, 20, 22, 58, 66, 68, 71, 91, 98, 100, 114, 117, 123, 129, 130, 131, 133, 144, 146, 147, 218
Sala, 14, 148
Sanskrit, 32, 60, 93-96
Sastry, 73
Schein, B., 4, 95, 122
Selkirk, E., 18, 109
Sezer, E., 78, 89
Sievers, 59, 190
Single Tier Hypothesis, 17, 107-114
Slovak, 7, 142-143
Smith, N., 31
Staalsen, P., 8
Steriade, D., 21, 35, 94, 95, 122
Stevens, K., 15, 25, 32, 49, 54, 75, 84, 86
Straka, G., 7
Strevens, P., 53

Sunwari, 14
Sutcliffe, E., 155, 189, 191, 231, 232
Swedish, 45
Swift, L.B., 78
Tarascan, 74
Tier Conflation, 120, 160, 174-176, 202
Tongue: topology, 25
Trigo, L., 13
Tucker, A.N., 73
Tulu, 114
Turkish, 78, 80, 93
Underspecification, 20, 21, 154, 205
Unified Features Theory, 15, 16, 98, 100
Vago, R., 10, 31, 35, 36, 77
Veogelin, C.F. & F.M., 73
von Soden, W., 112
Vowel Fronting, 7-9, 10, 11
Vowel Movement: complete, 154, 202
Wängler, H.-H., 38, 40
Ward, D., 138
Waugh, L.R., 7, 52
Westerman, D., 31
Whitney, W.D., 94, 122
Wierzchowska, B., 42, 84
Wood, S., 49, 50, 51
Yanuwa, 87
Yip, M., 17, 107, 109, 110
Younes, R., 120, 160
Zemlin, W., 28, 29

For Product Safety Concerns and Information please contact our EU representative GPSR@taylorandfrancis.com
Taylor & Francis Verlag GmbH, Kaufingerstraße 24, 80331 München, Germany

www.ingramcontent.com/pod-product-compliance
Lightning Source LLC
Chambersburg PA
CBHW071813300426
44116CB00009B/1291